More Enchanted Eating

FROM THE WEST SHORE

Published by Friends of the Symphony Publications

425 Western Avenue
P.O. Box 1603
Muskegon, Michigan 49443
231-726-3231

Library of Congress Catalog Number: 99-071398

ISBN: 0-9617142-1-2

Designed, Edited, and Manufactured by

Favorite Recipes® Press
an imprint of

FRP™

P.O. Box 305142
Nashville, Tennessee 37230
800-358-0560

Art Director: Steve Newman
Designer: Jim Scott
Project Manager: Linda A. Jones

Manufactured in the United States of America

First Printing: 2000 10,000 copies

To order additional copies, use the order forms
in the back of the book or write:

Friends of the Symphony Publications
P.O. Box 1603
Muskegon, Michigan 49443

Checks should be made payable to Friends of the Symphony Publications
for $23.95 plus $3.50 shipping and handling.
Michigan residents add $1.44 sales tax.

The Friends of the Symphony is the support organization for the West Shore Symphony Orchestra. Our members provide volunteer manpower, fund-raising activities, assistance with ticket sales, and educational programs for children.

Some Enchanted Eating, our 1986 cookbook, brought us bravos and continues to elicit applause. This sequel, our all-new **More Enchanted Eating**, brings you the latest favorites of today's fine West Shore chefs.

We invite you to visit our Western Michigan communities and to experience our sparkling waters, soaring dunes, and quiet forests. We give you our best wishes along with these, our best recipes.

Table of Contents

Executive Committee

CO-CHAIRPERSONS
Marleen DeLong
Kay Olthoff
Sue Schuiteman

TREASURER
Darlene Smith

EDITOR
Jill Sanders

TESTING COORDINATORS
Lila Manhart
Nancy VanderVere

PHOTOGRAPHY
W. Patrick Chambers Photography
Frederic A. Reinecke Photography
Muskegon County Convention
and Visitors Bureau

We would like to thank all whose contributions, diligence, and hard work helped to make **More Enchanted Eating** become a reality.

Shirley Almond
Jo Anacker
Jean Anderson
Andy Askam
Joe Auffrey
Bonnie Bailey
Pamela Smitter Baker
Sherri Balaskovitz
Shirley Barry
Donna Beauvais
Sharon Bedford
Jane Bednarz
Ellen Berens
Joan Bergmann
Barbara Berry
Ann Blais
Karen Blais
Arlee Bodnar
Inge Boelkins
Karen Booth
Barb Boyer
Kandace Boysen
Karen Brady
Jean Brayman
Jane Brown
Jill Brown
Sherry Brown
Linnea Brugman
Barbara Buth
Mort Butzman
Pat Byersmith
Jane Caplitz
Blanche Carlson
Beverly Lee Carroll
Vella Caruso
Rona Caswell
Mudgi Cavender
Debra Chase
Diane Clarke
Jane Clover
Marge Collinge
Lincoln Collins
Victoria Collins
Jeanne Comeau
Kristina Conley
Sara Cornwell
Cynthia Crane
Debi Cribley
Beverlie Curtis
Betsy Cutler
Jan Daniels
Janet Day
John Day
Judy DeHaan
Audrey DeHorn
Marleen DeLong
Susan DeLong
Alyce Dempsey
Anne Dickson
Marcia D'Oyly
Louise Dykema
Ann Eichmann
Brian Ellis
Mary Lou Eyke
Dorothy Far
Heather Faraci
Marty Ferriby
Ann Fish
Judy Fleener
Roberta Fleischmann
Bonnie Fox
Renee Galombeck
Marcia Garrigan
Jane Hagen Gates
Judy Gingras
Bonnie Gluhanich
Judith Gorham
Lori Goryl
Ron Gossett
Shirley Gossett
Sandra Green
Frances Gross
Mary Gust
Suzanne Gust
Karen Hahn
Ellen Hanichen
Mary Sue Hansen
Virginia Hansen

Acknowledgements

Madelon Hanson
Tom Harsay
Sophia Hartman
Anita Hasper
Joanne Hatch
The Hearthstone
Restaurant
Carolyn Heckle
Barbara Hermanson
Jeanne Hines
Genevieve Hornak
Joni Hornbeck
Susan Horsfall
Ruth Ann Hovey
Pat Hunt
Cynthia Hunting
Ellen Hurley
Warren Husid,
Chef, Baker College
Jeanne Ingalls
Deb Jackson
Flo Jackson
Barbara Johnson
Holly Johnson
Mary Ann Johnson
Steven Johnson,
Chef, Muskegon
Country Club
Liz Johnston
Andrea Kahn
Martha Keller
Mindy Kelner
Tammy Kerr
Henrietta Kibbey
Scott Klimpfbeck
Jacqueline Wilbur
Klooster
Ruth Kramer
Joan Krenz
Charlotte Krive
Bruce Krueger
Mary Krueger
Pat Kufta
Donna Lachniet
Jane LaMarca
Dorothy Landman
Clara Lang
Doris Lange
Karla Lange
Helen Larsen
Lynne Larsen
Phyllis Laurin
Jacquie Leary
Joan Leder
Betty Linacre
Donna Lundholm
Dorothy Luyendyk
Mary Lou Maher
Joe Manhart
Lila Manhart
Jean Manning
Jean Mast
Louise Matz
Caroline Mayberry
Rosalind Mayberry
Mary Jane McBeath
Alice McGuire
Ann McMillen
Lucille Meier
Gretchen Mellema
Lisa Menerick
Rosalie Meyer
Ellen Middlebrook
Christine Miegoc
Irene Miegoc
Alanna Miller
Ed Minty
Judith Minty
Carol Mogdis
Nancy Morgenstern
Jeanne Mudler
Barbara Mullally
Linda Munson
Barb Murphy
Veronica Muscat
Ruth Musil
Jennifer Naglekirk
Kathy Neff
Christine Neis
Deb Newson
Julie Noel
Fred Norris
Joanna Norris
Connie Obits
Bonnie Olson
Kay Olthoff
H. Kay Ostrom
Pat Parsons

Bev Pennington
Ardis Peters
Karen Peters
Nancy Peters
Earline Phillips
Pam Pimley
Ann Rogalla Portenga
Barbara Petrak Potuznik
Nancy Price
Andrea Bard Prue
Helen Pyle
Rafferty's Dockside
Judy Rahrig
Nancy Reggaert
Gretchen Cheney Rhoades
Nancy Ribecky
Jack Rice
Jennifer Richardson
Lois Ridley
Shirley Rieckhoff
Pennie Robertson
Patti Roy
Ann Russell
Bette Russell
Marilyn Ryan
Jill Sanders
Jean Schilleman
Joan Schlukebir
Marcia Schneeberger
Ruth Schrier
Toby Schrier
Bob Schuiteman
Mary Beth Schuiteman
Sue Schuiteman
Suzanne Schuiteman
Merle Scolnik
Bill Seeback
Ruth Seyferth
Charles Sheridan
Nancy Sheridan
Betty Silberman
Mary Kay Simon
Darlene Smith
Peggy Smith
Sue Snider
Ann Soles
Brenda Sprader
Diane Steverman
Margaret Stidham
Zinnie Stille
Therese Stone
Linda Strong
Yvonne Strutwa
Shirlee Swanson
Linda Talkington
Carol Thompson
Karen Thornton
Jack Tierney
Judy Tierney
Mary Topp
Mary Elizabeth Tyler
Mary Tyler
David Utzinger
Louanne Utzinger
Anamae Valk
Adelle VanDaalen
Joan Vandeberg
Carol VanderJagt
June Vandervelde
Nancy VanderVere
Nancy VanderVrede
Kay VanderWall
Bette Vanderwerp
Holly VanLeuven
Merri Lee VanLeuven
Vicki Verplank
Harriett Walsh
Yvonne Way
Thomas Webb,
Chef, Kirby Grill
Roxie Westgate
Bob White
Linda White
John Whitlock
Peggy Whitlock
Sue Wierengo
Judy Wilcox
Pat Wilkerson
Diane Williams
Mary Williams
Melanie Wilson
Roy Winegar
Linda Wishart
Scott Wishart
Kathleen Workman
Sheri Wray
Jane Wright
Diane Zappone

W. PATRICK CHAMBERS graduated from Grand Valley State University with a Bachelor of Science degree in photography and group social studies. He is a commercial photographer with his own business. Some of his favorite work is commercial in nature, yet it has been taking a welcomed twist toward fine arts. Currently, Patrick is very involved in architectural, food, jewelry, and documentary photography. He was a medical photographer at Hackley Hospital for eleven years and very much enjoyed his experiences there. Patrick is probably best known for his landscapes and lakescapes of the Muskegon area.

FREDERIC A. REINECKE is an award-winning commercial photographer. He believes that to truly capture the beatuy of an area, one must live there. He has taken hundreds of photos of Muskegon landmarks, capturing them at the most opportune time with the correct lighting and weather conditions to have the most desirable effect. Frederic is a graduate of Central Michigan University and has collections on display in major corporations and galleries.

Appetizers and Beverages

LAKE MICHIGAN SHORELINE

Spicy Bacon, Tomato and Broccoli Dip

Stores well

- **Serves 6 to 8**

Dip:
- **Must do ahead**
- **Chill up to 12 hours**

Tortillas:
- **Can do ahead**
- **Oven Temperature 375 degrees**
- **Bake 10 to 15 minutes**

DIP
2 cups water
1 teaspoon salt
3 cups chopped fresh broccoli
2 tablespoons olive oil
3/4 cup chopped onion
2 garlic cloves, minced
2 teaspoons oregano
1 (4-ounce) can chopped green chiles
1/4 cup grated Parmesan cheese
1/2 to 1 cup sour cream
Salt and pepper to taste
1 cup drained, chopped, seeded tomato
6 to 8 slices bacon, cooked, crumbled

TORTILLA TRIANGLES
1 package tortillas
Coarse salt

For the dip, bring the water to a boil in a saucepan. Add the salt and broccoli. Cook for 2 to 3 minutes or until tender; drain. Heat the olive oil in a small sauté pan. Add the onion. Sauté until softened. Add the garlic and oregano. Cook for 1 minute. Cool. Process the broccoli, sautéed onion, undrained chiles and Parmesan cheese in a food processor until smooth. Spoon into a bowl. Add as much sour cream as needed for the desired consistency, stirring constantly. Season with salt and pepper. Stir in the tomato and bacon. Chill, covered, for up to 12 hours.

For the tortilla triangles, brush the tortillas lightly with water and divide into stacks of 3 each. Cut into wedges and place on lightly oiled baking sheets. Sprinkle with coarse salt. Bake at 375 degrees for 10 to 15 minutes or until crisp and light brown. Store in an airtight container.

To serve, spoon the dip into a serving dish and serve with tortilla triangles.

Caramel Dip for Apples

Great with uncooked sweet potato wedges also

- **Serves 4 to 6**
- **Can do ahead**

1/2 cup (1 stick) butter
3 tablespoons brown sugar
1 teaspoon vanilla extract
1 cup sour cream

Melt the butter and brown sugar in a saucepan, stirring constantly. Cool. Add vanilla and sour cream and mix well. Spoon into a serving dish. Serve as a dip with apple wedges.

Note: Dip apple wedges in lemon juice to prevent browning. May prepare the caramel dip ahead of time and store, covered, in the refrigerator.

Crab Meat Dip

So delicious

- **Serves 6 to 8**
- **Oven Temperature 350 degrees**
- **Bake 18 to 20 minutes**

8 ounces cream cheese, softened
3/4 cup mayonnaise
1 (14-ounce) can artichoke hearts, drained, chopped
1/4 cup chopped onion
1/2 teaspoon salt
3 ounces Parmesan cheese, grated
1 (14-ounce) package imitation crab meat

Beat the cream cheese and mayonnaise in a mixer bowl until smooth. Add the artichoke hearts, onion, salt and Parmesan cheese and mix well. Stir in the crab meat. Spoon into a 9-inch pie plate. Bake at 350 degrees for 18 to 20 minutes or until heated through.

Note: Can use light cream cheese and fat-free mayonnaise in this recipe.

Greek Cucumber Yogurt Dip

Delicious

- **Serves 6 to 8**
- **Must do ahead**
- **Chill a few to 12 hours**

1 large slim cucumber, peeled, seeded, minced
3 to 4 garlic cloves, minced
1 large container plain yogurt
1/2 to 1 teaspoon lemon juice
Salt to taste

Press the minced cucumber in a fine sieve to extract the liquid. Combine the cucumber, garlic, yogurt, lemon juice and salt in a bowl and mix well. Chill, covered, for a few hours to 12 hours. Spoon into a serving dish and garnish with parsley. Serve as a dip with assorted bite-size fresh vegetables.

Note: Can also be served as an accompaniment to fish, lamb, chicken or roast beef. Can store in the refrigerator for 5 to 7 days. Can use sour cream instead of yogurt.

Gorgonzola Cheese Dip

Lower in fat, but not in lost flavor

- **Serves 6 to 8**
- **Must do ahead**
- **Chill 8 to 12 hours**

3 cups low-fat sour cream
2 teaspoons Worcestershire sauce
1 teaspoon dry mustard
1 cup crumbled Gorgonzola cheese

Blend the sour cream, Worcestershire sauce and dry mustard in a bowl. Stir in the Gorgonzola cheese. Chill, covered, for 8 to 12 hours. Serve as a dip with bite-size fresh vegetables, crackers or bread sticks.

Creamy Low-Fat Pesto Dip

Great as a dip or with pasta

- **Serves 12**
- **Must do ahead**
- **Chill**

1 cup nonfat cottage cheese
½ cup packed fresh basil
1 tablespoon pine nuts
¼ teaspoon salt
Dash of freshly ground black pepper
Dash of cayenne pepper

Blend the cottage cheese, basil, pine nuts, salt, black pepper and cayenne pepper in a food processor or blender until smooth. Chill, covered, in the refrigerator. Serve as a dip with assorted vegetable sticks or add to cooled cooked pasta for a summer salad.

Note: May add a small amount of minced garlic.

Pretzel Dip

Mustard lover's delight

- **Serves 6 to 8**

¼ cup dry mustard
2 tablespoons apple cider vinegar
1 tablespoon water
¼ cup sugar
1 egg yolk
8 ounces cream cheese, softened

Mix the dry mustard, vinegar and water in a small saucepan. Add the sugar and egg yolk. Cook over medium heat until thickened, whisking constantly with a wire whisk. Beat the cream cheese in a mixer bowl until light and fluffy. Add the mustard mixture and beat until smooth. Serve as a dip with pretzels.

Black Bean Mango Salsa

The "In Thing"

- **Serves 6 to 8**
- **Must do ahead**
- **Chill**

2 cups cooked black beans
1 red bell pepper, chopped
1/2 cup chopped mango or peach
1/4 cup chopped cilantro
1/2 cup chopped red onion
2 tablespoons lime juice
2 tablespoons olive oil
2 teaspoons cumin

Combine the black beans, red pepper, mango, cilantro, red onion, lime juice, olive oil and cumin in a bowl and mix well. Chill, covered, in the refrigerator.

Fresh Salsa

Light and Healthy

- **Serves 6 to 8**

4 jalapeño peppers
1 green bell pepper, quartered
4 tomatillos, peeled
5 Roma tomatoes, quartered
2 medium onions, quartered
2 garlic cloves, peeled
Juice of 1 lime
Cooked fresh sweet corn kernels (optional)

Process the jalapeño peppers, green pepper, tomatillos, Roma tomatoes, onions, garlic and lime juice in a food processor until of the desired degree of chunkiness. Stir in the corn. Serve with unsalted tortilla chips.

Super-Duper Salsa

The peaches enhance the flavor

Bring the vegetable oil, onion, tomatoes, peaches, tomato sauce, jalapeño peppers, green pepper and cilantro to a simmer in a saucepan. Simmer for 1 hour, stirring occasionally. Remove from the heat and stir in the vinegar. Serve over foods or as a dip.

- **Serves 6 to 8**
- **Must do ahead**
- **Can be frozen**

1 tablespoon vegetable oil
1 medium onion, chopped
4 medium tomatoes, chopped
2 medium peaches, peeled, chopped
1 (15-ounce) can tomato sauce
3 jalapeño peppers, seeded, chopped
1 green bell pepper, seeded, chopped
1 tablespoon crushed cilantro
1 tablespoon white vinegar

Pineapple Salsa

Fresh and Spunky Flavors

• **Serves 8**

1 whole pineapple, peeled, coarsely chopped
1 red bell pepper, coarsely chopped
1/2 cup coarsely chopped melon
3/4 cup coarsely chopped cilantro
1 (4-ounce) can green chiles, drained
1 tablespoon white wine vinegar

Combine the pineapple, red pepper, melon and cilantro in a large bowl. Add the green chiles and vinegar and mix well.

Cucumber Party Snacks

Refreshing

• **Serves 8 to 10**

8 ounces light cream cheese, softened
1/2 cup mayonnaise
1 envelope Italian salad dressing mix
1 loaf party rye bread, sliced
1 cucumber
Dillweed to taste

Combine the cream cheese, mayonnaise and salad dressing mix in a bowl and mix until smooth. Spread on the party rye bread slices. Cut the cucumber into thin slices. Arrange on the top of each slice of prepared party rye bread. Sprinkle lightly with dillweed.

Cheese Spread

Many ways to serve

- **Serves 8**
- **Must do ahead**
- **Chill several hours**

8 ounces extra-sharp Cheddar cheese, grated
1 medium onion, grated
Mayonnaise

Mix the cheese and onion in a bowl. Add enough mayonnaise to moisten, stirring until the mixture holds together. Chill, covered, in the refrigerator for several hours to blend the flavors. Serve with crackers, bagel chips or Triscuits.

Note: Can also use as a spread on bread and broil for an open-face cheese sandwich or use as a topping for hamburgers.

Variation: Stir in chopped ham or chopped green bell pepper.

Hungarian Cheese Spread

Flavorful

- **Serves 6 to 8**

8 ounces cream cheese, softened
1/4 cup (1/2 stick) butter, softened
1 tablespoon caraway seeds
5 green onions, finely chopped
1 tablespoon anchovy paste
1/4 teaspoon paprika

Beat the cream cheese and butter in a mixer bowl until smooth. Add the caraway seeds, green onions, anchovy paste and paprika and mix well. Spoon into a serving bowl. Serve with assorted crackers.

Note: Can shape into a ball or into the desired shaped mold.

Layered Cheese Spread

Party fare

- **Serves 20**
- **Must do ahead**

Herb Cream Cheese Layer

- **Chill**

Cheddar Cheese Layer

- **Chill 3 to 12 hours**

HERB CREAM CHEESE LAYER
1/2 cup fresh parsley leaves
1 tablespoon fresh thyme leaves, or 1/2 teaspoon dried thyme
1 tablespoon chopped fresh basil, or 1/2 teaspoon dried basil
1 tablespoon fresh tarragon leaves, or 1/2 teaspoon dried tarragon
1 garlic clove, coarsely chopped
16 ounces cream cheese, softened, chopped
1/2 cup (1 stick) butter, softened
1 teaspoon Worcestershire sauce
1/2 teaspoon red wine vinegar

CHEDDAR CHEESE LAYER
12 ounces sharp Cheddar cheese, shredded
1/4 cup milk
1/3 cup sour cream
1/4 cup (1/2 stick) butter, softened
2 tablespoons chopped fresh sage leaves, or 1/2 teaspoon dried sage
1 tablespoon chopped fresh chives
1 teaspoon Dijon mustard

For the herb cream cheese layer, line a 7- or 8-inch springform pan with plastic wrap, leaving an overhang. Process the parsley, thyme, basil, tarragon and garlic in a food processor until finely chopped. Add the cream cheese, 1/2 cup butter, Worcestershire sauce and vinegar and process until creamy and well mixed. Spread evenly in the prepared pan. Chill in the refrigerator.

For the Cheddar cheese layer, process the Cheddar cheese, milk, sour cream and 1/4 cup butter in a food processor until smooth and creamy. Add the sage, chives and mustard and process until well mixed. Spoon over the herb cream cheese layer and spread evenly. Chill, covered with plastic wrap, for 3 to 12 hours.

To serve, uncover the pan and invert onto a serving plate. Release the side; remove the bottom and plastic wrap. Spread the surface with a small spatula until smooth. Garnish with fresh herbs and edible flowers. Let stand at room temperature until of a spreading consistency before serving.

Jezebel Sauce

Keep on hand for unexpected guests

- **Yields 5 cups**
- **Must do ahead**
- **Chill 1 to 2 days**

18 ounces pineapple preserves
18 ounces apple jelly
1 (5-ounce) jar prepared horseradish, drained
1 small can dry mustard
1 tablespoon cracked pepper

Combine the preserves, jelly, horseradish, dry mustard and pepper in a bowl and whisk well using a wire whisk. Spoon into airtight containers. Chill for 1 to 2 days before serving. Store in the refrigerator.

To serve, spoon generously over an 8-ounce block of cream cheese. Serve with crackers.

Hummus

Very good

- **Serves 8 to 10**

TAHINI SAUCE
1/4 cup sesame seeds
1 teaspoon sesame oil
1 tablespoon lemon juice
1/2 teaspoon salt
1/2 cup water

HUMMUS
1 (24-ounce) can chick-peas, cooked, drained
3 ounces fresh lemon juice
4 garlic cloves, minced
3 ounces olive oil
2 tablespoons chopped fresh parsley
2 tablespoons chopped fresh mint
Salt and pepper to taste

For the sauce, blend the sesame seeds, sesame oil, 1 tablespoon lemon juice and 1/2 teaspoon salt in a blender or food processor until smooth. Add the water gradually, processing until of the desired consistency.

For the hummus, combine 4 ounces of the tahini sauce, chick-peas, 3 ounces lemon juice, garlic, olive oil, parsley, mint, salt and pepper to taste in a food processor container and process until smooth. Serve with fresh pita bread and fresh vegetable slices.

Sun-Dried Tomato Spread

Mold for a great presentation

- **Serves 8**

16 ounces cream cheese, softened
½ cup chopped, drained, oil-pack sun-dried tomatoes
8 green onions, chopped
½ cup chopped pecans
Worcestershire sauce to taste
Hot pepper sauce to taste

Beat the cream cheese in a mixer bowl until smooth. Add the sun-dried tomatoes, green onions, pecans, Worcestershire sauce and hot pepper sauce and mix well. Serve with crackers.

Vidalia Onion Spread

Delicious

- **Serves 10 to 12**
- **Oven Temperature 350 degrees**
- **Bake 10 to 15 minutes**

1 cup minced Vidalia onion
1 cup cubed Swiss cheese
1 cup mayonnaise

Mix the onion, cheese and mayonnaise in a bowl. Spoon into an ovenproof serving dish. Bake at 350 degrees for 10 to 15 minutes or until soft and creamy. Serve with crackers.

Note: Can vary the servings by using equal amounts of the ingredients.

Peanut Butter Spread

Never too old

- **Serves 12 to 14**

4 ounces Major Grey's chutney
3 ounces cream cheese, softened
1/4 teaspoon Worcestershire sauce
1/4 teaspoon seasoned salt
8 ounces chunky peanut butter
Dry red wine

Pour the chutney into a bowl and cut some of the larger pieces into smaller chunks. Add the cream cheese, Worcestershire sauce, seasoned salt and peanut butter and mix well. Stir in enough wine to moisten the mixture. Serve on crackers or icebox rye bread.

***Note:** Can store in the refrigerator for weeks.*

Carrot Pâté

Noteworthy

- **Serves 8**
- **Must do ahead**
- **Chill**

2 tablespoons olive oil
1 medium white onion, coarsely chopped
1 pound carrots, peeled, shredded
1 cup orange juice
2 tablespoons finely chopped orange peel
1/4 teaspoon salt
1/4 teaspoon freshly ground pepper
1/2 teaspoon curry powder
1/4 cup light mayonnaise
1 tablespoon coarse-grain prepared mustard or Dijon mustard

Heat the olive oil in a skillet over low heat. Add the onion. Cook for 7 minutes or until tender. Add the carrots, orange juice, orange zest, salt, pepper and curry powder and mix well. Simmer, covered, for 10 to 15 minutes. Uncover and increase the heat. Cook until the liquid evaporates, stirring frequently. Remove from the heat and cool.

Process in a food processor until smooth. Add the mayonnaise and mustard and mix well. Spoon into a serving dish. Chill, covered, until serving time. Serve on Belgium endive leaves, on pesticide-free tulip petals or with crackers.

Note: Can garnish with capers or black olive slices or stir into the pâté.

CHICKEN PÂTÉ

NOT MADE WITH LIVERS

- **Makes about 2 cups**
- **Must do ahead**
- **Chill 2 hours to 2 days**

3 tablespoons butter
2 medium skinless boneless chicken breasts, cut into 1/2-inch pieces (about 10 ounces)
Salt and pepper to taste
1 tablespoon chopped garlic
1/3 cup lightly salted roasted cashews (about 2 ounces)
1/3 cup mayonnaise
1/2 cup finely chopped onion
3/4 cup grated asiago cheese
1/2 teaspoon hot pepper sauce
1/4 cup chopped fresh basil

Line a small bowl with plastic wrap, leaving an overhang. Melt the butter in a large heavy skillet over medium-high heat. Sprinkle the chicken with salt and pepper. Add the chicken and garlic to the skillet. Sauté for 3 minutes or until the chicken is cooked through. Stir in the cashews. Remove from the heat and cool.

Spoon into a food processor container. Add the mayonnaise, onion, cheese and hot pepper sauce and process until smooth. Add the basil and process until blended. Spoon into the prepared bowl. Chill, covered, for 2 hours or for up to 2 days. Uncover and invert onto a serving plate.

Smoked Salmon Spread

Delicious

- **Serves 8**

1 pound smoked salmon or trout, flaked
1/2 cup sour cream
1/2 cup mayonnaise
1 sweet onion, finely chopped (about 1/2 cup)
1 tablespoon capers
2 teaspoons chopped fresh dill
2 teaspoons minced fresh parsley
1/2 teaspoon coarsely ground pepper

Process the salmon, sour cream, mayonnaise, onion, capers, dill, parsley and pepper in a food processor until blended. Spoon into a serving dish. Garnish with a sprig of fresh dill. Serve with water crackers or butter wafers.

***Note:** Can also smoke your own fish for use in this recipe for a fresh smoked flavor.*

Shrimp Taco

Very good

- **Serves 8**
- **Must do ahead**
- **Chill 1 hour**

8 ounces cream cheese, softened
1/4 cup milk
1/2 bottle chili sauce
1 (4-ounce) can cooked tiny shrimp, rinsed, drained, patted dry
5 scallions, chopped
3/4 cup chopped green bell pepper
1 (4-ounce) can sliced black olives, drained, patted dry
2 cups shredded Cheddar cheese

Beat the cream cheese and milk in a mixer bowl until smooth. Spread in an even layer on a serving platter. Spread the chili sauce over the cream cheese layer. Layer the shrimp, scallions, green pepper, black olives and Cheddar cheese in the order listed over the sauce. Chill, covered, for 1 hour before serving. Serve with tortilla chips.

Cocktail Cheesecake

Wonderful

- **Serves 16 to 20**
- **Can do ahead**
- **Oven Temperature 350 degrees**
- **Bake 45 to 60 minutes**

3/4 cup toasted bread crumbs
3/4 cup finely chopped toasted walnuts
3 tablespoons unsalted butter, melted
12 ounces asiago cheese, grated
20 ounces cream cheese, softened
4 eggs
1 medium garlic clove, minced
1 tablespoon minced fresh tarragon, or 1/4 teaspoon dried tarragon
Salt and pepper to taste

Process the bread crumbs, walnuts and butter in a food processor until combined. Press over the bottom and slightly up the side of an 8-inch springform pan.

Beat the asiago cheese and cream cheese in a mixer bowl until smooth. Add the eggs 1 at a time, beating well after each addition. Add the garlic and tarragon and mix well. Season with salt and pepper. Pour into the prepared pan.

Bake at 350 degrees for 45 to 60 minutes or until set and golden brown and puffed. Remove from the oven and let stand for 30 minutes.

To serve, remove the side of the pan and place on a serving plate. Garnish with parsley. Serve with crackers.

Note: Can store in the refrigerator for several days.

Southwestern Cheesecake

Eye-Appealing Appetizer

For the crust, combine the tortilla chips and butter in a bowl and mix well. Press in a lightly greased 9-inch springform pan. Bake at 325 degrees for 15 minutes. Cool on a wire rack.

For the filling, beat the cream cheese in a mixer bowl for 3 minutes. Add the eggs and beat well. Stir in the Jack cheese, green chiles and red pepper. Pour into the tortilla crust. Bake at 325 degrees for 30 minutes. Cool for 10 minutes. Remove the side of the pan. Chill, covered, in the refrigerator until serving time.

To serve, uncover and spread the top of the cheesecake with sour cream. Garnish with sliced red and yellow bell peppers, scallions and cilantro. Serve with crackers.

- **Serves 16 to 20**
- **Must do ahead**
- **Chill**

Crust

- **Oven Temperature 325 degrees**
- **Bake 15 minutes**

Filling

- **Oven Temperature 325 degrees**
- **Bake 30 minutes**

CRUST

1½ cups crushed tortilla chips
¼ cup (½ stick) butter, melted

FILLING

19 ounces cream cheese, softened
2 eggs
1½ cups shredded Jack cheese with peppers
1 (4-ounce) can green chiles, drained, chopped
¼ teaspoon ground red pepper
1 cup sour cream

GARNISHES

Sliced red and yellow bell peppers
Scallions
Chopped cilantro

Mini Blinis

Yummy

- **Serves 10 to 20**
- **Can do ahead**
- **Can be frozen**
- **Oven Temperature 400 degrees**
- **Bake 8 to 10 minutes**

BLINIS

16 ounces cream cheese, softened
1/2 cup sugar
2 egg yolks
2 (1-pound) loaves thinly sliced white bread, crusts trimmed
1 cup sugar
1 to 3 teaspoons cinnamon, or to taste
1 cup (2 sticks) butter, melted

CURRANT DIP

2 cups sour cream
2 tablespoons currant jelly

For the blinis, beat the cream cheese, 1/2 cup sugar and egg yolks in a mixer bowl until smooth and creamy. Roll each slice of bread with a rolling pin until flattened. Spread each slice with the cream cheese mixture and roll up.

Mix 1 cup sugar and cinnamon in a bowl. Roll each roll-up in the melted butter; roll in cinnamon-sugar. Cut each into halves or quarters. Place on baking sheets. Bake at 400 degrees for 8 to 10 minutes or until golden brown.

For the dip, mix the sour cream and jelly in a bowl. Serve as a dip with the blinis.

Note: Can freeze the unbaked blinis on the baking sheets and place in freezer bags to store for later use. The frozen blinis will need to be baked longer before serving.

Artichoke Phyllo Triangles

Seconds will be a must

- **Makes 30**
- **Oven Temperature 350 degrees**
- **Bake 20 minutes**

FILLING

1/4 cup olive oil
1 large onion, chopped
1 yellow bell pepper, seeded, finely chopped
3 to 4 garlic cloves, finely chopped
1 teaspoon basil
1 teaspoon oregano
1 teaspoon thyme
1/4 teaspoon red pepper flakes
3 medium tomatoes, finely chopped
1 (14-ounce) can artichoke hearts, drained, finely chopped
1 cup chopped black olives
Salt and black pepper to taste
3 eggs, lightly beaten
1/2 cup grated Parmesan cheese
1/2 cup dry bread crumbs
8 ounces shredded provolone cheese
1/4 cup minced parsley

PHYLLO AND ASSEMBLY

1 pound phyllo, thawed
Olive oil
Dry bread crumbs

For the filling, heat 1/4 cup olive oil in a large sauté pan. Add the onion. Sauté until softened. Add the yellow pepper. Sauté until softened. Stir in the garlic, basil, oregano, thyme, red pepper flakes, tomatoes and artichokes. Simmer until of a sauce consistency. Stir in the olives. Season with salt and black pepper. Cool to room temperature. Stir in the eggs. Mix the Parmesan cheese, 1/2 cup dry bread crumbs, provolone cheese and parsley in a bowl. Stir into the artichoke mixture. Adjust the seasonings.

For the phyllo, unwrap and cut into 3 long strips. Stack the strips and keep covered with plastic wrap. Brush 1 phyllo strip with olive oil and sprinkle with dry bread crumbs. Top with another phyllo strip. Brush lightly with olive oil and sprinkle with dry bread crumbs.

To assemble, place 1 to 1 1/2 tablespoons of the filling at 1 corner of the phyllo stack. Fold phyllo over filling to form a triangle. Continue folding as for a flag. Place the triangle seam side down on an oiled baking sheet. Brush lightly with olive oil. Repeat with the remaining phyllo and filling.

Bake at 350 degrees for 20 minutes or until golden brown. Cool on wire racks.

Spanish Cheddar Squares

Light and Healthy

- **Serves 16**
- **Oven Temperature 350 degrees**
- **Bake 35 to 40 minutes**

1½ cups egg substitute
¾ cup skim milk
1 tablespoon onion flakes
1 tablespoon grated Parmesan cheese
¼ teaspoon garlic powder
⅛ teaspoon ground pepper
¼ cup dry bread crumbs
¾ cup shredded fat-free Cheddar cheese
1 (10-ounce) package frozen chopped spinach, thawed, drained
¼ cup chopped pimentos (optional)

Combine the egg substitute, skim milk, onion flakes, Parmesan cheese, garlic powder and pepper in a bowl and mix well. Sprinkle the bread crumbs evenly in a lightly greased 8x8-inch baking dish. Layer ½ cup of the Cheddar cheese, spinach and egg substitute mixture in the prepared baking dish. Sprinkle with the remaining Cheddar cheese and pimentos.

Bake at 350 degrees for 35 to 40 minutes or until set. Let stand for 10 minutes. Cut into 2-inch squares. Serve immediately.

Party Pinwheels

Do-ahead Special

Beat the cream cheese and salad dressing mix in a mixer bowl until smooth. Stir in the green onions. Spread on each tortilla. Sprinkle with the red pepper, celery and black olives. Roll up. Wrap tightly in plastic wrap. Chill for 2 hours. Trim the ends of each roll-up. Cut each into 1-inch slices.

Note: Pimentos and green chiles can be substituted for the red bell pepper and celery.

- **Makes 24 to 32**
- **Must do ahead**
- **Chill 2 hours**

16 ounces cream cheese, softened
1 envelope ranch salad dressing mix
2 green onions, minced
3 or 4 (8-inch) flour tortillas
1/2 cup chopped red bell pepper
1/2 cup chopped celery
1 (4-ounce) can sliced black olives, drained

Stuffed Mushrooms

There won't be one left on the plate

- **Serves 6**
- **Oven Temperature 325 degrees**
- **Bake 15 minutes**

18 bite-size mushrooms
1 small onion, finely chopped
5 slices bacon, cooked, crumbled
Mayonnaise
Seasoned salt to taste
1/2 cup shredded sharp Cheddar cheese

Clean the mushrooms. Remove the stems and finely chop. Place the mushroom caps in a shallow baking pan. Mix the onion, mushroom stems and bacon in a bowl. Stir in just enough mayonnaise to hold the mixture together. Season with seasoned salt. Spoon into the mushroom caps. Sprinkle with cheese. Bake, covered with foil, at 325 degrees for 15 minutes.

***Note:** This recipe can be doubled or tripled. If you have more filling than the mushroom caps will hold, spread on crackers and bake.*

Pizza on the Grill

No, it does not fall through the grill

For the dough, dissolve the yeast in the warm water in a large bowl. Add the oil. Stir in the flour and salt. Divide into 2 or more portions. Roll each portion into a circle. The dough can stand at this point, but it doesn't have to rise. Place 1 circle on a grill rack. Grill for about 5 minutes or until heated through and turn over using a spatula or tongs.

For the sauce and toppings, spread the circle with 1/2 of the sauce. Add 1/2 of the toppings of choice. Grill until the cheese melts.

Repeat with the remaining dough circle, sauce and toppings.

- **Serves 12**
- **Grill**

DOUGH
1 envelope dry yeast
1 1/4 cups warm water
2 tablespoons vegetable oil
4 cups flour
1 teaspoon salt

SAUCE AND TOPPINGS
1 cup spaghetti sauce or pizza sauce
Shredded cheese
Pepperoni slices
Chopped green bell peppers
Chopped onions
Sliced olives

Clam and Ham Filling in Puff Pastry

Warm or cold, they're great

- **Serves 15**
- **Oven Temperature 325 degrees**
- **Bake 10 to 15 minutes**

1 (7-ounce) can minced clams, drained
8 ounces slivered ham, chopped
1/3 cup chopped onion
1 cup sour cream
1 cup mayonnaise
1 cup grated Parmesan cheese
1/4 cup chopped parsley
1/2 teaspoon pepper
15 miniature puff pastry shells

Combine the clams, ham, onion, sour cream, mayonnaise, Parmesan cheese, parsley and pepper in a bowl and mix well. Spoon into miniature puff pastry shells. Place on a baking sheet. Bake at 325 degrees for 10 to 15 minutes or until heated through.

Note: Can also spoon into miniature phyllo shells and microwave just until the filling is warm. Can serve the filling cold with crackers.

Seafood Tarts

You Can't Eat Just One

For the crust, mix the butter, cream cheese and 3 cups flour in a bowl to form a soft dough. Roll the dough into small balls. Place in miniature tart pans and press to form a cup. Chill in the refrigerator.

For the filling, combine the eggs, mayonnaise, 2 tablespoons flour and wine in a bowl and mix well. Stir in the shrimp, celery and green onions.

To assemble, fill the tart cups with the filling. Bake at 350 degrees for 30 to 35 minutes or until set.

- **Serves 72**
- **Must do ahead**
- **Chill**
- **Oven Temperature 350 degrees**
- **Bake 30 to 35 minutes**

CRUST
1 1/2 cups (3 sticks) butter, softened
12 ounces cream cheese, softened
3 cups flour

FILLING
2 eggs, beaten
1/2 cup mayonnaise
2 tablespoons flour
1/2 cup dry white wine
1 2/3 cups chopped cooked shrimp
1/3 cup chopped celery
1/3 cup chopped green onions

Meatballs

Super simple and bountiful

• **Serves 8**

1 pound bulk sausage
1 egg
$^1/_3$ cup cracker crumbs
$^1/_2$ teaspoon ground sage
$^1/_2$ cup catsup
1 teaspoon balsamic vinegar
1 tablespoon brown sugar
1 tablespoon soy sauce

Combine the sausage, egg, cracker crumbs and sage in a bowl and mix well. Shape into small balls. Cook in a skillet for 15 minutes or until brown and cooked through; drain.

Mix the catsup, balsamic vinegar, brown sugar and soy sauce in a bowl. Pour over the meatballs in the skillet. Simmer until the meatballs are candied. Serve hot.

***Note:** This recipe is a snap to make and can easily be multiplied to feed the entire symphony and their friends.*

Zesty Sausage

Fabulous appetizer

• **Serves 4**

1 (16-ounce) package kielbasa sausage
$1^1/_2$ cups white wine
1 teaspoon sugar
$^1/_4$ cup Dijon mustard
2 tablespoons parsley

Cut the sausage into 1-inch slices. Cut each slice into quarters. Place in 1 layer in a heavy skillet. Add the wine to cover. Bring to a boil. Boil until the wine is almost evaporated. Add the sugar and Dijon mustard. Cook until the sausage is glazed. Add the parsley and toss to mix well.

***Note:** Can also be served as a main dish with mashed potatoes and a mild vegetable such as yellow squash or zucchini.*

Deviled Shrimp

Tantalizing

For the dressing, combine the lemon juice, olive oil, vinegar, dry mustard, salt, cayenne pepper, black pepper, bay leaf and garlic in a bowl and mix well.

For the shrimp, cook the shrimp in boiling water to cover in a large saucepan for 4 minutes or until the shrimp turn pink. Drain the shrimp and place under cold running water until the shrimp are warm.

To assemble, pour the dressing over the warm shrimp in a serving bowl. Sprinkle with the red onion, lemon zest, black olives and pimento. Serve at room temperature.

- **Serves 6 to 8**

DRESSING
1/2 cup freshly squeezed lemon juice
1/4 cup olive oil
1 tablespoon white vinegar
1 tablespoon dry mustard
1 teaspoon salt
1/8 teaspoon cayenne pepper
Freshly ground black pepper to taste
1/2 bay leaf, ground
1 garlic clove, minced

SHRIMP AND ASSEMBLY
2 pounds shrimp, shelled, deveined
1/4 red onion, thinly sliced
Zest of 1 lemon
Black olives (optional)
Red pimento (optional)

Water Chestnut Appetizers

You'll crave more

- **Serves 8**
- **Oven Temperature 425 degrees**
- **Bake 20 minutes**
- **Oven Temperature 375 degrees**
- **Bake 20 minutes**

WATER CHESTNUTS
1 pound sliced bacon
3 (8-ounce) cans whole water chestnuts, drained

SAUCE
3/4 cup catsup
3/4 cup mayonnaise
1 1/2 cups sugar

For the water chestnuts, cut each slice of bacon into thirds. Wrap a piece of the bacon around each water chestnut and secure with a wooden pick. Arrange close together in a 9x13-inch baking pan. Bake at 425 degrees for 20 minutes or until cooked through; drain.

For the sauce, mix the catsup, mayonnaise and sugar in a bowl.

To assemble and serve, pour the sauce over the water chestnuts. Bake at 375 degrees for 20 minutes. Serve while still warm.

Appetizers

Baked Tortilla Chips

Serve with Hummus, Salsa or Guacamole

Mix the olive oil, garlic salt and ground cumin seeds in a bowl. Brush each tortilla with the olive oil mixture. Cut into bite-size pieces. Place on a baking sheet. Bake at 450 degrees for 5 minutes or until crisp.

- **Serves 8**
- **Oven Temperature 450 degrees**
- **Bake 5 minutes**

1/2 cup olive oil
1 tablespoon garlic salt, or to taste
1/2 tablespoon ground cumin seeds
1 (10-count) package flour tortillas

Cheese Coins

Great with Cocktails

Combine the butter and Cheddar cheese in a bowl and mix well by hand. Add the onion soup mix and flour and mix well by hand. Divide into 4 equal portions. Roll each portion into a log 1/2 inch in diameter. Wrap in plastic wrap and freeze.

To serve, thaw the logs slightly. Cut into 1/4-inch slices. Place close together on a nonstick baking sheet. Bake at 350 degrees for 20 minutes. Cool on a large nonrecycled paper bag. Store in an airtight container.

Variation: May also wrap the dough around small pimento-stuffed olives and bake.

- **Serves 12 to 16**
- **Must do ahead**
- **Freeze**
- **Oven Temperature 350 degrees**
- **Bake 20 minutes**

1/2 cup (1 stick) butter, softened
4 ounces sharp Cheddar cheese, shredded, at room temperature
1/2 envelope onion soup mix
1 cup flour

Lavender Lemonade

Refreshing

- **Serves 18**

1 (12-ounce) can frozen lemonade concentrate
1 gallon cold water
1/4 cup pesticide-free fresh or dried lavender flowers
2 cups boiling water

Combine the lemonade concentrate and cold water in a large pitcher and blend well. Steep the lavender in the boiling water in a saucepan for 10 minutes. Strain into the prepared lemonade. Serve over ice and garnish with mint sprigs.

Sunshine Anytime Punch

Great for brunches, graduation parties, etc.

- **Serves 18 to 20**
- **Must do ahead**
- **Freeze until firm**

4 cups sugar
6 cups water
2 (12-ounce) cans frozen orange juice concentrate, thawed
1 (12-ounce) can frozen lemonade concentrate, thawed
1 (46-ounce) can pineapple juice
5 large bananas, puréed
6 (1-quart) bottles lemon-lime soda

Bring the sugar and water to a boil in a saucepan. Boil for 1 minute. Cool.

Mix the orange juice concentrate and lemonade concentrate in a large container. Stir in the sugar-water. Add the pineapple juice and bananas and mix well. Pour into five 1-quart freezer containers. Freeze until firm.

To serve, pour lemon-lime soda over slightly thawed concentrate in a punch bowl 30 to 60 minutes before serving.

Margaritas

Adults only

- **Serves 8**

1 (8-ounce) can frozen limeade concentrate
1 (8-ounce) can tequila
1 (8-ounce) can beer

Combine the limeade concentrate, tequila and beer in a blender container. Add enough ice to fill the blender container. Process until mixed.

Kahlúa

Strictly adult

- **Makes 4 cups**
- **Must do ahead**

4 cups sugar
1/2 cup instant coffee
Dash of salt
3 cups water
1 cup 80-proof vodka
3 tablespoons vanilla extract

Mix the sugar and coffee powder in a 3-quart saucepan. Add the salt and water. Bring to a boil, stirring constantly until the sugar dissolves. Reduce the heat. Simmer for 1 hour. Remove from the heat. Stir in the vodka and vanilla. Cool. Pour into a sterilized bottle with a lid and cover.

Hot Cider

Great Way to Warm Up

- **Serves 20**

2 quarts apple cider
1 quart cranberry juice
2 cups orange juice
1 teaspoon whole cloves
1 teaspoon whole allspice
3 cinnamon sticks, broken
1 cup sugar

Combine the apple cider, cranberry juice and orange juice in the bottom of a large coffee maker. Place the cloves, allspice, cinnamon sticks and sugar in a percolator basket lined with a filter. Perk and serve hot.

***Note:** 1½ times this recipe fills a 30-cup percolator.*

Mulled Red Wine

Good for a Cool Night

- **Serves 16**

3 cups water
1½ cups sugar
6 cinnamon sticks
6 whole cloves
3 lemons, thinly sliced
1½ liters burgundy

Bring the water, sugar, cinnamon and cloves to a boil in a saucepan. Boil for 5 minutes. Add the lemons and remove from the heat. Let stand, covered, for 10 minutes. Add the wine. Return to the heat and heat gradually; do not boil. Strain into a punch bowl. Garnish with some of the thinly sliced lemons. Serve hot.

Soups

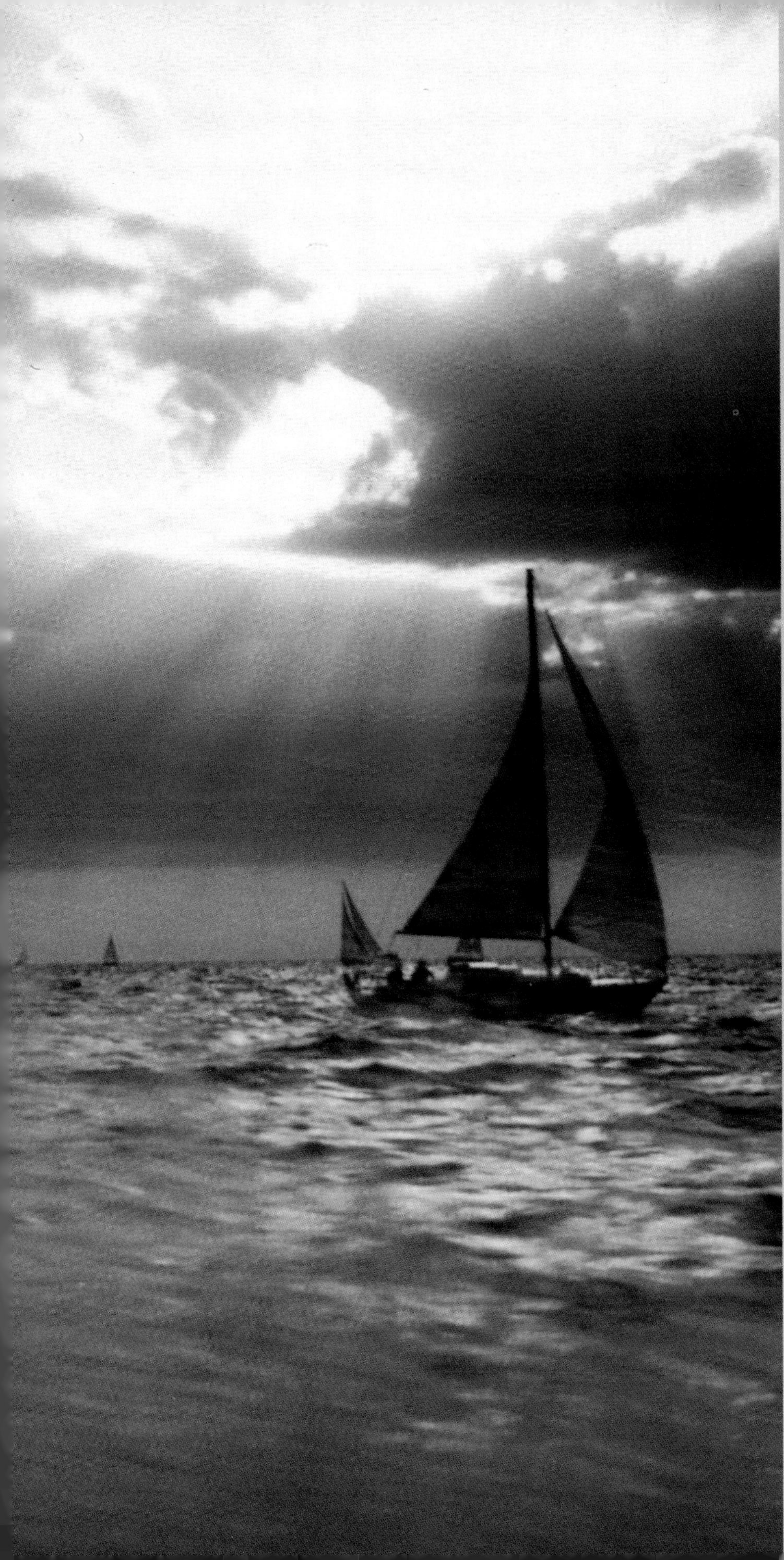

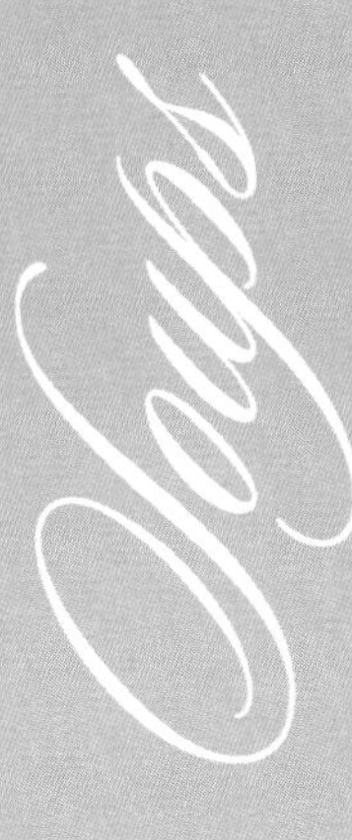

Evening Sail on
Lake Michigan

Frosted Ginger-Minted Two-Melon Soup

Beautiful presentation as soup or dessert

- **Serves 6 to 8**
- **Must do ahead**
- **Chill 3 hours or up to 2 days**

CANTALOUPE PURÉE
1 cantaloupe, peeled, seeded, cut into 1/2-inch to 1-inch pieces
2 tablespoons fresh lemon or orange juice
1 teaspoon fresh gingerroot, chopped

HONEYDEW MELON PURÉE
1 small honeydew melon, peeled, seeded, cut into 1/2-inch to 1-inch pieces
2 tablespoons fresh lime juice
4 fresh mint leaves

GARNISHES
Fresh mint sprigs
Citrus peel

For the cantaloupe purée, process the cantaloupe, lemon juice and gingerroot in a blender or food processor until smooth. Pour into a glass jar with a lid. Chill, covered, for 3 hours or up to 2 days.

For the honeydew melon purée, process the honeydew melon, lime juice and mint leaves in a blender or food processor until smooth. Pour into a glass jar with a lid. Chill, covered, for 3 hours or up to 2 days.

To serve, place each chilled purée in separate containers with pouring spouts. Pour equal amounts of each simultaneously into each clear glass serving bowl or champagne glass; the 2 purées will remain separated while being served and eaten. Garnish with fresh mint sprigs and citrus peel.

Fresh Asparagus Soup

Spring specialty

- **Serves 4 to 6**

2 pounds fresh asparagus, trimmed
1 small onion, chopped
1 teaspoon salt
1 (14-ounce) can chicken broth
1½ cups light cream
2 garlic cloves, minced, or to taste
Salt and pepper to taste

Combine the asparagus, onion, 1 teaspoon salt and ¾ cup chicken broth in a large saucepan. Cook for 10 minutes or until the asparagus is tender.

Process in a blender until smooth and creamy. Pour into a bowl. Stir in the cream, garlic and salt and pepper to taste. Add the remaining broth and mix well. Serve very hot or chilled.

***Note:** Do not substitute canned or frozen asparagus for the fresh asparagus.*

Broccoli Soup

Creamy and Smooth

• **Serves 6**

3 tablespoons margarine
1/2 cup chopped onion
1/2 cup chopped celery
1 (10-ounce) package frozen broccoli
1 cup water
2 tablespoons instant chicken bouillon
1 (12-ounce) can evaporated milk
1 1/2 cups milk

GARNISHES
Chopped fresh parsley
Slivered almonds

Melt the margarine in a skillet. Add the onion and celery. Sauté until the onion is transparent.

Cook the broccoli in the water in a saucepan until tender. Process the broccoli and sautéed vegetables in a blender until smooth. Pour into a bowl. Add the instant bouillon, stirring until dissolved. Add the evaporated milk and milk and mix well. Ladle into serving bowls and garnish with chopped parsley and almonds.

Note: Can thicken the soup with a small amount of cornstarch.

Butternut Squash and Apple Soup

Savory

Cut slashes into the whole squash with a knife. Place in a glass dish. Microwave on High for 20 minutes. Peel and remove the seeds.

Combine the squash, apples, onion, rosemary, marjoram, salt, white pepper, chicken broth, water, bread, cream and brown sugar in a saucepan and mix well. Bring to a boil and reduce the heat. Simmer for 30 minutes. Cool. Process in a food processor until smooth. Reheat to serve or serve cool. Sprinkle each serving with parsley.

Note: Can bake the squash in a 400-degree oven until tender.

- **Serves 8**

1 (1-pound) butternut squash
3 Granny Smith apples, peeled, cored, coarsely chopped
1 medium onion, coarsely chopped
1/4 teaspoon rosemary
1/4 teaspoon marjoram
Salt and white pepper to taste
3 (10-ounce) cans chicken broth
2 broth cans water
2 slices white bread, torn
1/4 cup heavy cream
1/4 cup packed brown sugar
1 tablespoon chopped fresh parsley

Hearty Cauliflower Soup

Betcha can't eat just one bowl

- **Serves 6 to 8**

4 cups caulifowerets
1 cup thinly sliced carrots
2 cups water
8 ounces fully cooked smoked kielbasa sausage, chopped
1/2 cup chopped onion
1/3 cup flour
1/8 teaspoon pepper
2 cup milk
8 ounces American cheese, cubed

Cook the cauliflowerets and carrots in the water in a saucepan until tender. Do not drain.

Brown the sausage and onion in a skillet over medium heat. Stir in the flour and pepper. Add the milk gradually. Bring to a boil. Cook for 2 minutes, stirring constantly. Add the undrained vegetables. Cook until heated through. Add the cheese, stirring until melted. Ladle into soup bowls.

Austrian Cream Cheese Soup

A Favorite from the Hearthstone Restaurant

- **Serves 6**

1/2 cup finely chopped celery
1/2 cup thinly sliced leek bulbs
2 large shallots, chopped
5 tablespoons margarine
2/3 cup flour
4 cups hot double-strength chicken broth
2 cups heavy cream
16 ounces cream cheese, cut into 1- to 2-inch cubes
1/2 teaspoon garlic powder
1/2 teaspoon white pepper

GARNISH
Sautéed leeks

Sauté the celery, leeks and shallots in margarine in a skillet for 15 minutes or until soft. Add the flour all at once. Cook until the flour turns golden brown, stirring constantly; do not burn. Add the hot chicken broth. Return to a boil, stirring constantly. Add the cream and return to a boil. Add the cream cheese and turn off the heat, stirring until the cream cheese melts. Season with garlic powder and white pepper.

Process the mixture in a food processor until smooth. Adjust seasonings. Ladle into soup bowls and garnish with additional sautéed leeks.

Note: Can add 1/2 to 1 cup chopped cooked ham to the soup after processing.

Corn Chowder

Delightful First Course

- **Serves 4 to 6**

2 ounces thick bacon, chopped
1 small onion, minced
1/4 green bell pepper, seeded, minced
3 large potatoes, chopped
  (about 3 cups)
2 cups boiling water
2 cups cooked fresh whole kernel
  corn
1 quart milk
1 tablespoon butter
2 teaspoons salt
1/4 teaspoon paprika

Sauté the bacon in a large skillet until brown and crisp. Remove the bacon to a bowl, reserving the pan drippings.

Add the onion and green pepper to the reserved drippings in the skillet. Sauté for 5 to 7 minutes or until the onion is translucent. Add the potatoes and boiling water. Simmer, covered, for 20 minutes or until the potatoes are tender. Add the corn, milk, butter, salt and paprika. Heat to just below the boiling point. Ladle into soup bowls. Sprinkle with the bacon and add an additional dab of butter.

***Note:** Can substitute an undrained 12-ounce can of whole kernel corn for the fresh corn.*

Gazpacho

Hard to resist

- **Serves 6**
- **Must do ahead**
- **Chill**

1 large cucumber, peeled, seeded, cut into 1/4-inch pieces
1/2 green bell pepper, finely chopped
1 pimento, finely chopped
1/2 large onion, finely chopped
3 tablespoons finely chopped parsley
2 tablespoons finely chopped fresh basil
1 large garlic clove, minced
1 cup Italian salad dressing
6 large tomatoes, peeled, seeded, chopped, or 1 (14-ounce) can tomatoes
1 cup tomato juice
Salt and pepper to taste

ASSEMBLY
Homemade croutons
Sour cream
Cucumber spears

Combine the cucumber, green pepper, pimento, onion, parsley, basil and garlic in a bowl and mix well. Stir in the salad dressing. Add the tomatoes and tomato juice. Season with salt and pepper to taste. Chill, covered, until serving time.

To assemble and serve, ladle into chilled serving bowls or stemmed glasses. Serve with homemade croutons, a spoonful of sour cream and a cucumber spear.

Note: Can substitute one 14-ounce can tomatoes for the fresh tomatoes, straining the juice and chopping the tomatoes first. For a more sweet-and-sour taste, add vinegar and sugar to taste.

Lentil Stew

Remarkable

- **Serves 8 to 10**

1 pound Italian sausage
$^1/_4$ cup olive oil
1 onion, chopped
2 ribs celery, chopped
1 bay leaf
1 garlic clove, chopped
1 carrot, chopped
1 pound dried lentils
1 (28-ounce) can whole tomatoes
2 quarts water
Salt and pepper to taste

Cook the sausage over medium-high heat in a stockpot until cooked through; drain. Remove the sausage to a warm platter. Cut into pieces.

Add the olive oil and onion to the stockpot. Sauté for 2 minutes or until the onion is translucent. Add the celery, bay leaf and garlic. Sauté for 2 minutes. Add the carrot.

Rinse the lentils. Add the lentils, undrained tomatoes and water to the stockpot. Add the sausage. Bring to a boil and reduce the heat. Simmer for 1 to $1^1/_2$ hours. Season with salt and pepper to taste. Remove the bay leaf. Serve over rice in a soup bowl.

***Note:** Can add one 10-ounce package frozen or fresh spinach.*

Mushroom Barley Soup

Unusual

- **Serves 6 to 8**

1/2 cup uncooked pearl barley
6 1/2 cups stock or water
3 to 4 tablespoons soy sauce
3 to 4 tablespoons dry sherry
1 cup (heaping) chopped onion
2 garlic cloves, minced
3 tablespoons butter
1 pound fresh mushrooms, sliced
1/2 to 1 teaspoon salt
Pepper to taste

Cook the barley in 1 1/2 cups of the stock in a stockpot until tender. Add the remaining stock, soy sauce and sherry.

Sauté the onion and garlic in the butter in a skillet until translucent. Add the mushrooms and salt. Sauté until the mushrooms are tender. Add to the barley. Season with pepper. Simmer, covered, over low heat for 20 minutes. Adjust the seasonings. Ladle into soup bowls.

Parsnip Soup

You'll never believe it's parsnips

- **Serves 4 to 6**

¼ cup (½ stick) butter or margarine
1 pound parsnips, peeled, thinly sliced
1 cup chopped celery
3 tablespoons flour
¼ cup chopped parsley
⅛ teaspoon white pepper
4 cups chicken broth
Salt to taste
Grated Parmesan cheese to taste

GARNISH
Sour cream

Melt the butter in a saucepan. Add the parsnips and celery. Cook, covered, over medium heat for 10 minutes, stirring occasionally.

Process the cooked vegetables, flour, parsley and white pepper in a blender or food processor until blended. Add 3 cups of the chicken broth. Process at high speed until smooth. Return to the saucepan. Stir in the remaining chicken broth. Simmer over low heat until heated through. Season with salt.

Ladle into soup bowls. Sprinkle with Parmesan cheese. Garnish each serving with a dollop of sour cream.

Split Pea, Bean and Barley Soup

A HEALTHY AND DELICIOUS VEGETARIAN SOUP

Heat the vegetable oil in a large heavy saucepan over medium heat. Add the onions. Sauté until the onions are translucent. Add the split green peas, lima beans, barley, water, bay leaf and celery seeds.

Bring to a boil and reduce the heat. Simmer for 1½ hours. Add the potato, carrot, celery, basil, salt, thyme and pepper. Simmer for 30 minutes or longer. Remove the bay leaf. Ladle into soup bowls.

- **Serves 6**

1 tablespoon vegetable oil
2 onions, chopped
½ cup dried split green peas, rinsed
¼ cup dried lima beans, rinsed
¼ cup barley, rinsed
5 cups water
1 bay leaf
1 teaspoon celery seeds
1 potato, peeled, chopped
1 carrot, chopped
1 rib celery, chopped
1 teaspoon basil
1 teaspoon salt
½ teaspoon thyme
¼ teaspoon pepper

Cajun Vegetable Chili

Delicious

- **Serves 6**

1 large onion, chopped
1 green bell pepper, chopped
1 red bell pepper, chopped
2 tablespoons olive oil
1 tablespoon minced garlic
2½ tablespoons chili powder
1 tablespoon cumin
1 (28-ounce) can peeled plum tomatoes, chopped
2 teaspoons thyme
2 (15-ounce) cans black-eyed peas
1 cup cooked corn
1 large bunch fresh spinach, trimmed, rinsed, chopped
Salt and pepper to taste
2 tablespoons lemon juice
Cooked white rice
½ cup nonfat plain yogurt
4 scallions, thinly sliced on the diagonal

Cook the onion, green pepper and red pepper in the olive oil in a large stockpot over low heat for 10 to 12 minutes or until the onion is transparent. Add the garlic, chili powder and cumin. Cook for 2 minutes. Add the tomatoes, thyme, black-eyed peas and corn. Cook for 20 minutes. Remove from the heat. Stir in the spinach, salt, pepper and lemon juice.

To serve, ladle over rice in a soup bowl. Add a dollop of yogurt and sprinkle with scallions.

Chocolate Chili

Unique

• **Serves 6 to 8**

1 large sweet onion
2 tablespoons olive oil
2 pounds ground sirloin
1 (15-ounce) can kidney beans, rinsed, drained
3 (10-ounce) cans tomato soup
1/2 (2-ounce) jar chili powder
1 (14-ounce) can beef broth
1/2 cup chocolate chips
1 jar raspberry salsa

Sauté the onion in the olive oil in a skillet. Brown the beef in a skillet; drain. Combine the onion and beef in a large saucepan. Add the kidney beans, tomato soup, chili powder, beef broth, chocolate chips and salsa.

Cook over medium heat until heated through, stirring frequently; watch carefully. Ladle into soup bowls.

Cincinnati Chili

Not like any other

- **Serves 6**
- **Can be made 3 days ahead**
- **Can be frozen**

2 large onions, chopped
3 tablespoons vegetable oil
4 garlic cloves, minced
3 pounds ground chuck
1/4 cup chili powder
2 teaspoons cumin
2 teaspoons sweet paprika
3/4 teaspoon cayenne pepper
1/4 teaspoon ground allspice
1/4 teaspoon cinnamon
1/4 teaspoon turmeric
1/4 teaspoon coriander
1/4 teaspoon cardamom
2 (8-ounce) cans tomato sauce
2 tablespoons baking cocoa
1 tablespoon molasses
3 cups canned beef broth
3 cups water
2 tablespoons cider vinegar
Salt and black pepper to taste

Cook the onions in the vegetable oil in a large stockpot over medium heat until softened. Add the garlic. Cook for 1 minute, stirring constantly. Add the ground chuck. Cook until brown and crumbly, stirring frequently. Add the chili powder, cumin, paprika, cayenne pepper, allspice, cinnamon, turmeric, coriander and cardamom. Cook for 1 minute, stirring constantly. Add the tomato sauce, baking cocoa, molasses, beef broth, water, vinegar, salt and black pepper. Bring to a boil and reduce the heat to low. Simmer for 1 1/2 hours or until thickened, stirring occasionally. The chili will not be thick.

Serve with spaghetti, finely grated mild Cheddar or colby cheese, cooked kidney beans, chopped onions, oyster crackers and hot sauce.

Note: Can chill, covered, for 8 to 12 hours to enhance the flavor. Can store in a freezer container in the freezer until ready to use.

White Chili

Hearty Winter Meal

- **Serves 5 to 6**
- **Must do ahead**

1 pound dried great Northern beans
6 cups water
6 cups chicken broth
1 large onion, chopped (1½ cups)
3 garlic cloves, minced
2 (4-ounce) cans diced green chiles
1 tablespoon oregano
1 tablespoon cumin
½ teaspoon salt
½ teaspoon red pepper
½ teaspoon black pepper
4 cups chopped cooked chicken
½ cup shredded Monterey Jack cheese

Sort and rinse the beans. Bring the beans and water to a boil in a Dutch oven and reduce the heat. Simmer, uncovered, for 2 minutes. Remove from the heat. Cover and let stand for 1 to 12 hours.

Drain the water from the beans. Add the chicken broth, onion, garlic, green chiles, oregano, cumin, salt, red pepper and black pepper. Bring to a boil and reduce the heat. Simmer, covered, for 1 hour. Stir in the chicken. Simmer, covered, for 30 to 60 minutes. Stir in the cheese just before serving. Serve with sliced chile peppers, additional cheese or sun-dried tomatoes.

Greek Lemon Chicken Soup

Sure cure for what ails you

- **Serves 8 to 10**

15 ounces skinless boneless chicken breasts, chopped
1/2 cup chopped onion
1 cup chicken stock
1 pound fresh or frozen chopped spinach
1 quart heavy cream
2 tablespoons cornstarch
1/2 cup lemon juice
Salt and pepper to taste

Sauté the chicken and onion in the chicken stock in a large saucepan until the chicken is cooked through. Add the spinach and cream. Simmer until tender.

Dissolve the cornstarch in the lemon juice. Stir into the soup. Cook until thickened, stirring constantly. Season with salt and pepper. Ladle into soup bowls.

Chicken Noodle Soup

Mama's prescription

For the broth, combine the chicken in a large saucepan with enough of the 3 quarts water to cover. Bring to a boil, skimming the foam from the surface. Reduce the heat. Add 3 ribs celery, onion, peppercorns and 1 tablespoon salt. Simmer for 30 to 45 minutes or until the chicken is tender. Remove the chicken from the broth to a platter with a slotted spoon. Cool slightly. Cut the chicken into 1-inch pieces, discarding the skin and bones. Strain the broth, reserving 2 quarts.

For the noodles, combine 1½ cups flour, baking powder and ½ teaspoon salt in a large bowl and mix well. Beat the eggs and 1 teaspoon cold water in a small bowl. Add to the flour mixture and mix to form a stiff dough, adding additional flour if needed. Roll the dough on a lightly floured surface until 1/16 inch thick. Cut into 2-inch squares.

For the vegetables, bring the reserved broth to a boil in a large saucepan. Add the potatoes, leeks, ¾ cup celery, carrot, parsley and saffron. Cook over medium-high heat for 5 minutes.

To assemble, add the noodle squares to the vegetable mixture, stirring gently. Cook for 12 to 15 minutes or until the noodles are tender. Add the chicken. Cook until heated through. Season with salt to taste, pepper and chicken seasoning.

Note: Can reduce the time to prepare this recipe by purchasing the noodles.

- **Serves 6 to 8**

CHICKEN BROTH
1 (4- to 5-pound) chicken, cut into pieces
3 quarts (or more) water
3 ribs celery with leaves, chopped
1 small onion, coarsely chopped
6 to 8 peppercorns
1 tablespoon salt

NOODLES
1½ cups (or more) flour
¾ teaspoon baking powder
½ teaspoon salt
2 eggs
1 teaspoon cold water

VEGETABLES AND ASSEMBLY
3 medium potatoes, peeled, cut into ½ to ¾-inch slices
2 to 3 medium leek bulbs, thinly sliced
¾ cup sliced celery
¾ cup sliced carrot
3 tablespoons minced fresh parsley
¼ teaspoon ground saffron
Salt and pepper to taste
Chicken seasoning to taste

Black Bean Soup

Gusto Flavor

- **Serves 6 to 8**
- **Must do ahead**

1 pound dried black beans
6 to 8 cups cold water
3 garlic cloves, minced
1 cup onion, chopped
1 cup celery, chopped
3 tablespoons olive oil
3 tablespoons finely chopped fresh parsley
2 bay leaves
1 teaspoon chili powder
1/2 teaspoon cumin
1/2 teaspoon salt
1/2 teaspoon fresh ground black pepper
2 skinless boneless chicken breasts
2 tablespoons olive oil
1 garlic clove, minced
1/2 teaspoon cayenne pepper
Paprika to taste
4 cups chicken broth

Sort and rinse the beans. Bring the beans and 6 cups water to a boil in a large saucepan and reduce the heat. Simmer for 1 hour, stirring occasionally.

Sauté 3 garlic cloves, onion and celery in 3 tablespoons olive oil in a skillet until tender. Do not overcook. Add to the beans with the parsley, bay leaves, chili powder, cumin, salt and black pepper. Add enough of the remaining water to cover. Simmer for 1 hour, stirring frequently.

Cut the chicken into 1-inch strips. Heat 2 tablespoons olive oil in a skillet. Add the chicken and 1 garlic clove. Sprinkle with cayenne pepper and a small amount of paprika. Sauté until the chicken is cooked through, but not brown. Tear the chicken into smaller pieces and add to the beans. Add enough of the broth to cover the bean mixture. Simmer for 2 to 4 hours or until the beans are tender, adding the remaining broth as needed and stirring occasionally. Discard the bay leaves before serving.

Mulligatawny Soup

Even Children Like This

Brown the turkey in the olive oil in a skillet. Add the onion, celery, uncooked rice, garlic and curry powder. Cook until the vegetables are tender-crisp, stirring frequently. Add the chicken broth, tomatoes, frozen mixed vegetables, parsley and nutmeg.

Simmer for 30 minutes, stirring occasionally. Ladle into soup bowls. Sprinkle each serving with 1/4 cup shredded cheese.

- **Serves 6 to 8**

1 1/2 pounds turkey or chicken breasts, chopped
2 tablespoons olive oil
1 medium onion, chopped
1 cup chopped celery
3/4 cup uncooked white rice
1 medium garlic clove
1 to 2 teaspoons curry powder
6 cups chicken broth or stock
1 (14-ounce) can crushed tomatoes
1 (16-ounce) package frozen mixed vegetables
1/4 cup chopped fresh parsley
1/4 teaspoon nutmeg
1 1/2 to 2 cups shredded cheese

ITALIAN SOUP

MAMA-MIA

• **Serves 6 to 8**

2 pounds Italian sausage
2 medium onions, chopped
4 small zucchini, sliced
4 carrots, chopped
2 garlic cloves, minced
10 cups chicken broth
2 (28-ounce) cans crushed tomatoes
1 cup dry white wine
1 cup uncooked orzo or rice
1 teaspoon oregano
2 teaspoons basil
Salt and pepper to taste

GARNISH
Shredded Italian cheese

Brown the sausage in a skillet; drain. Add the onions, zucchini, carrots and garlic. Cook until the vegetables are tender-crisp. Add the chicken broth, tomatoes, wine, orzo, oregano, basil, salt and pepper.

Bring to a boil and reduce the heat. Simmer for 30 minutes. Ladle into soup bowls. Garnish with shredded Italian cheese.

Easy New England Clam Chowder

Hearty

Sauté the bacon in a skillet until partially cooked through. Add the onion. Sauté until the onion is golden brown and the bacon is crisp; drain.

Add the potato soup and water. Stir in the clams, sour cream and parsley. Season with thyme, salt and pepper. Cook until heated through, stirring frequently. Ladle into soup bowls.

- **Serves 4**

4 ounces bacon, chopped
1 medium onion, chopped
2 (10-ounce) cans potato soup
2 soup cans water
2 (7-ounce) cans clams, drained
1 cup sour cream
1 teaspoon parsley flakes
Thyme to taste
Salt and pepper to taste

Spring Mussel Soup

Try with other seafood too

- **Serves 4**

2 pounds mussels, cleaned
1 cup dry white wine
1 sprig fresh lovage, coarsely chopped
2 ribs celery, coarsely chopped
1/2 onion, coarsely chopped
1 (2-inch) strip lemon peel
Pulp of 1/4 lemon
2 garlic cloves
1/8 teaspoon curry powder
1/4 teaspoon saffron threads
1/4 cup half-and-half
1/3 cup butter
12 snow peas
1 small zucchini, thinly sliced
3 ounces fresh spinach, trimmed, coarsely chopped
Chopped fresh chervil or parsley to taste

Place the mussels in a large saucepan with 1/2 of the white wine. Cook, covered, over high heat until the mussels open, stirring 1 to 2 times. Remove from the heat and pour into a colander, reserving the cooking liquid. Strain the reserved liquid through a fine sieve or several layers of cheesecloth into a saucepan. Add the lovage, celery, onion, lemon peel, lemon pulp, garlic, the remaining wine, curry powder, saffron and enough water to barely cover. Bring to a boil and reduce the heat. Simmer for 30 minutes. Reserve 8 mussels in the shell. Shuck the remaining mussels and set aside.

Strain the broth and return to the saucepan. Stir in the half-and-half and butter. Cook over high heat until the mixture is reduced slightly. Reduce the heat. Add the snow peas. Cook for 3 minutes. Add the zucchini and spinach. Cook for 2 minutes. Add the shucked and unshucked mussels just before serving. Cook just until heated through. Ladle into soup bowls and sprinkle with chervil. Serve with whole wheat peasant bread and chardonnay.

Note: *Do not eat any mussels that do not open easily after cooking. Clam juice or fish stock can be used in place of the water for a full-flavored broth. Frozen snow peas can be substituted for the fresh, just reduce the cooking time.*

Seafood Bisque

Gourmet Delight

Melt the butter in a skillet. Add the crab meat and shrimp. Sauté until the shrimp turn pink. Add the shallot. Add the flour, stirring until the butter is absorbed. Season with salt and pepper. Add the half-and-half.

Cook over low heat until creamy, stirring constantly. Do not boil. Stir in the sherry. Cook until heated through. Ladle into heated soup bowls. Sprinkle with Parmesan cheese and parsley.

- **Serves 4**

1/4 cup (1/2 stick) butter
8 ounces crab meat
8 ounces peeled shrimp, chopped
1 tablespoon chopped shallot or onion
1/4 cup flour
Salt and pepper to taste
1 quart half-and-half
1/4 cup sherry
1/4 cup freshly grated Parmesan cheese
1 tablespoon chopped parsley

CREOLE GUMBO

GOOD SOUTHERN FLAVOR

- **Serves 8**
- **Must do ahead**
- **Chill 24 hours**
- **Can be frozen**

ROUX
1/2 cup (1 stick) margarine
1 cup flour

GUMBO
1/2 cup (1 stick) margarine
2 cups chopped onions
1 cup sliced celery
1 cup chopped green bell pepper
2 cups cubed cooked ham
1 (16-ounce) package frozen cut okra
1 (8-ounce) can tomato sauce
1 (16-ounce) can tomatoes
3 cups (or more) water
6 chicken bouillon cubes
1 teaspoon pepper
2 teaspoons Worcestershire sauce
1 teaspoon Tabasco sauce, or to taste

ASSEMBLY
1 pound (or more) frozen, shelled, cooked shrimp
1 pound (or more) crab meat or crab meat substitute

For the roux, melt 1/2 cup margarine in a heavy skillet over low heat. Add the flour. Cook for 10 to 15 minutes or until the flour is dark brown, stirring constantly. Remove from the heat.

For the gumbo, melt 1/2 cup margarine in a 4-quart saucepan or stockpot. Add the onions, celery, green pepper and ham. Sauté until heated through. Add the frozen okra. Cook for 5 minutes. Add the tomato sauce, tomatoes, water, bouillon cubes, pepper, Worchestershire sauce, Tabasco sauce and the roux. Simmer for 30 minutes or until the vegetables are tender, stirring frequently and adding additional water if needed. Cool and chill, covered, for 24 hours.

To assemble and serve, reheat the gumbo over low to medium heat in a saucepan, stirring frequently. Add the shrimp and crab meat. Simmer for 5 to 8 minutes or until heated through. Ladle into soup bowls or serve over steamed rice.

***Note:** Can store in a freezer container in the freezer until ready to use.*

Salads

THE CHARLES E. HACKLEY HOUSE IS TRULY A UNIQUE EXAMPLE OF VICTORIAN ARCHITECTURE BUILT IN THE QUEEN ANNE STYLE. THE LUMBER BARON'S HOME FEATURES FIFTEEN STAINED GLASS WINDOWS, HANDCARVED WOOD BY THIRTEEN MASTER CARVERS, AS WELL AS INTERIOR STENCILING AND THE THIRTEEN-COLOR EXTERIOR PAINT SCHEME RE-CREATED FROM ORIGINAL PHOTOGRAPHS. THE HOME IS OPEN FOR TOURS.

Zesty Tomato Treats

Easy but so good on busy summer days

- **Serves 12**

6 medium tomatoes
1/2 cup mayonnaise-type salad dressing or mayonnaise
1/2 cup sour cream
2 tablespoons finely chopped onion
12 lettuce leaf cups
6 slices bacon, cooked, crumbled

Cut off both ends of the tomatoes. Cut the tomatoes horizontally into halves. Mix the mayonnaise-type salad dressing, sour cream and onion in a bowl. Place the lettuce cups on a large platter. Place a tomato half on each. Spoon the salad dressing onto each tomato half and sprinkle with the bacon. Garnish with parsley sprigs.

Artichoke and Pepper Salad

Great for a picnic

- **Serves 10 to 12**
- **Must do ahead**
- **Chill 1 hour**

2 green bell peppers
2 large red bell peppers
2 large yellow bell peppers
2 large purple bell peppers
1 (14-ounce) can quartered artichokes, drained
1 small red onion, finely chopped
1 (6-ounce) can pitted whole black olives, drained
1 (8-ounce) bottle zesty Italian salad dressing
Salt to taste
1/8 teaspoon freshly ground pepper
5 tablespoons crumbled bleu cheese

Rinse the bell peppers. Cut the bell peppers into halves and discard the seeds. Cut into 1-inch pieces. Cut the artichoke quarters into halves.

Combine the bell pepper pieces, artichokes, red onion and black olives in a large serving bowl. Add the salad dressing, salt and pepper and toss to mix. Chill, covered, for 1 hour. Sprinkle with the bleu cheese before serving.

***Note:** Can also add fresh tomato wedges, sliced tomatillos and yellow or red banana peppers. Can serve over romaine on individual serving plates.*

Asparagus Rice Salad

Fantastic

- **Serves 6 to 8**
- **Must do ahead**
- **Chill 8 to 12 hours**

DRESSING
1/4 cup French salad dressing
1 cup mayonnaise
2 tablespoons minced onion
1 teaspoon curry powder
3/4 teaspoon salt
3/4 teaspoon dry mustard

SALAD
2 cups cooked rice
3/4 to 1 cup chopped celery
3 cups cooked 1- to 2-inch asparagus pieces

For the dressing, combine the salad dressing, mayonnaise, onion, curry powder, salt and dry mustard in a bowl and mix well.

For the salad, combine the rice, celery and asparagus in a bowl. Add the dressing and toss to mix well. Chill, covered, for 8 to 12 hours.

Note: Can add chopped cooked chicken.

Broccoli Salad

Absolutely Delicious

For the dressing, mix the mayonnaise-type salad dressing, wine vinegar, sugar, dillweed and celery seeds in a bowl.

For the salad, fry the bacon in a skillet until crisp; drain. Crumble the bacon.

Cut the broccoli into florets. Combine the broccoli, red onion, celery, walnut pieces, bacon and raisins in a large bowl. Add the dressing and toss to mix well.

- **Serves 8**

DRESSING
1 cup mayonnaise-type salad dressing
2 tablespoons wine vinegar
1/2 cup sugar
Dillweed to taste (optional)
Celery seeds to taste (optional)

SALAD
8 ounces bacon
3 bunches broccoli crowns
1/2 cup coarsely chopped red onion
1/2 cup coarsely chopped celery
1/2 cup walnut pieces
1 cup golden raisins

Cucumber Thai Salad

Fresh, crispy, colorful

- **Serves 8**
- **Must do ahead**
- **Chill 1 hour**

1/3 cup white vinegar
1/3 cup sugar
1/2 teaspoon red pepper flakes
1/2 teaspoon salt
2 pounds cucumbers, quartered, seeded, sliced
1/4 cup finely chopped red onion
2 tablespoons chopped fresh cilantro
2 tablespoons chopped fresh mint
1/4 cup chopped roasted peanuts

Combine the vinegar, sugar, red pepper flakes and salt in a large bowl and stir until the sugar dissolves. Add the cucumbers, red onion, cilantro and mint and toss until coated.

Chill, covered, for 1 hour. Add the peanuts just before serving and toss to mix well.

STRING BEAN SALAD

LIGHT AND REFRESHING

For the dressing, combine the tomato sauce, salad oil, vinegar, water, sugar, salt, celery seeds and pepper in a jar with a tight-fitting lid. Cover and shake to mix well. Chill in the refrigerator.

For the salad, cook the green beans using the package directions; drain. Chill in the refrigerator. Combine the green beans, purple onion, green pepper and pimento in a bowl. Add the dressing and toss to mix well. Garnish with a quartered hard-cooked egg.

Note: Can use canned green beans instead of the frozen green beans.

- **Serves 6 to 8**
- **Must do ahead**
- **Chill**

DRESSING
1 (15-ounce) can tomato sauce
1/2 cup salad oil or olive oil
3/4 cup white vinegar
1/4 cup water
1 cup sugar
1 teaspoon salt
1 teaspoon celery seeds
1/2 teaspoon pepper

SALAD
1 (32-ounce) package frozen French-cut green beans
1 purple onion, sliced
1 green bell pepper, chopped
1 (2-ounce) jar chopped pimento, drained

GARNISH
Hard-cooked egg

White Bean Salad

Lemon adds the interest

- **Serves 6 to 8**

1 cup chopped onion
2 garlic cloves, minced
3 tablespoons olive oil
1 (14-ounce) can diced tomatoes, drained
2/3 cup chopped fresh parsley
1 (24-ounce) jar great Northern beans, rinsed, drained
2 tablespoons lemon juice
1 teaspoon salt
1/4 teaspoon pepper

Sauté the onion and garlic in the olive oil in a skillet over medium heat for 5 minutes. Add the tomatoes and parsley. Cook for 5 minutes. Add the white beans. Cook over low heat for 5 minutes, stirring occasionally. Stir in the lemon juice, salt and pepper. Serve hot or cold.

Dandy Greens

About one out of every four American cookbooks contains recipes using dandelions

Sauté the bacon in a skillet until crisp. Place the dandelion greens in a heat-proof salad bowl. Sprinkle with balsamic vinegar, salt and pepper. Pour the hot bacon and drippings over the top and toss to mix well. Add the avocado and toss again. Serve immediately.

- **Serves 2**

4 slices bacon, coarsely chopped
1 bunch dandelion greens, coarsely chopped
2 teaspoons balsamic vinegar
Salt and pepper to taste
1 avocado, chopped

Toasted Pecan and Romaine Salad

Cook-off Finalist

- **Serves 6**
- **Oven Temperature 350 degrees**
- **Bake 15 minutes**

SALAD
1/4 to 1/3 cup pecans
1 large bunch romaine, torn into bite-size pieces
1/4 cup grated fresh Parmesan, Romano or asiago cheese

DRESSING
1 envelope Italian salad dressing mix
1/2 cup olive oil
2 tablespoons balsamic vinegar
2 tablespoons raspberry vinegar
2 tablespoons water

For the salad, place the pecans in a shallow baking dish. Bake at 350 degrees for 15 minutes or until toasted. Cool. Combine the romaine, toasted pecans and Parmesan cheese in a salad bowl.

For the dressing, mix the dressing mix, olive oil, balsamic vinegar, raspberry vinegar and water in a bowl. Add to the salad and toss to mix well.

Christmas Cabbage Slaw

A non-creamy slaw

- **Serves 4 to 6**
- **Must do ahead**
- **Chill 2 to 6 hours**

2 cups finely shredded green cabbage
2 cups finely shredded red cabbage
1 cup jicama strips
1/4 cup chopped green bell pepper
1/4 cup thinly sliced green onions with tops
1/4 cup vegetable oil
1/4 cup lime juice
3/4 teaspoon salt
1/8 teaspoon freshly ground pepper
2 tablespoons coarsely chopped cilantro leaves

Combine the green cabbage, red cabbage, jicama, green pepper and green onions in a large bowl. Whisk the vegetable oil, lime juice, salt and pepper in a small bowl until blended. Stir in the cilantro. Pour over the cabbage mixture and toss lightly. Chill, covered, for 2 to 6 hours or until the flavors have blended.

Autumn Salad

Nice change

• **Serves 4 to 6**

DRESSING
1/4 cup salad oil
1/4 cup apple cider
1 tablespoon cider vinegar
1/4 teaspoon cinnamon
1/8 teaspoon ground cloves

SALAD
4 cups torn mixed greens
2 medium red or green apples, sliced
3/4 cup seedless red grapes

For the dressing, mix the salad oil, apple cider, cider vinegar, cinnamon and cloves in a bowl.

For the salad, combine the salad greens, apples and grapes in a salad bowl. Add the dressing and toss to mix. Serve immediately.

SPINACH AND GRAPEFRUIT SALAD

THE SECRET IS THE BLEU CHEESE

- **Serves 4**

2 tablespoons chopped pecans
8 cups torn spinach
2 cups grapefruit sections
2 cups sliced mushrooms
1/4 cup crumbled bleu cheese
1/2 cup raspberry vinaigrette

Sauté the pecans in a skillet over medium heat for 3 minutes or until brown. Place 2 cups spinach on each of 4 serving plates. Arrange 1/2 cup grapefruit and 1/2 cup mushrooms over the spinach on each plate. Sprinkle each with 1 tablespoon bleu cheese and 1 1/2 teaspoons pecans. Drizzle each with 2 tablespoons raspberry vinaigrette.

Spinach Strawberry Salad

Terrific dressing

- **Serves 12 to 15**

STRAWBERRY DRESSING
1 cup strawberry vinegar
1 cup olive oil
1 cup sugar

SALAD
1/2 package fresh spinach, trimmed
1/2 head lettuce
8 green onions, sliced
1 small package sliced fresh mushrooms
8 to 10 strawberries, sliced

For the dressing, combine the strawberry vinegar, olive oil and sugar in a bowl and stir until the sugar dissolves.

For the salad, tear the spinach and lettuce into bite-size pieces and place in a large salad bowl. Add the green onions, mushrooms and strawberries. Add the dressing and toss to mix well.

Orange Watercress Salad

Very Special

Arrange the Bibb lettuce, watercress and green onions on individual salad plates. Combine the orange juice, tarragon vinegar, olive oil, honey and dry mustard in a bowl and blend well. Drizzle over each salad. Arrange the oranges on top. Sprinkle with the pistachios.

- **Serves 4 to 6**

7 cups torn Bibb lettuce
2 cups torn trimmed watercress
1/4 cup sliced green onions
6 tablespoons orange juice
2 tablespoons tarragon vinegar
2 teaspoons extra-virgin olive oil
2 teaspoons honey
1/2 teaspoon dry mustard
2 cups orange sections (4 oranges)
2 tablespoons chopped pistachios

MANDARIN SALAD

EXQUISITE

- **Serves 6 to 8**
- **Must do ahead**
- **Chill**

DRESSING
1/4 cup vegetable oil
2 tablespoons vinegar
2 tablespoons sugar
1/2 teaspoon salt
1 tablespoon chopped fresh parsley
Dash of hot sauce

GLAZED ALMONDS
1 1/2 tablespoons sugar
1/2 cup sliced almonds

SALAD
1/4 head lettuce
1/4 head romaine
1 cup chopped celery
2 green onion tops, sliced
1 (11-ounce) can mandarin oranges, drained

For the dressing, combine the vegetable oil, vinegar, 2 tablespoons sugar, salt, parsley and hot sauce in a container with a tight-fitting lid and stir until the sugar is dissolved. Chill, covered, in the refrigerator.

For the almonds, melt 1 1/2 tablespoons sugar in a skillet over low heat. Add the almonds and stir until coated. Cool.

For the salad, tear the lettuce and romaine into bite-size pieces and place in a large salad bowl. Add the celery, green onions and mandarin oranges.

To serve, sprinkle with the glazed almonds. Drizzle with the dressing and toss to mix.

Salads

Warm Goat Cheese Salad with Dried Cherries and Pancetta Vinaigrette

Impressive

For the vinaigrette, brown the pancetta in the olive oil in a skillet over medium heat, stirring constantly. Remove about 3 tablespoons of the pan drippings, leaving about 1/3 cup in the skillet. Add the garlic to the skillet. Sauté until golden brown. Add the thyme and sherry vinegar and increase the heat to high. Boil for 1 minute.

For the salad, combine the mesclun and dried cherries in a large salad bowl. Crumble the goat cheese on top and sprinkle with the pepper. Add the hot vinaigrette and toss to mix. Serve immediately.

Note: Pancetta, Italian unsmoked cured bacon, is available at Italian markets, specialty food shops and some supermarkets.

• **Serves** 4

PANCETTA VINAIGRETTE
8 ounces pancetta, cut into 1/8x1-inch strips
1/4 cup olive oil
1 tablespoon finely chopped garlic
1 tablespoon finely chopped fresh thyme leaves
6 tablespoons sherry vinegar

SALAD
8 cups mesclun (mixed baby greens)
4 ounces dried cherries (about 1 cup)
6 ounces soft mild goat cheese
1/3 teaspoon freshly ground pepper, or to taste

Cherry Chicken Salad

Eye-Appealing

- **Serves 4**

MAYONNAISE
1 egg
1 teaspoon vinegar or lemon juice
9 ounces peanut oil
1/8 teaspoon salt
1/8 teaspoon pepper

SALAD
1/2 cup dried tart red cherries
2 cups chopped cooked chicken
1 cup coarsely chopped celery
1 large Granny Smith apple, coarsely chopped
1/4 cup finely chopped fresh parsley
1/2 cup walnuts or pecans, chopped
Salt and pepper to taste

For the mayonnaise, process the egg, vinegar, peanut oil, 1/8 teaspoon salt and 1/8 teaspoon pepper in a blender for 1 minute.

For the salad, cover the cherries with boiling water in a small bowl. Let stand for a few minutes or until plump; drain and pat dry. Combine the cherries, chicken, celery, apple and parsley in a large bowl. Add 1 cup of the mayonnaise and toss lightly. Sprinkle with the walnuts and salt and pepper to taste. Serve on lettuce leaves or with croissants.

Note: Curry powder to taste can be added to the mayonnaise for additional flavor.

Editors Note: In order to avoid raw eggs that may contain salmonella, pasteurize the egg before using. Mix 1 egg with 1 tablespoon lemon juice or vinegar and 1 tablespoon water in a small glass bowl. Microwave, covered, on High for 30 seconds or until the mixture begins to rise. Microwave for 5 seconds longer. Beat with a wire whisk until smooth. Microwave on High for 10 seconds or until the mixture rises again. Beat again. Mixture should be at 200 degrees. Cover the bowl and let stand for 1 minute before using.

Chinese Chicken Salad

Ideal on a Warm Summer Night

- **Serves 12**
- **Must do ahead**
- **Oven Temperature 325 degrees**
- **Bake 1 hour**
- **Chill**

SALAD
8 boneless skinless chicken breasts
Chicken broth
1 head savoy cabbage, shredded
1 bunch green onions, chopped
1/2 cup toasted almonds
1/2 cup toasted sesame seeds

DRESSING
1/2 cup rice vinegar
1 cup olive oil
6 tablespoons sugar
1 teaspoon salt
1 teaspoon pepper

ASSEMBLY
1 (3-ounce) can chow mein noodles

For the salad, place the chicken in a baking dish with a small amount of chicken broth. Bake, covered, at 325 degrees for 1 hour or until cooked through; drain immediately. Chill the chicken and cut into slices. Combine the chicken, cabbage, green onions, almonds and sesame seeds in a large bowl and toss to mix well.

For the dressing, combine the rice vinegar, olive oil, sugar, salt and pepper in a small bowl and stir until the sugar is dissolved.

To assemble, drizzle the dressing over the salad. Add the chow mein noodles and toss lightly.

Ranch Taco Chicken Salad

Low in Fat and Flavorful

- **Serves 6**

1 pound boneless skinless chicken breasts, sliced
1 tablespoon vegetable oil
1 tablespoon chili powder
1 (16-ounce) package salad greens
1 (8-ounce) jar salsa
1/2 cup fat-free ranch salad dressing
1 cup shredded nonfat Cheddar cheese
1/2 cup crushed baked tortilla chips

Sauté the chicken in the vegetable oil and chili powder in a large nonstick skillet over medium-high heat for 8 minutes or until the chicken is cooked through.

Combine the chicken, salad greens, salsa, salad dressing and Cheddar cheese in a large bowl and toss to mix. Sprinkle with crushed tortilla chips just before serving.

Shrimp and Crab Meat Salad

Exceptional

- **Serves 20**
- **Must do ahead**
- **Freeze 8 to 12 hours**
- **Chill 16 to 24 hours**

1 loaf white bread
Butter
4 to 6 hard-cooked eggs
1 sweet onion, sliced, chopped
1 (6-ounce) can crab meat, drained
1½ packages cooked small shrimp
1 teaspoon MSG
1 to 2 cups chopped celery
1 (8-ounce) can sliced water chestnuts, drained
2½ to 3 cups mayonnaise

Freeze the bread for 8 to 12 hours. Trim the crusts from the frozen bread and spread each slice with butter. Cut the bread into cubes and place in a bowl. Add the eggs and onion and toss to mix well. Chill, covered, for 8 to 12 hours.

Add the crab meat, shrimp, MSG, celery, water chestnuts and mayonnaise to the bread mixture and mix well. Chill, covered, for 8 to 12 hours. Serve over lettuce.

Crab Louis

Fisherman's Wharf classic

- **Serves 6**
- **Must do ahead**
- **Chill**

1/2 cup mayonnaise
1/2 cup sour cream
2 tablespoons chili sauce
2 tablespoons salad oil
1 tablespoon vinegar
1 tablespoon prepared horseradish
1 tablespoon fresh lemon juice
1 tablespoon fresh chopped parsley
2 teaspoons grated onion
1/2 teaspoon salt
4 drops of Tabasco sauce
1 medium head lettuce, shredded
1 pound fresh crab meat, cooked

GARNISHES
Sprigs of watercress or parsley
Lemon wedges
Hard-cooked eggs, quartered
Black olives
Tomatoes, quartered

Mix the mayonnaise, sour cream, chili sauce, salad oil, vinegar, prepared horseradish, lemon juice, parsley, onion, salt and Tabasco sauce in a bowl. Chill, covered, in the refrigerator. Arrange the lettuce on individual salad plates. Mound the crab meat on the lettuce. Spoon the mayonnaise mixture over the crab meat. Garnish with sprigs of watercress or parsley, lemon wedges, quartered hard-cooked eggs, black olives and quartered tomatoes.

Note: Can use thawed frozen Alaska king crab meat instead of the fresh crab meat. Pat dry and break into bite-size pieces. Chill until ready to use.

All Season Rice Salad

It's just the best

For the dressing, combine the vegetable oil, rice vinegar, soy sauce, Dijon mustard, sugar, garlic powder, Old Bay seasoning and pepper in a bowl and mix well.

For the salad, combine the rice, bean sprouts, celery, yellow pepper strips and red onion in a large bowl. Add the dressing and toss gently to coat. Chill, covered, until serving time.

- **Serves 6 to 8**
- **Must do ahead**
- **Chill**

DRESSING

1/3 cup vegetable oil
1/4 cup rice vinegar
2 tablespoons soy sauce
1 teaspoon Dijon mustard
1 1/2 tablespoons sugar
1 teaspoon garlic powder
1/4 teaspoon Old Bay seasoning
1/4 teaspoon pepper

SALAD

4 cups cooked rice
1 (14-ounce) can bean sprouts, drained
1 1/2 cups sliced celery
1 cup diagonally sliced yellow bell pepper strips
1/2 cup chopped red onion

Bleu Cheese Dressing

You'll never want any other

- **Makes 2½ cups**

1 cup sour cream
1 cup mayonnaise
1 tablespoon lemon juice
1 teaspoon Worcestershire sauce
1 teaspoon garlic powder
1 teaspoon onion salt
Dash of Tabasco sauce
¼ teaspoon salt
¼ teaspoon pepper
4 ounces bleu cheese, crumbled

Combine the sour cream, mayonnaise, lemon juice, Worcestershire sauce, garlic powder, onion salt, Tabasco sauce, salt and pepper in a bowl and blend well. Stir in the bleu cheese. Pour into an airtight container. Store, covered, in the refrigerator.

Fresh Herb Dressing

Nice blend of flavors

Combine the orange juice, honey, salt, pepper, chervil, chives, tarragon and parsley in a bowl and whisk well. Store, covered, in the refrigerator.

- **Makes ¾ cup**

½ cup freshly squeezed orange juice
2 tablespoons honey
Pinch of salt
Pepper to taste
1 teaspoon finely chopped fresh chervil
1 teaspoon finely chopped fresh chives
1 teaspoon finely chopped fresh tarragon
1 teaspoon finely chopped fresh parsley

ITALIAN VINAIGRETTE

GOOD BLEND OF FLAVORS

- **Makes 1 cup**

1/2 cup light olive oil
1/4 cup plus 2 tablespoons vegetable oil
3 tablespoons white wine vinegar
1/4 teaspoon basil
1/4 teaspoon oregano
1/4 teaspoon minced garlic
1 tablespoon sugar
Dash of cumin

Combine the olive oil, vegetable oil, white wine vinegar, basil, oregano, garlic, sugar and cumin in a bowl. Whisk until the sugar is dissolved. Store, covered, in the refrigerator.

Brunch and Lunch

LAKE MICHIGAN

Thai Steamed Eggs

Good combination of flavors

• **Serves 4**

4 eggs, beaten
2 green onions, thinly sliced
3 ounces shrimp, cooked, peeled, finely chopped
1 red chile, seeded, thinly sliced
1 tablespoon chopped cilantro leaves
1/3 cup coconut milk
2 teaspoons fish or oyster sauce

GARNISHES
Sprigs of cilantro
Red chile rings

Process the eggs, green onions, shrimp, red chile, cilantro, coconut milk and fish sauce in a blender until blended.

Pour into 4 well-greased heatproof ramekins. Place in a steaming basket and place over boiling water in a saucepan. Steam, covered, for 10 to 12 minutes or until set. Remove from the heat. Let stand for 1 to 2 minutes.

Invert onto warm individual serving plates. Garnish with sprigs of cilantro and red chile rings.

Spinach Cheese Casserole

Makes an excellent quiche when baked in a pie shell

- **Serves 8 to 10**
- **Oven Temperature 350 degrees**
- **Bake 1 hour**

6 tablespoons flour
2 pounds cottage cheese
6 eggs
1/2 cup (1 stick) margarine, melted
1 (10-ounce) package frozen chopped spinach, thawed, drained
1 package Old English cheese slices, diced

Mix the flour into the cottage cheese in a bowl. Add the eggs, margarine, spinach and Old English cheese and mix well. Pour into a nonstick baking dish. Bake at 350 degrees for 1 hour.

Green Chile Strata

Different and good

- **Serves 8 to 10**
- **Oven Temperature 350 degrees**
- **Bake 45 minutes**

1 (2-pound) package frozen Tater Tots
8 eggs, beaten
4 cups milk
Salt and pepper to taste
2 (4-ounce) cans chopped green chiles, drained
8 ounces shredded cheese

Place the Tater Tots in a 9x12-inch baking dish. Beat the eggs, milk, salt and pepper in a bowl. Stir in the green chiles. Pour over the Tater Tots. Sprinkle the cheese on top. Bake at 350 degrees for 45 minutes or until set. Serve with salsa.

Note: Can easily be reheated.

Tahoe Brunch

Great for the Ski Trip

- **Serves 6 to 8**
- **Must do ahead**
- **Chill 12 hours**
- **Oven Temperature 350 degrees**
- **Bake 1 hour**

2 to 3 tablespoons butter or margarine, softened
12 slices white bread, crusts trimmed
1/2 cup (1 stick) butter or margarine
8 ounces sliced fresh mushrooms
2 cups thinly sliced yellow onion rings
Salt and pepper to taste
1 pound mild Italian sausage links
12 ounces Cheddar cheese, grated
5 eggs
2 1/2 cups milk
1 tablespoon Dijon mustard
1 teaspoon dry mustard
1 teaspoon nutmeg
Chopped fresh parsley

Spread the softened butter on the bread. Melt 1/2 cup butter in a large skillet. Add the mushrooms and onion rings. Cook until tender. Season with salt and pepper. Cook the sausage in a skillet until brown and cooked through. Cut into bite-size pieces.

Layer 1/2 of the bread, 1/2 of the mushroom mixture, 1/3 of the cheese and 1/2 of the sausage in a 9x13-inch baking dish. Repeat the layers. Sprinkle with the remaining cheese.

Beat the eggs, milk, Dijon mustard, dry mustard and nutmeg in a bowl. Pour over the layers. Chill, covered, for 12 hours. Sprinkle with parsley. Bake, uncovered, at 350 degrees for 1 hour or until bubbly. Serve immediately.

***Note:** Can substitute whole wheat or rye bread for the white bread. Can use Swiss or Monterey Jack cheese.*

Brunch Sausage Ring

Perfect for a Buffet

Combine the sausage, apples, bread crumbs, onion and eggs in a large bowl and mix well. Press into a bundt pan or large ring mold. Place in a preheated 400-degree oven. Reduce the oven temperature to 350 degrees. Bake for 1 hour; drain. Unmold onto a serving platter. Top with spiced apples and sprigs of fresh parsley.

- **Serves 8 to 12**
- **Oven Temperature 400 degrees**
- **Oven Temperature 350 degrees**
- **Bake 1 hour**

2 pounds bulk lean pork sausage
2 cups chopped apples
2 cups dry bread crumbs
1/2 cup finely chopped onion
2 eggs, lightly beaten
Spiced apples
Sprigs of fresh parsley

Holiday Eggs

Quick and Easy

Brown the sausage in a large skillet, stirring until crumbly; drain. Beat the eggs in a large bowl. Add the milk and cheese and mix well. Unroll the crescent roll dough in a 9x13-inch baking dish, pressing to seal perforations. Pour the egg mixture over the dough. Sprinkle with the sausage. Bake at 400 degrees for 15 minutes or until set.

***Note:** Can use reduced-fat cheese, skim milk and egg substitute. Can substitute 2 cups cubed cooked ham for the sausage.*

- **Serves 8**
- **Oven Temperature 400 degrees**
- **Bake 15 minutes**

1 pound bulk pork sausage
4 eggs
2/3 cup milk
2 cups shredded Cheddar cheese
1 (8-count) can crescent rolls

Spinach-Filled Turkey Roll

Wonderful at Brunch

- **Serves 6 to 8**
- **Oven Temperature 350 degrees**
- **Bake 55 to 60 minutes**

2 pounds ground turkey
½ cup finely chopped onion
⅔ cup mayonnaise
4 slices bread, crumbled
3 eggs, lightly beaten
2 tablespoons parsley
½ teaspoon seasoned salt
Pinch of pepper
Pinch of garlic powder
1 teaspoon instant chicken bouillon
1 (10-ounce) package frozen chopped spinach, thawed, drained
½ cup shredded part-skim mozzarella cheese

Combine the ground turkey, onion, mayonnaise, bread, eggs, parsley, seasoned salt, pepper, garlic powder and instant bouillon in a bowl and mix well. Pat into an 8x12-inch rectangle on a sheet of foil.

Squeeze any excess moisture from the spinach. Spread the spinach over the ground turkey mixture. Sprinkle with the cheese. Roll up the rectangle from the short side to enclose the filling, lifting the foil to aid in the rolling process. Place seam side down on a foil-lined 10x15-inch baking pan. Bake at 350 degrees for 55 to 60 minutes or until cooked through. Let stand for 10 minutes before serving.

Bell Pepper Frittata

Beautiful Dish for a Brunch

Sauté the garlic, purple onion, red peppers and yellow pepper in 1 tablespoon olive oil in a large skillet until tender; drain and pat dry. Sauté the squash and zucchini in 1 tablespoon olive oil in a skillet until tender; drain and pat dry. Sauté the mushrooms in 1 tablespoon olive oil in a skillet until tender; drain and pat dry.

Combine the eggs, cream, salt and pepper in a bowl and whisk well. Stir in the sautéed vegetables, ½ of the bread cubes, cream cheese and Swiss cheese.

Press the remaining bread cubes over the bottom of a lightly greased 10-inch springform pan. Place the pan on a baking sheet. Pour the vegetable mixture over the bread cubes. Bake at 325 degrees for 1 hour, covering with foil after 45 minutes to prevent excessive browning. Serve warm.

- **Serves 8**
- **Oven Temperature 325 degrees**
- **Bake 1 hour**

3 garlic cloves, minced
1 large purple onion, sliced
2 red bell peppers, cut into thin strips
1 yellow bell pepper, cut into thin strips
1 tablespoon olive oil
2 yellow squash, thinly sliced
2 zucchini, thinly sliced
1 tablespoon olive oil
1 (8-ounce) package fresh mushrooms, sliced
1 tablespoon olive oil
6 eggs
¼ cup heavy cream
2½ to 3 teaspoons salt
2 teaspoons freshly ground pepper
8 slices sandwich bread, cubed
8 ounces cream cheese, cubed
2 cups shredded Swiss cheese

Green Chile Omelet

Wonderfully tasty and easy

- **Serves 8**
- **Must do ahead**
- **Chill 8 to 12 hours**
- **Oven Temperature 350 degrees**
- **Bake 45 to 50 minutes**

2 (4-ounce) cans chopped mild green chiles, drained
Seasoned salt to taste
2 pounds Monterey Jack cheese, shredded
Butter
12 eggs
1/4 cup evaporated milk
Pepper to taste

Place 1/2 of the green chiles in a greased 9x13-inch baking pan. Sprinkle with seasoned salt. Sprinkle 1/2 of the cheese over the green chiles and dot with butter. Repeat the layers with the remaining green chiles, cheese and butter. Chill, covered, for 8 to 12 hours.

Beat the eggs in a bowl. Add the evaporated milk and pepper and mix well. Pour over the layers. Bake at 350 degrees for 45 to 50 minutes or until a knife inserted in the center comes out clean. Serve with salsa.

Party Jarlsberg Spinach Quiche

Perfect for a Crowd

- **Serves 12 to 15**
- **Oven Temperature 375 degrees**
- **Bake 45 minutes**

PASTRY
3 cups flour
1 teaspoon salt
3/4 cup (1 1/2 sticks) butter
1 egg, lightly beaten
7 tablespoons cold water

QUICHE
2 cups shredded Jarlsberg cheese
1 (10-ounce) package frozen chopped spinach, thawed, drained
2 cups heavy cream
2 cups milk
6 eggs
1 medium onion, minced
1/2 cup flour
1 1/2 teaspoons salt
1/2 teaspoon pepper
1 1/2 teaspoons nutmeg

For the pastry, combine 3 cups flour and 1 teaspoon salt in a large bowl. Cut in the butter until crumbly. Add 1 egg and cold water and mix until a soft dough forms. Roll the dough into a 15x19-inch rectangle on a lightly floured surface. Place in a 12x18-inch baking pan and trim and flute the edges.

For the quiche, sprinkle the Jarlsberg cheese and spinach over the pastry. Combine the cream, milk, 6 eggs, onion, 1/2 cup flour, 1 1/2 teaspoons salt, pepper and nutmeg in a large bowl and mix well. Pour over the spinach. Bake at 375 degrees for 45 minutes or until set.

Basil Tomato Tart

Wonderful distinctive flavor

- **Serves 4**
- **Oven Temperature 375 degrees**
- **Bake 35 to 40 minutes**

1 (1-crust) pie pastry
1½ cups shredded mozzarella cheese
5 Roma tomatoes
1 cup loosely packed fresh basil
4 garlic cloves
½ cup mayonnaise or mayonnaise-type salad dressing
¼ cup grated Parmesan cheese
⅛ teaspoon white pepper

Unfold the pie pastry. Place in a 9-inch quiche dish or glass pie plate and trim and flute the edge. Prebake using the package directions. Sprinkle the prebaked pastry with ½ cup of the mozzarella cheese. Cool.

Cut the tomatoes into wedges; drain on paper towels. Arrange over the mozzarella cheese in the prebaked pie pastry. Process the basil and garlic in a food processor until coarsely chopped. Sprinkle over the tomatoes.

Combine the remaining mozzarella cheese, mayonnaise, Parmesan cheese and white pepper in a medium bowl and mix well. Spoon over the top and spread evenly to the edge. Bake at 375 degrees for 35 to 40 minutes or until bubbly and the top is golden brown. Garnish with additional basil leaves.

Puffy German Pancake

Children of All Ages Watch Through the Oven Window

- **Serves 6**
- **Oven Temperature 425 degrees**
- **Bake 20 to 25 minutes**

1/3 cup butter or margarine
5 eggs
1 1/4 cups milk
1 1/4 cups flour

Place the butter in a 9x13-inch baking dish. Bake at 425 degrees until the butter is melted, tilting the dish to coat the bottom.

Process the eggs in a blender at high speed for 1 minute. Add the milk and flour. Stir with a spoon. Process at medium speed for 30 seconds. Pour into the hot melted butter. Bake at 425 degrees for 20 to 25 minutes or until puffy and brown. Loosen the pancake from the side of the dish with a knife or spatula. Cut into oblong pieces.

Serve with toppings such as syrup, jam, fruit compote, confectioners' sugar with a squeeze of lemon, fresh berries, canned pie filling or crisp bacon.

***Note:** For 3 to 4 servings, reduce the butter to 1/4 cup, reduce the eggs to 4, and reduce the flour and milk to 1 cup each. Bake in a 2-quart baking dish.*

Baked Oatmeal

Wonderful

- **Serves 6 to 8**
- **Oven Temperature 400 degrees**
- **Bake 45 minutes**

2 cups rolled oats
4 cups milk
1/4 cup packed brown sugar
1 1/2 teaspoons cinnamon
1/4 teaspoon vanilla extract
3/4 cup raisins
1/2 cup chopped pecans or walnuts
1 large apple, finely chopped

Combine the oats, milk, brown sugar, cinnamon and vanilla in a large bowl and mix well. Stir in the raisins, pecans and apple. Pour into a 3-quart baking dish sprayed with nonstick cooking spray. Bake, uncovered, at 400 degrees for 45 minutes. Serve hot with warm milk and extra brown sugar.

Note: Can be prepared in a slow cooker.

Maple Syrup

Try on Ice Cream, Too

- **Serves 10 to 12**

2 cups water
1 cup sugar
1/2 cup packed brown sugar
1 tablespoon corn syrup (optional)
1/2 teaspoon maple extract
1/2 teaspoon vanilla extract

Combine the water, sugar, brown sugar and corn syrup in a saucepan. Boil for 10 minutes. Remove from the heat. Stir in the maple and vanilla extracts. Serve hot or cold over pancakes, waffles or French toast. Store in the refrigerator for 1 month or longer.

Fruit and Nut Maple Granola

Trendy

- **Makes 9 cups**
- **Can be frozen**
- **Oven Temperature 325 degrees**
- **Bake 30 to 35 minutes**

4 cups regular rolled oats
1 cup chopped walnuts or pecans
1/2 cup whole almonds
1 cup whole-bran cereal
1/4 cup sesame seeds
1/2 cup sunflower kernels
1 cup dried cherries, dried cranberries, dried blueberries or raisins
1/2 cup snipped dried apricots
1/2 cup vegetable oil
1/2 cup maple syrup
1/4 teaspoon salt

Combine the rolled oats, walnuts, almonds, whole-bran cereal, sesame seeds, sunflower kernels, dried cherries and dried apricots in a large bowl and toss to mix. Combine the vegetable oil, maple syrup and salt in a bowl and mix well. Drizzle over the oat mixture and toss to coat. Spread evenly in a greased 10x15-inch baking pan.

Bake at 325 degrees for 30 to 35 minutes or until light brown, stirring after 20 minutes. Invert onto a large sheet of foil and cool. Store at room temperature in tightly covered jars or sealable plastic bags for up to 2 weeks.

***Note:** For longer storage, seal the granola in freezer bags and store in the freezer.*

Chicken Crepes-Northern States

Best ever

- **Serves 12**
- **Oven Temperature 350 degrees**
- **Bake 25 minutes**

CREPES
1 cup flour
1 to 1½ cups milk
2 eggs
1 tablespoon vegetable oil
¼ teaspoon salt

FILLING
6 tablespoons (¾ stick) butter
¼ cup minced onion
6 tablespoons flour
2 cups milk or chicken stock
1 cup half-and-half
½ cup grated Parmesan cheese
1 teaspoon salt
½ teaspoon thyme
8 ounces sliced fresh mushrooms
2 tablespoons (¼ stick) butter
1 tablespoon lemon juice
2 cups chopped cooked chicken

For the crepes, combine 1 cup flour, 1 to 1½ cups milk, eggs, vegetable oil and ¼ teaspoon salt in a bowl and beat until blended. Heat a lightly greased 6-inch skillet and remove from the heat. Add ¼ cup of the batter to the skillet, tilting to coat the skillet. Return to the heat. Cook until brown on the bottom and "blistered" on the top. Invert the skillet over a paper towel and tap lightly to remove the crepe. Repeat with the remaining batter, greasing the skillet as needed. Layer crepes alternately with waxed paper.

For the filling, melt 6 tablespoons butter in a medium saucepan. Add the onion. Sauté until tender. Blend in 6 tablespoons flour. Cook until frothy, stirring constantly. Add 2 cups milk and half-and-half. Cook until the mixture comes to a boil and is thickened, stirring constantly. Stir in the Parmesan cheese, 1 teaspoon salt and thyme. Sauté the mushrooms in 2 tablespoons butter in a skillet until tender. Stir in the lemon juice. Combine ½ of the sauce, mushroom mixture and chicken in a bowl and mix well.

To assemble, spoon ¼ cup of the chicken filling down the center of each crepe and roll up. Arrange in a greased baking dish. Pour the remaining sauce over the top. Bake at 350 degrees for 25 minutes or until bubbly.

STROMBOLI

GREAT WITH SOUP

- **Serves 8**
- **Oven Temperature 350 degrees**
- **Bake 25 to 35 minutes**

2 (8-count) cans crescent rolls
4 ounces thinly sliced ham
4 ounces thinly sliced provolone cheese
4 ounces Genoa salami
4 ounces Swiss cheese
4 ounces pepperoni
1 large jar roasted red bell peppers
3 tablespoons grated Parmesan cheese
3 eggs
Pepper to taste

Unroll 1 can of crescent roll dough. Line the bottom of a 9x13-inch baking pan with the dough, pressing to seal the perforations. Layer the ham, provolone cheese, Genoa salami, Swiss cheese and pepperoni in the prepared dish. Sprinkle with the red peppers and Parmesan cheese.

Beat the eggs and pepper in a bowl. Pour most of the egg mixture over the layers. Unroll the remaining can of crescent roll dough, pressing to seal the perforations. Place over the top. Brush with the remaining egg mixture.

Bake, covered, at 350 degrees for 25 minutes. Bake, uncovered, for 10 minutes longer or until brown. Cut into squares to serve.

Note: Can add a layer of fresh spinach under the red peppers.

Seafood Casserole

Delightful for a Ladies Luncheon

- **Serves 6**
- **Oven Temperature 450 degrees**
- **Bake 15 minutes**

2 cups cooked peeled shrimp and/or crab meat
2 cups thinly sliced celery
2 cups croutons
1 cup mayonnaise or mayonnaise-type salad dressing
1/2 cup slivered almonds, toasted
2 tablespoons lemon juice
2 teaspoons minced onion
1/2 teaspoon salt
1/2 cup shredded Swiss or Cheddar cheese

Combine the shrimp, celery, 1 cup of the croutons, mayonnaise, almonds, lemon juice, onion and salt in a bowl and mix well. Spoon into six 1-cup baking dishes or shell ramekins. Sprinkle with the remaining croutons and cheese. Bake at 450 degrees for 15 minutes or until bubbly.

Note: Can substitute chopped cooked chicken for the shrimp and/or crab meat.

Georgia Reuben

Tasty

- **Serves 1**
- **Grill**

2 or 3 slices turkey
1 slice Havarti or Provolone cheese
1/4 cup shredded cabbage
2 tablespoons Russian salad dressing
2 slices whole-grain bread
1 to 2 tablespoons margarine

Layer the turkey, cheese, cabbage and salad dressing on 1 slice of bread. Top with the remaining bread slice. Heat the margarine in a skillet. Add the sandwich. Grill until golden brown on each side, turning once.

Pesto Pockets

Saturday Lunch Special

- **Makes 20**
- **Oven Temperature 400 degrees**
- **Bake 8 to 10 minutes**

2 (10-count) cans biscuits
1/4 cup pesto
1/2 cup shredded mozzarella cheese
1 egg white, beaten
1 teaspoon water

Separate the biscuit dough. Flatten each into a 4-inch circle on a lightly floured surface. Spread about 1/2 teaspoon pesto on 1/2 of each circle, spreading to within 1/2 inch of the edge. Sprinkle 1/2 of the mozzarella cheese over the pesto on each circle. Mix the egg white and water together. Brush the edge of each circle with the egg wash. Fold each circle in half and crimp edge with a fork; prick the top once.

Place the pockets on a greased baking sheet. Brush the tops with the remaining egg wash. Sprinkle each with the remaining mozzarella cheese. Bake at 400 degrees for 8 to 10 minutes or until golden brown. Serve warm.

Untidy Toms

Healthy barbecue sandwiches

- **Serves 6 to 8**
- **Must do ahead**

1 medium onion, chopped
2 tablespoons (1/4 stick) butter
2 tablespoons vinegar
2 tablespoons sugar
1/4 cup lemon juice
Pepper to taste
1 cup tomato sauce
1 tablespoon Worcestershire sauce
1 teaspoon prepared mustard
1/2 cup chopped celery with leaves
2 to 3 cups chopped cooked turkey or cooked ground turkey

Sauté the onion in the butter in a skillet until translucent. Place in a slow cooker. Add the vinegar, sugar, lemon juice, pepper, tomato sauce, Worcestershire sauce, mustard, celery and turkey and mix well. Cook on High for 1 hour. Cook on Low for 3 hours longer or until of the desired consistency and the flavors are blended. Serve on buns.

Breads

Restored train depot, now home of the Muskegon County Convention and Visitors Center

Southern Biscuits

GOOD ANYTIME

- **Serves 4**
- **Oven Temperature 400 degrees**
- **Bake 10 to 12 minutes**

2 cups flour
1 tablespoon baking powder
1 teaspoon salt
1/4 cup vegetable oil
3/4 to 1 cup milk

Mix the flour, baking powder and salt in a bowl. Add the vegetable oil and 3/4 cup milk and mix lightly to form a soft dough, adding additional milk if needed. Knead lightly on a floured surface. Pat the dough 1 inch thick. Cut with a biscuit cutter. Place on a baking sheet. Bake at 400 degrees for 10 to 12 minutes or until golden brown.

Note: Store any leftover biscuits in an airtight container. Wrap in foil and reheat when ready to serve.

Variations: For Cheesy Biscuits, add 1/2 cup shredded mild or sharp Cheddar cheese and 1 teaspoon paprika before adding the milk.

For Strawberry Shortcake, add 1/4 cup sugar before adding the milk. Serve baked biscuits with sweetened sliced strawberries and light cream, ice cream or frozen yogurt.

Brandied Fruit Bread

Nontraditional

Soak the cherries in the brandy in a bowl for 30 minutes. Process the butter and sugar in a food processor until creamy. Add the banana, apples and cherry mixture and process until blended. Add the eggs, sour cream and vanilla and process well.

Mix the flour, baking powder, baking soda, salt and nutmeg in a large bowl. Add the processed mixture and stir just until moistened. Stir in the walnuts. Pour into a buttered 5x9-inch loaf pan. Bake at 350 degrees for 1 hour or until the loaf tests done. Cool in the pan for 10 to 15 minutes. Invert onto a wire rack to cool completely.

- **Makes 1 loaf**
- **Oven Temperature 350 degrees**
- **Bake 1 hour**

1/4 cup chopped dried cherries
1/4 cup apricot brandy
1/4 cup (1/2 stick) butter, softened
3/4 cup sugar
1 medium ripe banana, mashed
1 large Granny Smith apple, cored, peeled, chopped
1 large Delicious apple, cored, peeled, chopped
2 eggs, beaten
1/4 cup sour cream
1 teaspoon vanilla extract
2 1/2 cups flour
2 teaspoons baking powder
1/2 teaspoon baking soda
1/2 teaspoon salt
1/4 teaspoon nutmeg
1 cup chopped walnuts

Orange Raspberry Bread

Very moist and easy to prepare

- **Makes 1 loaf**
- **Oven Temperature 350 degrees**
- **Bake 55 to 60 minutes**

2 cups flour
1 teaspoon baking powder
1/2 teaspoon salt
2 tablespoons (1/4 stick) butter, softened
1 cup sugar
1 cup orange juice
1 teaspoon baking soda
1/2 cup vegetable oil
1 egg
1/2 cup chopped walnuts
1 cup raspberries

Mix the flour, baking powder and salt together. Cream the butter and sugar in a mixer bowl. Add the orange juice, baking soda, vegetable oil and egg and mix well. Stir in the flour mixture. Fold in the walnuts and raspberries. Pour into a greased 5x9-inch loaf pan. Bake at 350 degrees for 55 to 60 minutes or until the loaf tests done. Cool on a wire rack.

Poppy Seed Bread

Search no more

- **Makes 3 small loaves**
- **Oven Temperature 350 degrees**
- **Bake 35 to 40 minutes**

4 eggs, beaten
1/2 cup vegetable oil
1 cup water
1 (4-ounce) package lemon instant pudding mix
1 (2-layer) package lemon cake mix
1/4 cup (scant) poppy seeds
1 teaspoon vanilla extract
1 teaspoon almond extract

Combine the eggs, vegetable oil, water, lemon pudding mix, lemon cake mix, poppy seeds, vanilla and almond extracts in a mixer bowl and mix well. Pour into 3 greased 3x5-inch loaf pans. Bake at 350 degrees for 35 to 40 minutes or until the loaves test done. Cool on wire racks.

Cream Cheese Pumpkin Bread

Autumn Treat

For the batter, mix the flour, 1½ cups sugar, baking soda, cinnamon, salt and nutmeg in a large bowl. Combine the pumpkin, margarine, 1 egg and water in a bowl and mix well. Add to the flour mixture and stir just until moistened.

For the filling, beat the cream cheese, ¼ cup sugar and 1 egg in a mixer bowl until smooth.

To assemble, spoon ½ of the batter into a greased and floured 5x9-inch loaf pan. Pour the filling over the batter. Drop the remaining batter by spoonfuls over the filling. Swirl with a knife to marbleize. Bake at 350 degrees for 70 minutes. Cool in the pan for 5 minutes. Invert onto a wire rack to cool completely.

- **Makes 1 loaf**
- **Oven Temperature 350 degrees**
- **Bake 70 minutes**

BATTER
1¾ cups flour
1½ cups sugar
1 teaspoon baking soda
1 teaspoon cinnamon
½ teaspoon salt
¼ teaspoon nutmeg
1 cup mashed cooked pumpkin
½ cup (1 stick) margarine
1 egg
⅓ cup water

FILLING
8 ounces cream cheese, softened
¼ cup sugar
1 egg

Chocolate Chip Muffins

A sure hit

- **Makes 1 dozen**
- **Oven Temperature 400 degrees**
- **Bake 20 to 25 minutes**

BATTER
2 cups flour
1/2 cup sugar
1 tablespoon baking powder
1/2 teaspoon salt
3/4 cup miniature chocolate chips
1 egg, beaten
3/4 cup milk
1/3 cup vegetable oil

TOPPING
3 tablespoons sugar
2 tablespoons brown sugar

For the batter, combine the flour, 1/2 cup sugar, baking powder, salt and miniature chocolate chips in a medium bowl. Add the egg, milk and vegetable oil and stir just until moistened. The batter will be lumpy.

For the topping, combine 3 tablespoons sugar and brown sugar in a small bowl.

To assemble, spoon the batter into paper-lined muffin cups, filling 2/3 full. Sprinkle with the topping. Bake at 400 degrees for 20 to 25 minutes or until golden brown. Remove immediately from the muffin cups. Serve warm.

Lemon Raspberry Muffins

They'll melt in your mouth

For the batter, mix 2 cups flour, ½ cup sugar, baking powder, baking soda and salt in a large bowl. Combine the yogurt, vegetable oil, lemon peel and eggs in a small bowl and mix well. Add to the flour mixture and stir just until moistened. Fold in the raspberries.

For the topping, combine ⅓ cup sugar and ¼ cup flour in a small bowl. Cut in the butter until crumbly.

To assemble, spoon the batter into greased miniature muffin cups, filling ¾ full. Sprinkle with the topping. Bake at 400 degrees for 11 to 13 minutes or until light golden brown and a wooden pick inserted in the center comes out clean. Cool in the pan for 5 minutes before serving.

- **Makes 3 dozen**
- **Oven Temperature 400 degrees**
- **Bake 11 to 13 minutes**

BATTER
2 cups flour
½ cup sugar
2 teaspoons baking powder
½ teaspoon baking soda
½ teaspoon salt
1 cup lemon yogurt
½ cup vegetable oil
1 teaspoon grated lemon peel
2 eggs
1 cup fresh or frozen raspberries

TOPPING
⅓ cup sugar
¼ cup flour
2 tablespoons (¼ stick) butter or margarine

Morning Muffins

Delicious served from the oven

- **Makes 16 muffins**
- **Oven Temperature 350 degrees**
- **Bake 20 minutes**

2 cups flour
1 1/4 cups sugar
2 teaspoons baking soda
2 teaspoons cinnamon
1/2 teaspoon salt
1/2 cup chopped nuts
1/2 cup raisins
1/2 cup flaked coconut
1 large apple, peeled, chopped
2 cups grated carrots
3 eggs, beaten
1 cup unsweetened applesauce
2 teaspoons vanilla extract

Mix the flour, sugar, baking soda, cinnamon and salt in a large bowl. Fold in the nuts, raisins, coconut, apple and carrots. Combine the eggs, applesauce and vanilla in a bowl and mix well. Fold into the flour mixture. Spoon into paper-lined muffin cups sprayed with nonstick cooking spray. Bake at 350 degrees for 20 minutes.

Overnight Oatmeal Muffins

Old-Fashioned Goodness

- **Makes 1 dozen**
- **Must do ahead**
- **Chill 8 to 12 hours**
- **Oven Temperature 400 degrees**
- **Bake 18 to 20 minutes**

3/4 cup all-purpose flour
1 cup quick-cooking oats
1/2 cup packed brown sugar
1/2 cup whole wheat flour
1/2 teaspoon baking soda
1/2 teaspoon baking powder
1/2 teaspoon salt
1 teaspoon cinnamon
3/4 cup buttermilk
1/4 cup vegetable oil
1 egg
1/2 cup finely chopped apple
1/2 cup raisins
1/2 cup chopped nuts

Mix the all-purpose flour, oats, brown sugar, whole wheat flour, baking soda, baking powder, salt and cinnamon in a large bowl. Add the buttermilk, vegetable oil and egg and mix well. Fold in the apple, raisins and nuts. Chill, covered, for 8 to 12 hours. The batter will become stiffer.

Spoon the batter into greased or paper-lined muffin cups. Bake at 400 degrees for 18 to 20 minutes or until the muffins test done. Serve warm or cool.

***Note:** Can add enough milk to 2 teaspoons vinegar to measure 3/4 cup and use instead of the buttermilk.*

Pumpkin Apple Streusel Muffins

Good-tasting

- **Makes 2 dozen**
- **Oven Temperature 350 degrees**
- **Bake 35 minutes**

BATTER
2½ cups flour
2 cups sugar
1 tablespoon pumpkin pie spice
1 teaspoon baking soda
½ teaspoon salt
2 eggs, lightly beaten
1 cup solid-pack pumpkin
½ cup vegetable oil
2 cups finely chopped peeled apples

STREUSEL TOPPING
¼ cup sugar
2 tablespoons flour
½ teaspoon cinnamon
4 teaspoons butter

For the batter, mix 2½ cups flour, 2 cups sugar, pumpkin pie spice, baking soda and salt in a large bowl. Combine the eggs, pumpkin and vegetable oil in a bowl and mix well. Add to the flour mixture and stir just until moistened. Stir in the apples.

For the topping, mix ¼ cup sugar, 2 tablespoons flour and cinnamon in a small bowl. Cut in the butter until crumbly.

To assemble, spoon the batter into greased or paper-lined muffin cups, filling ¾ full. Sprinkle with the streusel topping. Bake at 350 degrees for 35 minutes or until a wooden pick inserted in the center comes out clean.

Note: Can make 6 giant muffins by baking in 6 large muffin cups, but increase the baking time to 40 to 45 minutes.

Herbed Cheese Beer Bread

One slice won't do

Combine the beer, self-rising flour, sugar, basil, rosemary, oregano and garlic powder in a bowl and mix well. Stir in the cheese. Spoon into a greased 5x9-inch loaf pan. Brush with melted butter. Bake at 375 degrees for 45 to 50 minutes or until the loaf tests done.

- **Makes 1 loaf**
- **Oven Temperature 375 degrees**
- **Bake 45 to 50 minutes**

12 ounces lager beer
3 cups self-rising flour
1/4 cup sugar
2 tablespoons snipped fresh basil leaves
2 tablespoons snipped fresh rosemary leaves
2 tablespoons snipped fresh oregano leaves
2 teaspoons garlic powder
1 1/2 cups shredded sharp Cheddar cheese
1/4 cup (1/2 stick) butter, melted

Wheat Germ Bread

Sweet and Moist

- **Makes 2 loaves**
- **Must do ahead**
- **Oven Temperature 375 degrees**
- **Bake 40 to 45 minutes**

1½ cups boiling water
6 tablespoons shortening
½ cup honey
1 tablespoon salt
2 envelopes dry yeast
½ cup warm (105 to 115 degrees) water
2 eggs
1 cup fresh wheat germ
5½ cups flour
Melted butter

Combine the boiling water, shortening, honey and salt in a large mixer bowl and stir until the shortening is melted. Cool to lukewarm.

Dissolve the yeast in the warm water. Add the yeast mixture, eggs, wheat germ and ½ of the flour to the shortening mixture. Beat for 2 minutes at medium speed. Stir in the remaining flour with a spoon. The dough will be sticky. Spread the dough evenly in 2 well-greased 5x9-inch loaf pans. Pat the tops with floured hands until smooth. Let rise in a warm place until the dough is 1 inch from the top of the pans.

Bake at 375 degrees for 40 to 45 minutes or until dark brown and the loaves sound hollow when tapped. Remove from the pans immediately. Brush the tops of the loaves with melted butter. Cool before serving.

***Note:** Fresh wheat germ may be purchased at your favorite health food store.*

Swedish Braids

Mom's Easter treat

For the bread, dissolve the yeast in the lukewarm water. Combine the hot scalded milk, sugar, butter and salt in a large mixer bowl, stirring to mix well; cool to lukewarm. Add the yeast mixture, eggs, cardamom seeds and 2 cups of the flour and beat until smooth. Add enough of the remaining flour a small amount at a time to make a soft dough. Knead on a lightly floured surface for 8 to 10 minutes or until smooth and elastic. Place in a lightly greased bowl, turning to coat the surface. Let rise, covered, in a warm place for 1 to 1½ hours or until doubled in bulk.

Divide the dough into 4 equal portions. Divide each portion into thirds. Roll each into a 10-inch strip. Braid 3 of the strips at a time together. Place on greased baking sheets. Let rise until doubled in bulk. Bake at 375 degrees for 20 to 25 minutes or until golden brown.

For the almond glaze, combine the confectioners' sugar, almond extract and milk in a mixer bowl and beat until smooth.

To assemble and serve, drizzle the almond glaze over the warm loaves. Decorate with red candied cherries for flowers and green candied cherries cut to resemble leaves.

- **Makes 4 braided loaves**
- **Must do ahead**
- **Oven Temperature 375 degrees**
- **Bake 20 to 25 minutes**

BREAD
2 envelopes dry yeast
½ cup lukewarm water
2 cups milk, scalded
1 cup sugar
½ cup (1 stick) butter
1 teaspoon salt
2 eggs
1 teaspoon cardamom seeds, finely crushed
8½ to 9 cups flour

ALMOND GLAZE
2 cups sifted confectioners' sugar
½ teaspoon almond extract
3 tablespoons milk

ASSEMBLY
Red and green candied cherries

FEATHER ROLLS

LIGHT AND LUSCIOUS

- **Makes $2\frac{1}{2}$ to 3 dozen**
- **Must do ahead**
- **Oven Temperature 350 degrees**
- **Bake 20 minutes**

2 envelopes dry yeast
1/2 cup sugar
1/4 cup lukewarm water
1 cup milk, scalded
3/4 teaspoon salt
1/2 cup (1 stick) butter or margarine
2 eggs, beaten
4 cups flour

Dissolve the yeast and 1/2 teaspoon of the sugar in the lukewarm water. Combine the hot scalded milk, remaining sugar, salt, butter and eggs in a large bowl and mix well. Cool to lukewarm. Add the yeast mixture and flour and mix to form a sticky dough.

Let rise, covered, in a warm place for 2 hours or until doubled in bulk. Invert onto a floured surface. Let rest for 15 minutes. Shape the dough a small portion at a time into 1 1/2- to 3-inch rectangles and fold over in half. Place on a greased baking sheet. Let rise, covered, for 1 hour or until doubled in bulk. Bake at 350 degrees for 20 minutes or until golden brown.

Cinnamon Rolls

Worth the Effort

- **Makes 32 large rolls**
- **Must do ahead**
- **Oven Temperature 375 degrees**
- **Bake 20 minutes**

DOUGH
2 envelopes dry yeast
1/2 cup lukewarm water
1/2 cup sugar
2 teaspoons salt
2 cups milk, scalded, cooled
2 eggs, beaten
6 to 6 1/2 cups bread flour
1/2 cup shortening, melted, cooled

CINNAMON FILLING
1 cup (2 sticks) butter, softened
2 cups sugar
2 tablespoons cinnamon

TOPPINGS
3 tablespoons brown sugar
3 tablespoons dark corn syrup

VANILLA GLAZE
1 cup sifted confectioners' sugar
3 tablespoons evaporated milk
1/2 teaspoon vanilla extract
Pinch of salt

For the dough, dissolve the yeast in the lukewarm water in a bowl. Dissolve 1/2 cup sugar and 2 teaspoons salt in the milk in a large bowl. Stir in the yeast mixture. Add the eggs and mix well. Add 3 cups of the flour gradually, mixing well by hand. Add the shortening and mix well. Add enough of the remaining flour to form a soft dough. Invert onto a floured surface. Let rest, covered, for 10 minutes.

Knead the dough for 10 minutes or until smooth and elastic, adding only enough of the remaining flour to keep the dough from becoming sticky. Place in a large greased bowl, turning to coat the surface. Cover with a damp cloth. Let rise for 2 hours or until doubled in bulk. Punch the dough down. Cover and let rise for 45 minutes.

For the cinnamon filling, combine the butter, 2 cups sugar and cinnamon in a small bowl and mix well.

To assemble, divide the dough into 2 equal portions. Roll each portion into a 12x15-inch rectangle on a lightly floured surface. Spread each rectangle with 1/2 of the cinnamon filling. Roll up each from the long side as for a jelly roll; seal the edges. Cut each roll-up into 16 slices. Arrange cut side up in buttered 9x13-inch baking pans.

For the toppings, sprinkle the rolls with brown sugar; drizzle with corn syrup. Let rise, covered, for 1 hour. Bake, uncovered, at 375 degrees for 20 minutes. Cool in the pans for 1 minute. Invert onto baking sheets, leaving the pans on top of the rolls for 1 minute. Remove the pans.

For the vanilla glaze, combine the confectioners' sugar, evaporated milk, vanilla and pinch of salt in a bowl and mix until smooth. Drizzle over the warm rolls.

Finnish Coffee Cakes

Moist and Dense, but Not Too Sweet

- **Makes 4 braided loaves**
- **Must do ahead**
- **Oven Temperature 370 degrees**
- **Bake 20 minutes**

1 teaspoon cardamom seeds
1 cup sugar
2 envelopes dry yeast
1/2 cup warm water
1 1/2 cups warm milk
1 teaspoon salt
3 eggs, beaten
1/2 cup (1 stick) butter, melted
7 to 7 1/2 cups bread flour
1 cup strong brewed coffee, cooled
Sugar

Peel the cardamom seeds. Process with 1 cup sugar in a food processor until ground. Dissolve the yeast in the warm water in a bowl. Mix the warm milk, salt, sugar mixture, eggs and butter in a large bowl. Let cool to lukewarm. Add the yeast mixture and mix well. Beat in 3 cups of the bread flour. Stir in 3 more cups of the bread flour. Invert onto a surface sprinkled with 1/2 of the remaining bread flour. Knead until smooth and elastic, adding the remaining flour only if the dough remains sticky. Place in a greased bowl, turning to coat the surface. Let rise, covered, for 1 1/2 hours or until a little more than doubled in bulk. Punch the dough down. Let rise for 1 hour or until doubled in bulk.

Invert onto a floured surface. Cover and let rest for 10 minutes. Divide into 4 equal portions. Shape 1 portion into 3 balls. Roll each ball into a long rope. Braid the ropes to form a loaf. Repeat with the remaining dough portions.

Place 2 braided loaves on each of 2 greased baking sheets. Let rise, covered, in a warm place until doubled in bulk. Bake, uncovered, at 370 degrees for 20 minutes or until golden brown. Brush with the strong coffee and sprinkle with sugar. Remove to wire racks to cool.

Note: Since cardamom seeds can be hard to find, 1 1/2 teaspoons fresh cardamom powder can be substituted. Cardamom powder loses its flavor quickly.

Variation: Each of the 4 portions of dough can be shaped into 12 rolls instead of 1 braided loaf.

Easy Caramel Pecan Pull-Aparts

Delicious

- **Serves 6 to 8**
- **Oven Temperature 350 degrees**
- **Bake 30 to 35 minutes**

1 cup packed brown sugar
1/2 cup (1 stick) butter
2 tablespoons water
1/2 cup pecans
2 (8-count) cans crescent rolls
1/4 cup sugar
1 teaspoon cinnamon

Combine the brown sugar, butter and water in a saucepan. Bring to a slow boil and remove from the heat. Stir in the pecans. Remove the dough from the cans, retaining the log shape. Cut each log into 10 equal slices. Toss with a mixture of sugar and cinnamon. Layer the dough slices and caramel mixture 1/2 at a time in a greased bundt pan. Bake at 350 degrees for 30 to 35 minutes or until brown. Cool slightly. Invert onto a warm platter to serve.

Orange Toast

Good anytime

- **Makes 5 dozen**
- **Oven Temperature 250 degrees**
- **Bake 1 hour**
- **Can be frozen**

3/4 cup sugar
3/4 cup (1 1/2 sticks) butter or margarine, softened
2 tablespoons orange juice
3 tablespoons finely grated orange peel
1 loaf thinly sliced white or whole wheat bread

Combine the sugar, butter, orange juice and orange peel in a bowl and mix well. Spread on 1 side of each slice of bread. Cut each slice diagonally into halves. Place on ungreased baking sheets. Bake at 250 degrees for 1 hour. Cool. Store in an airtight container at room temperature or in the freezer.

Note: Do not use light butter or margarine in this recipe. Recipe can easily be doubled.

Vegetables and Side Dishes

WINTER SPLENDOR
ON LAKE MICHIGAN

Asparagus with Honey Garlic Sauce

A Nice Variation

- **Serves 5**

1 pound fresh asparagus
1/2 cup Dijon mustard
1/2 cup dark ale or beer
1/2 cup honey
1 garlic clove, minced
1/2 teaspoon thyme
1/2 teaspoon salt

Trim the asparagus and rinse. Cook the asparagus in boiling water to cover in a skillet for 3 to 5 minutes or until tender-crisp. Do not overcook. Drain and rinse under cold water.

Combine the Dijon mustard, dark ale, honey, garlic, thyme and salt in a bowl and mix well. Place the asparagus in a serving bowl. Pour the sauce over the asparagus.

Chinese Broccoli

Something different

Rinse the broccoli. Trim the florets from the stalk. Cut the stalk into thin strips. Combine the butter, water and soy sauce in a large skillet. Bring to a boil. Stir in the broccoli florets, broccoli stalk, celery and water chestnuts. Return to a boil. Cook, covered, for 5 to 10 minutes or until tender-crisp.

Toast the sesame seeds in a small skillet until light brown, shaking the skillet constantly. Add to the broccoli mixture and stir to mix well. Serve with additional soy sauce.

- **Serves 4**

1 1/2 pounds broccoli
1/4 cup (1/2 stick) butter
1/4 cup water
2 tablespoons soy sauce
1 cup thinly sliced celery
1 (5-ounce) can sliced water chestnuts, drained
2 tablespoons sesame seeds

Cabbage Crown

Nutritious and Attractive

- **Serves 6 to 8**
- **Oven Temperature 375 degrees**
- **Bake 45 minutes**
- **Oven Temperature 400 degrees**
- **Bake 5 minutes**

FILLING

5 tablespoons olive oil
2 onions, chopped
5 large garlic cloves, minced
1 small head cabbage, finely chopped (about 2 pounds)
2 teaspoons chopped fresh dill, or 1 teaspoon dried dill
1/2 teaspoon salt
Freshly grated black pepper to taste
1/2 teaspoon paprika
1/2 to 1 teaspoon grated lemon peel
1 cup sour cream
2 tablespoons freshly grated Romano or Parmesan cheese

CROWN

8 ounces (10 sheets) phyllo dough
1 cup (2 sticks) unsalted butter, melted

For the filling, heat the olive oil in a large skillet. Add the onions and garlic. Sauté until the onions are translucent. Increase the heat slightly. Add the cabbage. Cook until tender, stirring constantly and adding additional olive oil if needed. Pour into a colander to drain. Place the drained cabbage mixture in a large bowl. Add the dill, salt, black pepper, paprika and lemon peel. Let stand until cool. Add the sour cream and Romano cheese and mix well.

For the crown, cut the phyllo dough into thirds lengthwise. Stack the strips and cover with clear plastic wrap. Brush 1 strip of the phyllo dough with melted butter. Drape gently into a large greased bundt pan, letting the middle of the phyllo dough hang down in a "U" shape and letting the ends fall over the outside edge and center of the pan. Repeat with the remaining phyllo dough, brushing with melted butter and draping to overlap each strip by 1/2 inch all the way around the inside of the pan.

To assemble, pour the filling into the prepared pan. Cut a "+" through the phyllo dough covering the center of the tube. Fold the cut ends away from the center of the tube down over the filling. Brush with melted butter. Fold the overhanging ends from the outer edge of the pan over the filling to enclose, tucking the edges under. Brush with butter. Bake at 375 degrees for 45 minutes or until golden brown. Let stand until cool. Invert and unmold onto a baking sheet. Increase the oven temperature to 400 degrees. Bake for 5 minutes or until the phyllo dough is crisp. Remove from the oven. Cool for 15 minutes before serving.

Sweet-and-Sour Cabbage

The Old-Fashioned German Flavor

- **Serves 4 to 6**

1 head red cabbage, chopped
1 apple, sliced
1 small onion, chopped
1/2 cup vinegar
1/2 cup sugar
1/2 cup beer
1/4 cup (1/2 stick) margarine
3/4 cup water
1/2 teaspoon salt
1/4 teaspoon pepper

Combine the cabbage, apple, onion, vinegar, sugar, beer, margarine, water, salt and pepper in a large saucepan. Bring to a boil and reduce the heat to low. Simmer for 30 to 40 minutes or until tender.

Glazed Carrots

Tried and True

- **Serves 8**

10 medium carrots
Salt to taste
2 tablespoons sugar
1 teaspoon cornstarch
1/2 teaspoon salt
1/2 teaspoon ginger
1/2 cup orange juice
1/4 cup (1/2 stick) butter

Scrape the carrots and cut into slices. Place in water to cover in a saucepan. Season with salt to taste. Cook for 20 minutes or until tender; drain.

Combine the sugar, cornstarch, 1/2 teaspoon salt and ginger in a small saucepan. Add the orange juice. Boil for 1 minute or until thickened, stirring constantly. Stir in the butter. Pour over the carrots and toss until coated.

Great Carrots

Good with Ham

- **Serves 6 to 8**
- **Must do ahead**
- **Chill 8 to 12 hours**
- **Oven Temperature 350 degrees**
- **Bake until heated through**

3 pounds carrot sticks
1 cup (2 sticks) butter
2 cups sugar
Juice of 4 lemons
1 onion, finely chopped

Cook the carrot sticks in water to cover in a saucepan until tender-crisp; drain. Do not overcook.

Melt the butter in a saucepan. Add the sugar, lemon juice and onion. Heat until the sugar is dissolved, stirring constantly. Pour over the carrots in a large bowl. Chill, covered, for 8 to 12 hours.

To serve, spoon the carrots into a baking dish. Bake at 350 degrees until heated through.

Scalloped Corn

Grandma's Original

Combine the egg yolks, flour, milk, salt, sugar, butter and corn in a bowl and mix well. Beat the egg whites in a mixer bowl until soft peaks form. Fold into the corn mixture. Spoon into a 1- or 1½-quart baking dish. Bake at 350 degrees for 45 minutes.

- **Serves 4 to 6**
- **Oven Temperature 350 degrees**
- **Bake 45 minutes**

2 egg yolks, lightly beaten
2 tablespoons flour
½ cup milk
Pinch of salt
1 tablespoon sugar
1 to 2 tablespoons butter
1 (17-ounce) can cream-style corn
2 egg whites

Stuffed Fried Eggplant

Rich and Wonderful

- **Serves 4**
- **Oven Temperature 350 degrees**
- **Bake 30 to 40 minutes**

EGGPLANT
2 to 3 eggs
Salt and pepper to taste
1/2 to 3/4 cup grated Parmesan cheese
2 eggplant, cut into thin slices
1/2 cup flour
Vegetable oil for frying

FILLING
2 pints ricotta cheese
2 to 3 eggs, beaten
Salt and pepper to taste
1/2 cup grated Parmesan cheese

ASSEMBLY
3 to 4 cups spaghetti sauce
8 ounces mozzarella cheese, sliced 1/4 inch thick, torn into pieces
Grated Parmesan cheese to taste

For the eggplant, beat 2 to 3 eggs with salt, pepper and 1/2 to 3/4 cup Parmesan cheese in a bowl. Dip the eggplant in the flour; dip in the egg mixture. Fry in medium-hot vegetable oil in a skillet until golden brown.

For the filling, mix the ricotta cheese, 2 to 3 eggs, salt, pepper and 1/2 cup Parmesan cheese in a bowl.

To assemble, spoon a thin layer of spaghetti sauce in a baking dish. Place a spoonful of the filling and some mozzarella cheese in the center of each eggplant slice. Fold each in half and place in the prepared dish. Cover with the remaining spaghetti sauce. Sprinkle with Parmesan cheese to taste. Bake at 350 degrees for 30 to 40 minutes or until bubbly.

Eggplant with Feta Cheese

A non-eggplant lover's favorite

- **Serves 4 to 6**

1 large eggplant, or 2 small eggplant
3 medium onions, sliced lengthwise
1/4 cup virgin olive oil
2 garlic cloves, minced
6 fresh tomatoes, chopped
1/4 cup chopped fresh parsley
Salt and pepper to taste
3/4 cup crumbled feta cheese

Cut the unpeeled eggplant into small pieces. Sauté the onions in the olive oil in a skillet until translucent. Add the garlic. Sauté for a few minutes. Add the eggplant, tomatoes, parsley, salt and pepper. Cook for 30 to 45 minutes or until the eggplant is tender, stirring occasionally. Pour into a serving bowl. Sprinkle with the feta cheese.

Note: Can use one 29-ounce can diced tomatoes for the fresh tomatoes.

Onion Shortcake

A vegetable, not a dessert

- **Serves 4**
- **Oven Temperature 425 degrees**
- **Bake 25 to 30 minutes**

1 large sweet onion, sliced
1/4 cup (1/2 stick) butter
1 cup sour cream
1/4 teaspoon dillseeds
1 cup shredded sharp Cheddar cheese
1 (8-ounce) package corn muffin mix
1/3 cup milk
1 egg
1 cup cream-style corn
2 drops of Tabasco sauce
1/4 teaspoon salt

Sauté the onion in the butter in a skillet over low heat. Add the sour cream, dillseeds and 1/2 cup of the Cheddar cheese and mix well.

Combine the corn muffin mix, milk, egg, corn, Tabasco sauce and salt in a bowl and mix well. Spoon into a buttered 9x9-inch baking dish. Spread the onion mixture over the batter. Sprinkle with the remaining Cheddar cheese. Bake at 425 degrees for 25 to 30 minutes or until cooked through. Serve warm.

Note: Can double the recipe and add more cheese if desired. Skim milk, reduced-fat cheese and light sour cream can be used to reduce caloric intake. Do not use no-fat products in this recipe.

Garden-Style Mashed Potatoes

Effortless

- **Serves 6**
- **Can do ahead**

6 white potatoes
Butter
Milk
½ cup chopped cabbage
½ cup chopped or shredded carrot
¼ cup finely chopped onion
½ cup finely chopped celery
Olive oil
4 leaves fresh sage, chopped
⅛ teaspoon nutmeg
Salt and pepper to taste

Cook the potatoes in water to cover until tender; drain. Add a small amount of butter and milk and beat until smooth.

Sauté the cabbage, carrot, onion and celery in a small amount of olive oil until tender. Add the sage. Add to the potatoes and mix well. Season with the nutmeg, salt and pepper.

***Note:** To prepare ahead, spoon into a greased baking dish and dot with butter. When ready to serve, place under a broiler to warm.*

Baked Mashed Potatoes

Do Ahead and Skip the Last Minute Rush

- **Serves 9**
- **Can do ahead**
- **Oven Temperature 375 degrees**
- **Bake 30 to 45 minutes**

4 pounds russet potatoes
Salt to taste
6 ounces cream cheese, chopped
3/4 cup sour cream
1 1/2 teaspoons finely chopped garlic
Pepper to taste
3 tablespoons butter, melted

Peel the potatoes and cut into 1-inch pieces. Cook in salted boiling water to cover in a saucepan for 20 minutes or until tender; drain. Add the cream cheese and beat until smooth. Beat in the sour cream and garlic. Season with salt and pepper to taste. Spoon into a glass baking dish. Drizzle with the butter. Bake, uncovered, at 375 degrees for 30 minutes or until heated through.

***Note:** Can assemble 1 day ahead and store, covered, in the refrigerator. Bake for 45 minutes or until heated through.*

Festive Potatoes

Attractive

- **Serves 4**

4 large potatoes
1 cup chopped red bell pepper
1 cup chopped zucchini
1/4 cup chopped onion
4 tablespoons (1/2 stick) butter
1/2 cup hot milk
3/4 teaspoon sea salt
1/4 teaspoon white pepper

Scrub the potatoes and prick with a fork. Arrange in a circle on a microwave-safe paper towel in the microwave. Microwave on High for 20 to 22 minutes or until tender.

Combine the red pepper, zucchini, onion and 2 tablespoons of the butter in a microwave-safe dish. Microwave on High for 4 to 6 minutes or until tender.

Cut the potatoes into halves lengthwise. Scoop out the centers and place in a bowl, reserving the potato shells. Add the hot milk, remaining 2 tablespoons butter, sea salt and white pepper to the potatoes and beat until light and fluffy. Stir in the vegetables. Spoon into the potato shells. Place on a microwave-safe 12-inch platter. Microwave on High for 5 to 6 minutes or until heated through.

Garlic Roasted Potatoes

Dresses up the plate

- **Serves 4**
- **Oven Temperature 400 degrees**
- **Bake 1 hour**

8 red potatoes
1/2 cup olive oil
3 large garlic cloves, finely minced
Salt and pepper to taste

Scrub the potatoes and pat dry. Cut a small slice off 1 end of each potato so the potatoes will stand upright. Insert a skewer lengthwise into the potato to 1/4 inch from the bottom. Cut the potato crosswise to the skewer into 1/4-inch slices. Remove the skewer. Repeat with the remaining potatoes.

Mix the olive oil and garlic in a bowl. Brush the potatoes with 1/2 of the olive oil mixture. Arrange the potatoes upright on a greased baking sheet. Sprinkle with salt and pepper. Bake at 400 degrees for 30 minutes. Brush with the remaining olive oil mixture. Bake for 30 minutes or until the potatoes are tender and golden brown.

To serve, place the potatoes upright on serving plates and push down on the potatoes in one direction to fan the slices slightly.

Potato Kugel

An old stand-by

- **Serves 6 to 8**
- **Oven Temperature 350 degrees**
- **Bake 1 hour**

4 cups grated potatoes, drained
3 eggs
1 large onion, grated
1½ teaspoons salt
¼ teaspoon pepper
¼ cup (½ stick) butter, melted
⅓ cup flour
6 sprigs of parsley, chopped

Combine the potatoes, eggs, onion, salt, pepper, butter, flour and parsley in a bowl and mix well. Spoon into a greased 9-inch cast-iron skillet. Bake at 350 degrees for 1 hour or until set and golden brown. Cut into wedges to serve.

Note: This recipe is wonderful sliced the next day and fried. May use bacon or chicken drippings instead of the butter.

Creamy Baked Potatoes

Great for a buffet

- **Serves 6 to 8**
- **Can do ahead**
- **Can be frozen**
- **Oven Temperature 350 degrees**
- **Bake 30 minutes**

6 medium potatoes, peeled, chopped
1 teaspoon salt
1/4 teaspoon pepper
1 cup sour cream
3 ounces cream cheese, softened
1 tablespoon butter
Paprika to taste

Boil the potatoes in water to cover in a saucepan until tender; drain. Add the salt, pepper, sour cream and cream cheese and beat until smooth. Spoon into a buttered baking dish. Dot with butter and sprinkle with paprika. Bake at 350 degrees for 30 minutes.

Note: The potato mixture will thicken as it is baked. The recipe can be assembled a day ahead and refrigerated until ready to bake. The recipe can also be assembled and frozen, but thaw before baking.

Easy German Potato Salad

Tasty and easy

- **Serves 8 to 12**
- **Must do ahead**

8 large red potatoes
1 pound sliced lean bacon, cooked, crumbled
3/4 cup finely chopped onion
1/3 cup bacon drippings
2 tablespoons flour
2 tablespoons sugar
1 1/2 teaspoons salt
1 teaspoon celery seeds
2 teaspoons chopped fresh parsley
Dash of pepper
3/4 cup water
3/4 cup apple cider vinegar

Scrub the potatoes. Cook in boiling water to cover in a saucepan until tender; drain. Peel the potatoes and cut into pieces. Combine the potatoes and bacon in a bowl.

Sauté the onion in the bacon drippings in a skillet until tender. Add the flour, sugar, salt, celery seeds, parsley, pepper, water and apple cider vinegar. Bring to a boil, stirring constantly. Boil for 1 minute. Stir in the potato mixture and remove from the heat. Let stand for 1 hour to blend the seasonings before serving.

Green Bean Potato Salad

A DIFFERENT TWIST

- **Serves 10**
- **Must do ahead**
- **Chill**

SALAD
3 pounds tiny new potatoes
Salt to taste
1 pound fresh green beans, cut into 1-inch pieces

DILL DRESSING
3/4 cup vegetable oil
1/4 cup red wine vinegar
1 teaspoon salt, or to taste
1/2 teaspoon pepper, or to taste
1 tablespoon snipped fresh dill
1 tablespoon Dijon mustard

ASSEMBLY
Red leaf lettuce
Alfalfa or radish sprouts

For the salad, scrub the potatoes. Peel a strip around the center of each potato. Boil in salted water to cover in a saucepan for 10 to 15 minutes or until tender; drain. Let stand until cool. Cook the green beans, partially covered, in a small amount of water for 10 to 15 minutes or until tender. Rinse under cold water and drain. Combine the potatoes and green beans in a bowl.

For the dressing, process the vegetable oil, red wine vinegar, 1 teaspoon salt, pepper, dill and Dijon mustard in a blender until blended.

To assemble, pour the dill dressing over the salad. Chill, covered, in the refrigerator. Line a serving platter with red leaf lettuce. Spoon the salad into the center and surround with alfalfa sprouts.

Potato Pancake with Smoked Salmon and Sour Cream

Delicious

Mix the sour cream, shallots, dill and lemon juice in a bowl and mix well. Chill, covered, until ready to use.

Toss the potatoes with 1 tablespoon of the butter in a bowl. Season with salt and pepper. Heat a 10-inch ovenproof skillet over medium heat. Add the remaining butter and swirl to coat the skillet. Add the potatoes, flattening with a spatula to form a large pancake. Cook for 2 minutes. Reduce the heat. Cook for 5 minutes longer or until the bottom is golden brown. Slide the pancake onto a plate; place skillet on top of pancake and invert back into skillet. Cook for 4 minutes or until golden brown on the bottom. Bake at 425 degrees for 10 minutes or until the pancake is crisp.

To serve, place the pancake on a serving platter. Spread with the sour cream mixture and top with the salmon. Sprinkle with the chives and serve.

- **Serves 8**
- **Must do ahead**
- **Chill**
- **Oven Temperature 425 degrees**
- **Bake 10 minutes**

1/4 cup sour cream
2 tablespoons minced shallots
2 tablespoons minced fresh dill
1 tablespoon fresh lemon juice
2 1/2 cups grated peeled russet potatoes
2 tablespoons (1/4 stick) butter, melted
Salt and pepper to taste
3 ounces thinly sliced salmon
1 tablespoon chopped fresh chives

Potato Pie

Excellent

- **Serves 8**
- **Can do ahead**
- **Oven temperature 425 degrees**
- **Bake 50 minutes**

1 pound cottage cheese
2 cups mashed cooked potatoes
1/2 cup sour cream
2 eggs
2 teaspoons salt
1/8 teaspoon cayenne pepper
1/2 cup sliced scallions
1 (10-inch) unbaked pie shell
3 tablespoons freshly grated Parmesan cheese

Process the cottage cheese in a food processor just until smooth. Beat the mashed potatoes and cottage cheese in a mixer bowl. Add the sour cream, eggs, salt and cayenne pepper and mix well. Stir in the scallions.

Spoon into the pie shell. Sprinkle with Parmesan cheese. Bake at 425 degrees for 50 minutes or until golden brown.

Note: The pie shell and filling can be made in advance and refrigerated until ready to assemble and bake.

Pommes de Terre avec Gruyère

A French impression

- **Serves 4**
- **Oven Temperature 350 degrees**
- **Bake 40 minutes**

3 potatoes
1 large Granny Smith apple
Butter or margarine
Salt and pepper to taste
Gruyère cheese, thinly sliced
1 cup heavy cream

Peel the potatoes and cut into thin slices. Cut the unpeeled apple into thin slices. Coat the inside of 4 ramekins with butter. Alternate layers of the potatoes and apple in the prepared ramekins, adding pats of butter and salt and pepper between each layer. Arrange several slices of Gruyère cheese over the layers. Pour the cream over the top. Place the ramekins on a baking sheet or in a glass baking dish. Bake at 350 degrees for 40 minutes. Serve hot.

Swedish Rutabagas

Try it—you'll like it

- **Serves 6**

2 medium rutabagas
2 tablespoons (1/4 stick) butter or margarine
2 tablespoons brown sugar
1/2 teaspoon ginger
1/2 teaspoon salt
1/8 teaspoon pepper

Peel the rutabagas and chop into pieces. Cook in water to cover in a saucepan until tender; drain. Add the butter, brown sugar, ginger, salt and pepper. Cook for 2 to 3 minutes or until the brown sugar is dissolved and the butter melts, stirring frequently.

Summer Squash Casserole

Nice flavor

- **Serves 6**
- **Can do ahead**
- **Can be frozen**
- **Oven Temperature 350 degrees**
- **Bake 20 to 30 minutes**

1 cup water
2 pounds summer squash, sliced
1 teaspoon salt
1/8 teaspoon sugar
1/4 cup (1/2 stick) butter
1 1/4 cups cubed Cheddar cheese
1 cup sour cream
1/3 cup grated Parmesan cheese
1/2 cup chopped onion
1/4 cup dry white wine, such as Vermouth
Salt and pepper to taste
1 cup fresh bread crumbs
3 tablespoons butter

Bring the water to a boil in a saucepan. Add the squash, 1 teaspoon salt and sugar. Cook, covered, for 20 minutes; drain. Add 1/4 cup butter and mash well. Stir in the Cheddar cheese, sour cream, Parmesan cheese, onion, wine, salt and pepper to taste. Spoon into an 11-inch gratin dish or baking dish.

Mix the bread crumbs and 3 tablespoons butter in a bowl. Sprinkle over the squash mixture. Bake at 350 degrees for 20 to 30 minutes or until the top is golden brown.

Note: Can prepare ahead and store, covered, in the freezer until ready to use.

Spicy Sweet Potato Bean Burrito

Exceptional Flavor

- **Serves 4 to 6**
- **Oven Temperature 375 degrees**
- **Bake 10 to 15 minutes**

1 teaspoon olive or canola oil
1 large onion, finely chopped
2 garlic cloves, minced
2 (15- to 16-ounce) cans kidney, adzuki or garbanzo beans
1 cup water
1½ tablespoons chili powder
1½ teaspoons prepared mustard
1 teaspoon cumin
1½ tablespoons soy sauce
8 (10-inch) soft flour tortillas
3 sweet potatoes, cooked, mashed (about 2 cups)
3 green onions, finely chopped

GARNISHES
Chopped avocado
Salsa
Yogurt

Heat the olive oil in a 4-quart saucepan over medium heat. Add the onion. Sauté until transparent. Stir in the garlic. Add the beans, water, chili powder, mustard and cumin. Bring to a boil over medium-high heat. Cover and reduce the heat to low. Simmer for 15 to 19 minutes or until the beans are soft. Stir in the soy sauce. Mash with a potato masher or large slotted spoon. Simmer, uncovered, over medium-low heat for 25 minutes or until the excess liquid has evaporated. Adjust the seasonings.

Spread ⅔ cup of the bean mixture down the middle of each tortilla. Top each with ½ cup mashed sweet potatoes and sprinkle with the green onions. Fold up bottom edge of each 2 inches; fold sides over to cover filling and roll up. Place seam side down on a baking sheet sprayed with nonstick cooking spray. Bake at 375 degrees for 10 to 15 minutes or until crisp.

Serve with toppings of choice such as shredded lettuce, grated carrots, alfalfa sprouts, minced onions or chopped celery. Garnish with avocado, salsa and yogurt.

Parsley Tomatoes

Nice side dish for a picnic-style menu

- **Serves 8**
- **Must do ahead**
- **Chill for up to 2 days**

8 medium-firm tomatoes
1/2 cup chopped fresh parsley
1 garlic clove, minced
1 teaspoon salt
1 teaspoon sugar
1/4 teaspoon pepper
1/4 cup olive oil
2 tablespoons tarragon vinegar or wine vinegar
2 teaspoons Dijon mustard

Core the tomatoes and turn upside down. Cut vertically into 1/2-inch slices to but not through the bottom. Spoon about 1 teaspoon of the parsley between each of the slices. Place in a shallow dish.

Combine the garlic, salt, sugar, pepper, olive oil, tarragon vinegar and Dijon mustard in a bowl and mix well. Pour over the tomatoes. Chill, covered, for up to 2 days before serving. Let stand for 20 minutes before serving.

***Note:** Tomatoes can be sliced and layered in a shallow dish, sprinkling parsley between each layer.*

Marinated Sliced Tomatoes

Perfect with grilled food

- **Serves 6**
- **Must do ahead**
- **Chill 1 hour**

4 large tomatoes
1/4 cup olive oil
1 tablespoon lemon juice
1/2 teaspoon minced garlic
1/2 teaspoon salt
1/2 teaspoon oregano leaves
1/2 teaspoon basil

Peel the tomatoes and cut into slices. Arrange in a shallow dish. Combine the olive oil, lemon juice, garlic, salt, oregano and basil in a bowl and mix well. Pour over the tomatoes. Chill, covered, for 1 hour.

STUFFED ZUCCHINI

FULL-FLAVORED

- **Serves 4**
- **Oven Temperature 350 degrees**
- **Bake 30 minutes**

2 (8-inch-long) zucchini
Salt to taste
8 ounces lean ground beef
1 tablespoon dry bread crumbs, rolled oats or crushed croutons
2 teaspoons catsup
1/2 teaspoon Worcestershire sauce
1 tablespoon minced onion
1 tablespoon chopped fresh parsley
1/2 teaspoon celery salt
Dash of garlic powder
Dash of pepper
1 egg, beaten
3 tablespoons grated Parmesan cheese

Rinse the zucchini and trim the ends. Cut the zucchini into halves lengthwise. Cook in boiling salted water in a saucepan until tender. Plunge into cold water immediately to stop the cooking process; drain and cool.

Scoop the zucchini pulp into a bowl, leaving 1/4-inch shells. Drain the shells cut side down on paper towels. Chop the pulp finely. Add the ground beef, bread crumbs, catsup, Worcestershire sauce, onion, parsley, celery salt, garlic powder, pepper and egg to the pulp in a bowl and mix well. Spoon into the zucchini shells. Sprinkle with the Parmesan cheese. Bake, uncovered, at 350 degrees for 30 minutes or until the filling is cooked through.

Vegetable Mélange

Use any vegetables you have on hand

- **Serves 6 to 8**
- **Oven Temperature 425 degrees**
- **Bake 37 to 42 minutes**

2 medium russet potatoes, cut into 1-inch pieces
2 medium carrots, cut into 1/2-inch slices
1 tablespoon olive oil
1 teaspoon chopped fresh basil
1 teaspoon chopped fresh oregano
1/4 teaspoon salt
1/4 teaspoon pepper
2 garlic cloves, minced
1 large zucchini, cut into 1/2-inch pieces
1 large red bell pepper, cut into 1-inch pieces
2 cups shredded 4-cheese blend

GARNISH
Sprigs of basil

Place the potatoes and carrots in a greased 9x13-inch baking dish. Drizzle with the olive oil. Sprinkle with the basil, oregano, salt, pepper and garlic. Toss lightly to coat.

Bake at 425 degrees for 20 minutes. Stir in the zucchini and red pepper. Bake for 15 to 20 minutes or until tender. Sprinkle with the cheese. Bake for 2 minutes or until the cheese melts. Garnish with basil sprigs.

Sautéed Summer Mushrooms

Great with Steak

- **Serves 2**

1 tablespoon butter
8 ounces mushrooms, cut into quarters
1 teaspoon finely chopped lemon thyme
2 tablespoons red wine
Salt and pepper to taste

Melt the butter in a medium sauté pan over medium heat. Add the mushrooms and lemon thyme. Sauté for 5 minutes. Add the red wine. Sauté until the pan juices have almost evaporated. Season with salt and pepper. Serve immediately.

Mushroom Cheese Pie

Makes a Delightful Accompaniment to Beef

- **Serves 6 to 8**
- **Oven Temperature 400 degrees**
- **Bake 25 to 30 minutes**

1 recipe (2-crust) pie pastry
1 pound sliced mushrooms
2 tablespoons olive oil
3/4 cup shredded sharp Cheddar cheese
1/2 teaspoon salt
Dash of pepper
1/2 teaspoon dry mustard

Line a pie plate with 1 of the pie pastries.

Combine the mushrooms with the olive oil in a bowl and toss to coat. Add the Cheddar cheese, salt, pepper and dry mustard and toss to mix well. Spoon into the prepared pie plate. Cover with the remaining pie pastry, trimming and fluting the edge and cutting vents. Bake at 400 degrees for 25 to 30 minutes or until golden brown.

Mushroom Rice Pilaf

Great with any Entrée

- **Serves 12**

1 cup (2 sticks) butter or margarine
2½ cups uncooked long grain white rice
1 cup coarsely chopped onion
8 ounces fresh mushrooms, sliced
2 (10-ounce) cans chicken broth
1 cup water
½ teaspoon thyme leaves
⅛ teaspoon pepper
½ cup chopped fresh parsley

Melt the butter in a 6-quart Dutch oven. Add the rice and stir until coated with the butter. Add the onion and mushrooms. Sauté for 5 minutes or until the onion is tender. Stir in the chicken broth, water, thyme and pepper. Bring to a boil and reduce the heat.

Simmer, covered, for 25 to 30 minutes or until the liquid is absorbed and the rice is tender. Add the parsley and toss lightly with a fork.

Golden Rice

Nice accompaniment

Bring the chicken broth, salt, butter and turmeric to a boil in a saucepan. Add the rice. Return to a boil and reduce the heat.

Simmer, covered, for 30 to 40 minutes or until tender. Add the orange peel, parsley and grapes. Cover and let stand for 1 minute. Toss with a fork and serve immediately.

- **Serves 8**

4 cups chicken broth
1/4 teaspoon salt
2 tablespoons (1/4 stick) butter
1/8 teaspoon turmeric
2 cups uncooked long grain rice
2 teaspoons grated orange peel
2 tablespoons chopped fresh parsley
2 cups grape halves

Rice Pilaf

Colorful

- **Serves 4 to 6**

1 tablespoon olive oil
1/4 cup chopped shallots
2 tablespoons pine nuts
1 cup uncooked basmati or long grain rice
2 to 3 carrots, grated
1 tablespoon grated orange peel
1/4 teaspoon cardamom
2 1/4 cups chicken broth, heated
1/2 teaspoon honey
1/8 teaspoon salt

Heat the olive oil in a saucepan over medium heat. Add the shallots and pine nuts. Cook for 4 to 6 minutes. Add the rice, carrots, orange peel and cardamom. Cook for 2 minutes, stirring frequently. Add the warm chicken broth, honey and salt. Simmer, tightly covered, for 25 to 30 minutes or until the liquid is absorbed.

Bulgur Wheat Sauté

Great change from potatoes and rice

Cook the bulgur, onion, garlic, celery, carrots and green pepper in the butter in a medium skillet over low heat for 10 to 15 minutes or until the onion is tender, stirring frequently. Stir in the water and instant bouillon. Bring to a boil and reduce the heat. Simmer, covered, for 15 to 30 minutes or until the bulgur is cooked through. Stir in the parsley.

- **Serves 8**

1 cup coarsely ground bulgur
1/3 cup chopped onion
1 garlic clove, minced
1/3 cup chopped celery
1/3 cup sliced carrots
1/3 cup chopped green bell pepper
1 tablespoon butter or margarine
2 cups water
2 1/2 teaspoons instant beef bouillon
2 tablespoons chopped fresh parsley

Baked Pineapple

Perfect accompaniment for meat or serve as a dessert

- **Serves 4**
- **Oven Temperature 325 degrees**
- **Bake 25 minutes**

1 whole pineapple
1/3 cup butter or margarine
1/4 cup packed brown sugar
3 tablespoons dark rum
1/2 teaspoon cinnamon
1/8 teaspoon ground cloves
Nutmeg to taste
Maraschino cherries

Remove the top of the pineapple and reserve for garnish. Cut the pineapple vertically into quarters and remove the core. Slice the pineapple from the rinds and cut into 1-inch slices, leaving the pineapple in the rinds. Place in a baking dish.

Heat the butter, brown sugar, rum, cinnamon and cloves in a saucepan until the butter is melted, stirring occasionally. Brush generously over the pineapple. Bake at 325 degrees for 25 minutes. Sprinkle with nutmeg and top with maraschino cherries. Garnish the center with the reserved pineapple top. Serve warm.

White Fruit Tango

Tasty and refreshing

- **Serves 4 to 6**
- **Must do ahead**
- **Chill 1 hour**

2 cups chopped fresh pineapple
2 cups chopped peeled Asian pears
2 cups chopped jicama
Juice of 1/2 lime, or to taste
1/4 cup Triple Sec
1 teaspoon freshly ground white pepper
1/2 cup coarsely chopped fresh cilantro

Combine the undrained pineapple, undrained pears, jicama and lime juice in a bowl. Add the Triple Sec and white pepper. Chill, covered, in the refrigerator for 1 hour. Add the cilantro just before serving.

Mango Chutney

A delightful addition to chicken or fish, easy and inexpensive to make

- **Makes 2½ to 3 cups**

1 mango, chopped
1 small red onion, chopped
1 medium red bell pepper, chopped
1 medium green bell pepper, chopped
½ cup packed brown sugar
¾ to 1 cup red wine vinegar
1 (8-ounce) can pineapple chunks
2 tablespoons cornstarch
¼ cup water
Pinch of cinnamon
Pinch of nutmeg

Sauté the mango, red onion, red pepper and green pepper in a nonstick skillet for 5 minutes. Add the brown sugar, vinegar and undrained pineapple. Bring to a boil. Dissolve the cornstarch in the water. Add to the mango mixture and reduce the heat to low. Simmer for 10 minutes, stirring frequently. Stir in the cinnamon and nutmeg.

Cranberry Relish

Holiday favorite

- **Serves 6 to 10**
- **Can do ahead**

1 (12-ounce) package fresh cranberries, rinsed
2 oranges, peeled, cut into small pieces
1 cup walnut pieces
1½ cups sugar

Combine the cranberries, oranges, walnuts and sugar in an 1½-quart microwave-safe dish. Microwave, covered, on High for 20 minutes, stirring after 10 minutes. Serve warm or cold.

Note: Can store in the refrigerator for 1 to 2 weeks.

Horseradish Sauce

Easy and Quick

- **Makes 1/2 to 3/4 cup**
- **Must do ahead**
- **Chill**

1/2 small jar prepared horseradish
2 tablespoons sour cream
Pinch of garlic powder
1 tablespoon mayonnaise
2 drops of vinegar

Combine the horseradish, sour cream, garlic powder, mayonnaise and vinegar in a bowl and mix well. Chill, covered, in the refrigerator.

Dilled Mustard

Try It as a Spread or Marinade

- **Makes 3/4 cup**
- **Must do ahead**

1/2 cup water
2 tablespoons mustard seeds
2 tablespoons vinegar
1 tablespoon brown sugar
1/2 teaspoon dillweed
1/4 teaspoon salt

Combine the water, mustard seeds, vinegar, brown sugar, dillweed and salt in a bowl and mix well. Let stand for 3 hours. Process in a blender for 2 minutes or until the mustard seeds are finely ground. Store, covered, in the refrigerator.

Pasta

Quiet Time

Alfredo

Just like in Rome

• **Serves 4**

WALNUTS
1 to 2 tablespoons butter
4 to 6 ounces coarsely chopped walnuts or slivered almonds

PASTA
12 ounces pasta
6 to 8 tablespoons (3/4 to 1 stick) butter, melted

SAUCE AND ASSEMBLY
6 tablespoons (3/4 stick) butter
2 cups half-and-half
3 egg yolks
8 ounces freshly grated Parmesan cheese
Salt and freshly ground pepper to taste

For the walnuts, melt 1 to 2 tablespoons butter in a medium skillet. Add the walnuts. Sauté over medium heat until the walnuts are toasted and the butter is brown.

For the pasta, cook the pasta using the package directions until al dente; rinse and drain. Place in a warm buttered bowl. Add 6 to 8 tablespoons melted butter and toss to coat well.

For the sauce, melt 6 tablespoons butter in a saucepan. Add the half-and-half. Cook until heated through; do not boil. Beat the egg yolks in a bowl. Whisk a small amount of the hot mixture into the egg yolks; whisk the egg yolks into the hot mixture. Add 1/2 of the Parmesan cheese, whisking constantly.

To serve, pour the sauce over the hot pasta and toss to mix well. Place in 4 pasta bowls. Top with the buttered walnuts. Sprinkle with the remaining Parmesan cheese. Season with salt and pepper to taste.

Spinach Lasagna

Light as You Like It

- **Serves 6**
- **Oven Temperature 350 degrees**
- **Bake 1 hour**

12 ounces 1 percent cottage cheese
1 cup drained, thawed frozen spinach
1/2 cup grated regular or fat-free Parmesan cheese
2 eggs, or 1/2 cup egg substitute
4 cups regular or light spaghetti sauce
8 ounces uncooked lasagna noodles
2 cups shredded part-skim mozzarella cheese

Combine the cottage cheese, spinach, 1/2 of the Parmesan cheese and eggs in a bowl and mix well.

Reserve some of the spaghetti sauce for the top. Layer the remaining spaghetti sauce, uncooked lasagna noodles, spinach mixture and mozzarella cheese 1/2 at a time in a 9x13-inch baking dish. Top with the reserved spaghetti sauce. Sprinkle with the remaining Parmesan cheese.

Bake, covered, at 350 degrees for 1 hour. Cool for 10 minutes before serving.

Ruffled Dill Pasta Salad

Delectable

- **Serves 4 to 6**
- **Must do ahead**
- **Chill several hours**

PASTA
8 ounces pasta ruffles, cooked, drained
½ red onion, slivered
1 red bell pepper, slivered
1 green bell pepper, slivered
1 yellow bell pepper, slivered
1 small cucumber, seeded, cut into chunks
Pitted black olives
2 pounds imitation crab meat chunks
Leaf lettuce, torn

CREAMY DILL DRESSING
4 ounces sour cream
½ cup mayonnaise
1 teaspoon milk
2 teaspoons parsley flakes
1 teaspoon dillweed
1 teaspoon Beau Monde seasoning
½ teaspoon garlic salt
½ teaspoon onion salt

For the pasta, combine the pasta, red onion, bell peppers, cucumber, black olives, imitation crab meat and lettuce in a bowl and toss to mix well.

For the dressing, mix the sour cream, mayonnaise, milk, parsley flakes, dillweed, Beau Monde seasoning, garlic salt and onion salt in a bowl.

To assemble, pour ½ of the dressing over the pasta and toss until coated. Chill, covered, for several hours. Add the remaining dressing and toss to mix well. Serve immediately.

Noodles Norfolk

Poultry loves to be accompanied by this

- **Serves 8 to 12**
- **Oven Temperature 250 degrees**
- **Bake 40 minutes**

12 ounces wide noodles, cooked, drained
1 cup chopped fresh parsley
1 pint large-curd cottage cheese
1 pint sour cream
1 tablespoon Worcestershire sauce
Dash of Tabasco sauce
1 bunch green onions, chopped
1/2 cup shredded sharp Cheddar cheese
1/2 teaspoon paprika

Combine the hot noodles, parsley, cottage cheese, sour cream, Worcestershire sauce, Tabasco sauce and green onions in a bowl and mix well.

Spoon into a greased 6x9-inch baking dish. Sprinkle with Cheddar cheese and paprika. Bake, uncovered, at 250 degrees for 40 minutes or until heated through.

Heavenly Pasta

Name says it all

- **Serves 6**
- **Must do ahead**
- **Marinate 4 to 12 hours**

4 pounds fresh tomatoes, chopped
1/2 cup chopped sun-dried tomatoes
1/2 bunch fresh spinach, trimmed, torn
8 ounces Brie cheese, rind removed, chopped
1/2 cup chopped fresh basil
1 tablespoon parsley
4 garlic cloves, minced
1/2 cup extra-virgin olive oil
1/2 teaspoon freshly ground pepper
1 pound uncooked linguini
Grated Parmesan cheese to taste

Combine the tomatoes, sun-dried tomatoes, spinach, Brie cheese, basil, parsley, garlic, olive oil and pepper in a bowl and mix well. Marinate at room temperature for 4 to 12 hours.

Cook the pasta using the package directions until al dente; drain. Add the tomato mixture and toss to mix well. Spoon into heated pasta bowls and sprinkle with Parmesan cheese.

Note: For easier handling, place the Brie cheese in the freezer for 15 to 20 minutes prior to chopping.

Pasta

MINT PASTA

NICE FLAVOR

Heat the olive oil in a heavy saucepan over medium-low heat. Add the onions. Cook for 25 to 30 minutes or until soft and caramelized to a dark gold color, stirring occasionally.

Bring the water to a boil in a large saucepan. Add the pasta. Cook until al dente; drain.

Combine the chicken stock and caramelized onions in a large bowl. Add the hot pasta, bacon bits, Parmesan cheese and mint and toss to mix well. Sprinkle with pine nuts.

- **Serves 4**

2 teaspoons olive oil
2 large onions, sliced
4 quarts water
8 ounces pasta
1 cup chicken stock
3 tablespoons bacon bits
3 tablespoons freshly grated Parmesan cheese
1 cup mint leaves
2 tablespoons pine nuts, toasted

Tomato Mozzarella Sauce over Fusilli

Guaranteed to Please

- **Serves 4**
- **Must do ahead**
- **Marinate 30 minutes**

2 pounds ripe plum tomatoes, diced
8 ounces fresh mozzarella cheese, cubed
1/2 cup chopped fresh basil
6 tablespoons extra-virgin olive oil
1/4 cup balsamic vinegar
4 garlic cloves, minced
1/4 teaspoon red pepper flakes
Salt and pepper to taste
12 ounces fusilli
1/4 cup pine nuts, toasted

Combine the tomatoes, mozzarella cheese, basil, olive oil, balsamic vinegar, garlic, red pepper flakes, salt and pepper in a bowl and mix well. Marinate at room temperature for 30 minutes.

Cook the pasta using the package directions until al dente; drain. Add the tomato mixture. Toss over low heat until the mozzarella cheese begins to melt. Spoon into heated pasta bowls or onto plates and sprinkle with pine nuts.

Tortellini with Feta Cheese, Tomato and Basil

Great dish to toss together at the last minute

Heat the olive oil in a large skillet over medium-high heat. Add the leeks. Sauté until soft. Stir in the chicken broth and lemon juice. Add the tortellini. Cook until most of the liquid has evaporated. Do not overcook.

Add the tomatoes, basil and feta cheese. Season with salt. Toss until the mixture is combined. Serve immediately with Parmesan cheese.

- **Serves 6**

5 tablespoons light olive oil
2 cups thinly sliced leeks
1/2 cup chicken broth
2 tablespoons lemon juice
9 ounces fresh cheese tortellini, cooked, drained
2 large tomatoes, peeled, seeded, cut into 1/2-inch pieces
16 fresh basil leaves, julienned
5 ounces feta cheese, cut into 1/4-inch pieces
Salt to taste
Grated Parmesan cheese or asiago cheese (optional)

Roasted Vegetables and Pasta

Colorful and Tasty

- **Serves 4 to 6**
- **Oven Temperature 450 degrees**
- **Bake 25 minutes**

6 ounces uncooked rigatoni
1 envelope herb and garlic onion soup mix
2 teaspoons thyme
1/2 cup olive oil
1 1/2 pounds assorted vegetables, thickly sliced
1/2 cup white wine vinegar
1/3 cup pine nuts, toasted
Freshly ground pepper to taste

Cook the pasta using the package directions, omitting the salt and vegetable oil; drain. Rinse and drain again. Place in a large bowl.

Combine the soup mix and thyme in a bowl. Stir in 1/4 cup of the olive oil. Add the vegetables and toss to coat. Spread evenly in a 10x15-inch baking pan. Bake at 450 degrees for 25 minutes, stirring after 15 minutes. Add to the pasta and toss to mix well.

Combine the remaining olive oil, white wine vinegar and pine nuts in a bowl. Pour over the pasta mixture and toss to coat well. Sprinkle with pepper. Serve immediately.

Note: Use assorted vegetables such as zucchini, summer squash, red or green bell peppers, carrots, celery, mushrooms or eggplant.

Vegetarian Puttanesca

Cook-off Winner

Combine the garlic, tomatoes, olive oil, basil, red pepper flakes, olives, capers, cilantro and Parmesan cheese in a large bowl and mix well. Spoon over the hot pasta in a serving bowl.

***Note:** Can substitute 1 cup drained cooked black beans for the Greek olives.*

• **Serves 4**

2 large garlic cloves
1 pound fresh tomatoes, seeded, coarsely chopped
1/4 cup extra-virgin olive oil
1/2 teaspoon basil or oregano
1/4 teaspoon hot red pepper flakes
10 Greek olives, pitted, chopped
2 tablespoons drained capers
1/4 cup chopped fresh cilantro leaves
2 tablespoons freshly grated Parmesan cheese
16 ounces penne, rigatoni or favorite pasta, cooked, drained

Reuben Pasta

Top notch

- **Serves 4 to 6**
- **Must do ahead**
- **Chill 8 to 12 hours**

1½ cups trio twist pasta
1 cup shredded Swiss cheese
1 cup shredded corned beef
16 ounces sauerkraut, drained
¾ cup Russian salad dressing
½ teaspoon caraway seeds

Cook the pasta using the package directions until al dente; drain. Add the Swiss cheese, corned beef, sauerkraut, salad dressing and caraway seeds and toss to mix well. Chill, covered, for 8 to 12 hours.

***Note:** Can use a mixture of ½ cup mayonnaise and 3 tablespoons catsup instead of the Russian salad dressing. Can substitute shredded cabbage for the sauerkraut.*

Baked Spaghetti

Omit ground beef for a hearty vegetarian meal

- **Serves 12**
- **Can do ahead**
- **Can be frozen**
- **Oven Temperature 350 degrees**
- **Bake 30 to 35 minutes**

16 ounces thin spaghetti
2 teaspoons salt
1 pound ground beef
1 cup chopped onion
1 cup chopped yellow bell pepper
1 (4-ounce) can green chiles, or chopped fresh jalapeño peppers
8 ounces sliced fresh mushrooms, or 1 (4-ounce) can mushroom stems and pieces
1 tablespoon butter or margarine
1 (2-ounce) can sliced black olives, drained
1 (28-ounce) can crushed Italian-style tomatoes
2 teaspoons oregano
1/4 cup balsamic vinegar
2 tablespoons sugar
2 cups shredded Cheddar cheese
1 (10-ounce) can low-fat cream of mushroom soup
1/4 cup water
1/4 cup grated Parmesan cheese

Cook the spaghetti with 1 teaspoon of the salt using the package directions; drain. Brown the ground beef with the remaining 1 teaspoon salt in a skillet, stirring until crumbly; drain.

Sauté the onion, yellow pepper, green chiles and mushrooms in the butter in a skillet until tender. Add the olives, tomatoes, oregano, balsamic vinegar, sugar and ground beef and mix well. Simmer, uncovered, for 10 minutes.

Layer the spaghetti, ground beef mixture and Cheddar cheese 1/2 at a time in a greased 3-quart oblong baking dish. Mix the mushroom soup and water in a bowl until smooth. Pour over the layers. Sprinkle with Parmesan cheese. Bake, uncovered, at 350 degrees for 30 to 35 minutes or until heated through.

Note: Can prepare ahead of time and store, covered, in the freezer.

Fettuccini with Lamb, Mushrooms and Shallots

Unique to serve

- **Serves 2**
- **Must do ahead**

2 tablespoons olive oil
5 ounces button mushrooms, thinly sliced
3 ounces shiitake mushrooms, stemmed, sliced
4 garlic cloves, thinly sliced
2 medium to large shallots, thinly sliced
1 teaspoon thyme
2/3 cup dry white wine
Salt and pepper to taste
4 ounces fettuccini
1/3 cup dry white wine
1/2 cup beef stock
1/2 cup chopped green onions
1/2 cup chopped fresh parsley
1 tablespoon olive oil
6 ounces boneless lamb sirloin steak, trimmed, cut diagonally into slices
1/2 red bell pepper, chopped
Freshly grated Parmesan cheese to taste

Heat 2 tablespoons olive oil in a large heavy skillet over high heat. Add 1/2 of the button mushrooms, 1/2 of the shiitake mushrooms, garlic, shallots and thyme. Sauté for 4 minutes or until golden brown. Add 2/3 cup white wine. Simmer for 5 to 10 minutes or until the mushrooms are tender and almost all of the liquid has evaporated. Season with salt and pepper. Cover and let stand at room temperature for up to 4 hours.

Cook the pasta using the package directions until al dente.

Add the remaining mushrooms and 1/3 cup white wine to the mushroom mixture in the skillet. Bring to a boil and reduce the heat. Simmer for 3 minutes or until the mushrooms are slightly limp. Stir in the beef stock, green onions and parsley.

Heat 1 tablespoon olive oil in a small heavy skillet over high heat. Add the lamb. Cook until of the desired degree of doneness.

To serve, drain the pasta and place on individual serving plates. Spoon the mushroom mixture over the pasta. Top with the lamb and red bell pepper. Sprinkle with Parmesan cheese.

Rigatoni with Spicy Chicken and Vegetables

Tempting

- **Serves 4**

1 cup chopped onion
2 garlic cloves, finely chopped
4 Roma tomatoes, chopped
1 zucchini, chopped
1 yellow squash, chopped
1 green bell pepper, sliced
4 boneless skinless chicken breasts, cut into strips
2 (6-ounce) cans spicy hot vegetable juice cocktail
12 ounces rigatoni, cooked, drained

Sauté the onion and garlic in a skillet sprayed with nonstick cooking spray over medium heat. Add the tomatoes, zucchini, squash, green pepper and chicken. Sauté for 5 minutes. Add 1/2 of the vegetable juice cocktail.

Cook until the chicken is cooked through, adding the remaining vegetable juice cocktail as needed for the desired consistency. Serve over the hot cooked pasta.

Pasta with Chicken and Feta Cheese

Leftovers are especially good

- **Serves 4**

2 cups drained, cooked roasted bell pepper and garlic rotini pasta
1 cup quartered cherry tomatoes
4 ounces feta cheese with basil and tomato, crumbled
1/2 cup Caesar salad dressing
1/3 cup lightly packed fresh basil leaf strips
1/4 cup chopped red onion
2 boneless skinless chicken breasts, grilled or broiled, cut into 1/4-inch slices

Combine the pasta, cherry tomatoes, crumbled feta cheese, salad dressing, basil and red onion in a large bowl and toss to mix well. Arrange the chicken over the top. Serve warm or chilled. Serve with crusty bread and a fresh fruit salad.

Note: Can use plain rotini or penne pasta.

Garlic Lovers Tuna and Yogurt Pasta

Tantalizing aroma

For the sauce, blend the yogurt, garlic and 1/2 teaspoon salt in a bowl.

For the pasta, heat the butter and olive oil in a saucepan. Add the onions. Sauté until soft; do not brown. Add the tomatoes, salt and pepper to taste. Simmer for 20 minutes, adding a small amount of water if needed. Remove from the heat. Stir in the tuna. Pour over the hot pasta in a large bowl and toss until the pasta is coated.

To serve, spoon the pasta onto serving plates. Drizzle with the yogurt sauce and sprinkle with Parmesan cheese.

- **Serves 4 or 5**

YOGURT SAUCE
1 cup plain yogurt
2 garlic cloves, minced
1/2 teaspoon salt

PASTA
3 tablespoons butter
3 tablespoons olive oil
3 medium onions, finely chopped
5 tomatoes, peeled, seeded, chopped
Salt and pepper to taste
1 (12-ounce) can water-pack white albacore tuna, drained, flaked
12 ounces thin spaghetti, cooked, drained
Grated Parmesan cheese to taste

LINGUINI WITH WHITE CLAM SAUCE

VERY QUICK AND EASY TO PREPARE

- **Serves 4**

2 (6-ounce) cans chopped clams
1/2 cup (1 stick) butter or margarine
3 garlic cloves, minced
1/2 cup chopped fresh parsley
1/2 teaspoon oregano
1/2 teaspoon basil
1/2 teaspoon pepper
8 ounces linguini, cooked, drained
Grated Parmesan cheese to taste

Drain the clams, reserving the juice. Heat the butter in a skillet. Add the garlic. Sauté for 3 minutes. Stir in the parsley, oregano, basil, pepper and reserved clam juice. Cook, uncovered, over low heat for 5 minutes. Add the clams. Cook for 3 minutes.

Spoon over the hot linguini and sprinkle with Parmesan cheese. Serve with a green salad, crusty bread and fresh fruit.

Shrimp in Angel Hair Pasta

Never use your stove top

Grease an 8x12-inch baking dish with the butter. Combine the eggs, half-and-half, yogurt, Swiss cheese, feta cheese, parsley, basil and oregano in a large bowl and mix well.

Layer 1/2 of the pasta, salsa, 1/2 of the shrimp and remaining pasta in the prepared dish. Spread the egg mixture over the layers and top with the remaining shrimp. Sprinkle with Monterey Jack cheese. Bake at 350 degrees for 30 minutes or until bubbly. Garnish with snow peas.

Note: Recipe can be assembled 1 day in advance and stored, covered, in the refrigerator until baking time.

- **Serves 6**
- **Can do ahead**
- **Oven Temperature 350 degrees**
- **Bake 30 minutes**

1 tablespoon butter
2 eggs
1 cup half-and-half
1 cup plain yogurt
1/2 cup shredded Swiss cheese
1/3 cup crumbled feta cheese
1/3 cup chopped parsley
1/4 cup chopped fresh basil, or 1 teaspoon crushed dried basil leaves
1 teaspoon crushed dried oregano leaves
9 ounces uncooked fresh angel hair pasta
1 (16-ounce) jar mild chunky salsa
1 pound medium shrimp, peeled, deveined
1/2 cup shredded Monterey Jack cheese

GARNISH
Snow peas

Antipasto Salad

Pack into your picnic basket

- **Serves 6 to 8**
- **Must do ahead**
- **Chill 8 to 12 hours**

1 cup bite-size pieces cauliflower
1 cup bite-size pieces broccoli
1 (6-ounce) can sliced black olives
3 ounces sliced pepperoni
2 to 3 cups cooked spiral pasta
4 ounces shredded mozzarella cheese
1½ cups Italian salad dressing
¼ cup grated Parmesan cheese

Combine the cauliflower, broccoli, black olives, pepperoni, pasta, mozzarella cheese and salad dressing in a large bowl and toss to mix well.

Marinate, covered, in the refrigerator for 8 to 12 hours, turning the bowl several times. Sprinkle with Parmesan cheese just before serving.

Ham and Pasta Salad

Excellent dressing

Cook the pasta using the package directions until al dente; drain. Add the broccoli florets, caulifloweret s, carrots, green pepper, green onions and ham. Drizzle the salad dressing over the salad. Sprinkle with the salad dressing mix and toss to coat. Spoon into a large airtight container. Chill, covered, for 2 days, turning upside down every day.

- **Serves 6 to 8**
- **Must do ahead**
- **Chill 2 days**

16 ounces spiral pasta
4 cups broccoli florets
4 cups cauliflowerets
6 carrots, grated
1 large green bell pepper, chopped
1 cup chopped green onions
4 cups chopped cooked ham
1 (16-ounce) bottle Italian salad dressing
2 envelopes zesty Italian salad dressing mix

Black Bean and Orzo Salad

Good taste, low-fat and quick—what more could you ask for

Cook the orzo in 4 cups boiling water in a saucepan until al dente; drain.

Mix the orzo, black beans and salsa in a bowl. Chill, covered, in the refrigerator.

- **Serves 4**
- **Must do ahead**
- **Chill**

1/2 cup orzo
4 cups water
1 (15-ounce) can black beans, rinsed
1/4 cup medium salsa, or to taste

Black Bean and Pasta Salad

Southwest-Inspired

- **Serves 4 to 6**
- **Must do ahead**
- **Chill several hours to 1 day**

SOUTHWEST DRESSING
3/4 cup chopped fresh cilantro
1/2 cup skimmed chicken broth
3 tablespoons orange juice
3 tablespoons red wine vinegar
1 teaspoon cumin
1/2 teaspoon chili powder, or to taste
1 tablespoon olive oil
Salt to taste

SALAD
12 ounces radiatore or other medium-size pasta
1 tablespoon olive oil
1 (15-ounce) can black beans, rinsed, drained
1 red bell pepper, chopped
1 green bell pepper, chopped
1 cup chopped peeled jicama
1/2 cup chopped red onion
Salt and chili powder to taste

GARNISH
Chopped jalapeño peppers

For the dressing, process the cilantro, chicken broth, orange juice, red wine vinegar, cumin and 1/2 teaspoon chili powder in a blender. Pour into a small bowl and whisk in 1 tablespoon olive oil and salt to taste. Chill, covered, in an airtight container for several hours or for up to 1 day.

For the salad, cook the pasta using the package directions until al dente; rinse and drain. Place in a large bowl. Add 1 tablespoon olive oil and toss until the pasta is coated. Add the black beans, red pepper, green pepper, jicama and red onion and toss to combine. Chill, covered, in an airtight container for several hours or for up to 1 day.

To serve, let the salad and dressing return to room temperature. Whisk the dressing. Drizzle over the salad in a serving bowl and toss gently to combine. Season with salt and chili powder to taste. Garnish with chopped jalapeño peppers.

California Pasta Salad

The Best Pasta Salad in the World

For the salad, combine the pasta, black beans, red pepper, yellow pepper, sun-dried tomatoes, green onions, celery and mozzarella cheese in a large bowl and toss to combine.

For the dressing, combine the cilantro, basil, garlic, Dijon mustard, balsamic vinegar, red wine vinegar and olive oil in a bowl and whisk well. Stir in the bleu cheese. Season with salt and pepper.

To serve, drizzle the dressing over the salad and toss to coat.

- **Serves 6 to 8**

SALAD

1 pound ruote (wagon wheels) pasta, cooked, drained
2 (15-ounce) cans black beans, rinsed, drained
1 red bell pepper, chopped
1 yellow bell pepper, chopped
1/2 cup chopped sun-dried tomatoes
1 bunch green onions, thinly sliced
4 ribs celery, chopped (optional)
12 ounces mozzarella cheese, cubed

BLEU CHEESE DRESSING

2 tablespoons chopped fresh cilantro
3 tablespoons chopped fresh basil
2 garlic cloves, minced
1 tablespoon Dijon mustard
1 tablespoon balsamic vinegar
2 tablespoons red wine vinegar
1 cup olive oil
1/2 to 1 cup crumbled bleu cheese
Salt and pepper to taste

Feta Cheese and Pasta Salad

Zippy

- **Serves 6 to 8**
- **Must do ahead**
- **Chill 3 to 12 hours**

OREGANO DRESSING

1/2 teaspoon anchovy paste
2 medium garlic cloves, minced
1 teaspoon finely chopped fresh oregano, or 1/2 teaspoon dried oregano
1/2 teaspoon Dijon mustard
2 tablespoons red wine vinegar
1/4 teaspoon kosher salt
1/4 teaspoon freshly ground black pepper
2/3 cup extra-virgin olive oil

SALAD

1 pound pipe rigate, fusili or shell pasta
8 ounces feta cheese, crumbled
3 ounces thinly sliced pepperoni, cut into strips (optional)
2 medium tomatoes, seeded, coarsely chopped
1/2 cup coarsely chopped seeded pepperoncini
1 cup black or Greek olives, sliced lengthwise

For the dressing, combine the anchovy paste, garlic, oregano, Dijon mustard, red wine vinegar, kosher salt and pepper in a bowl and whisk well. Add the olive oil in a fine stream, whisking constantly.

For the salad, cook the pasta using the package directions until al dente; drain. Rinse in cold water and drain again. Combine the feta cheese, pepperoni, tomatoes, pepperoncini and black olives in a large bowl. Add the pasta and toss to mix.

To assemble and serve, pour the oregano dressing over the salad and toss until coated. Chill, covered, for 3 to 12 hours to enhance the flavor. Allow the salad to return to room temperature before serving.

Tortellini Salad

The dressing is the secret

For the dressing, combine the olive oil, vinegar, Dijon mustard, salt, sugar, garlic and pepper in a container with a lid. Cover and shake to mix well.

For the salad, cook the tortellini using the package directions; drain. Add a small amount of the dressing or additional olive oil and toss to coat. Add the broccoli, cherry tomatoes, carrots, green pepper, sun-dried tomatoes and remaining dressing and toss to combine. Spoon into a serving bowl.

- **Serves 8 to 10**

ITALIAN SALAD DRESSING
3/4 cup olive oil
1/4 cup vinegar
2 teaspoons Dijon mustard
1/2 teaspoon salt
1/2 teaspoon sugar
2 garlic cloves, minced
Freshly ground pepper to taste

SALAD
12 to 16 ounces tortellini
1 bunch broccoli, cut into bite-size pieces
1 package cherry tomatoes, cut into halves
3 to 4 carrots, thinly sliced
1 green or red bell pepper, cut into thin strips
1/3 cup chopped oil-pack sun-dried tomatoes

Pasta Salad Supreme

Velvety texture

- **Serves 6 to 8**
- **Must do ahead**
- **Chill 1 hour or longer**

SALAD
8 ounces pasta
4 ounces fresh mushrooms
3 carrots, grated
2 ribs celery, finely chopped
2 scallions, finely chopped
2 ounces dilled Havarti cheese, grated
Chopped green or black olives to taste
Chopped pimento to taste
Sliced pepperoni to taste
Chopped summer sausage to taste

SALAD SUPREME DRESSING
1 cup mayonnaise
2 tablespoons Salad Supreme seasoning
$1/2$ teaspoon seasoned pepper
2 tablespoons grated Parmesan cheese

For the salad, cook the pasta using the package directions; drain. Combine the pasta, mushrooms, carrots, celery, scallions, Havarti cheese, green olives, pimento, pepperoni and summer sausage in a bowl and toss to mix.

For the dressing, mix the mayonnaise, Salad Supreme seasoning, seasoned pepper and Parmesan cheese in a bowl.

To assemble and serve, add the dressing to the salad and stir to coat. Chill, covered, for 1 hour or longer before serving.

Meats

Moorings along
Muskegon Lake

Tournedos Eva

First class

- **Serves 6**

Béarnaise Sauce

- **Can do ahead**

BÉARNAISE SAUCE
1 cup dry white wine
2 tablespoons chopped fresh tarragon
1 tablespoon finely chopped shallot
3 egg yolks
1 cup melted clarified butter
Salt and ground red pepper to taste

BEEF AND SHRIMP
2½ tablespoons butter
1 garlic clove, minced
6 (4-ounce) beef tenderloin fillets
Salt and black pepper to taste
4 ounces fresh sliced mushrooms
8 ounces medium peeled shrimp or crab meat
2 tablespoons dry white wine

For the sauce, combine 1 cup white wine, tarragon and shallot in a double boiler. Cook over boiling water over medium-high heat until the liquid is reduced to 2½ tablespoons. Remove from the heat. Whisk in the egg yolks. Cook over simmering water for 5 minutes or until thickened, whisking constantly. Remove from the heat. Add the hot clarified butter a few drops at a time, whisking constantly for 4 minutes or until the sauce is smooth. Season with salt and red pepper to taste.

For the beef and shrimp, melt 2½ tablespoons butter in a large heavy skillet over medium-high heat. Add the garlic. Add the beef immediately. Cook for 2 to 3 minutes per side for rare or to the desired degree of doneness. Season with salt and black pepper to taste. Remove to a heated plate. Add the mushrooms to the skillet. Cook for 5 minutes or until tender and the liquid evaporates. Add the shrimp and 2 tablespoons white wine. Stir-fry until the shrimp turn pink.

To serve, place the beef on heated individual serving plates. Spoon the mushroom mixture over the beef. Top with the sauce and serve immediately.

Note: The béarnaise sauce can be prepared up to several hours ahead of serving and stored in an airtight container.

Editors Note: To clarify butter, melt the butter in a small saucepan over low heat until foamy. Remove from the heat and let stand until the milk solids settle to the bottom of the saucepan and the salt crystals settle on the top. Skim off the salt crystals and carefully pour the butter oil into a separate container. Discard the milk solids that have settled in the bottom.

Steak Diane

Great flavor

Season both sides of the steak with salt and pepper. Melt 2 tablespoons butter in a heavy skillet. Add the Dijon mustard and shallot. Cook over medium heat for 1 minute. Add the steaks. Cook for 3 to 5 minutes per side for medium-rare or until done to taste. Remove the steaks to a warm platter and keep warm.

Add 1 tablespoon butter, lemon juice, Worcestershire sauce and chives to the pan drippings in the skillet. Cook for 2 minutes. Add the brandy. Pour over the steaks. Sprinkle with parsley.

- **Serves 2**

2 (6-ounce) filet mignons
1/8 teaspoon salt
1/8 teaspoon pepper
2 tablespoons (1/4 stick) butter
1 teaspoon Dijon mustard
2 tablespoons minced shallot
1 tablespoon butter
1 tablespoon fresh lemon juice
1 1/2 teaspoons Worcestershire sauce
1 tablespoon minced fresh chives
1 teaspoon brandy
1 tablespoon minced fresh parsley

- **Serves 6 to 8**
- **Must do ahead**
- **Marinate 24 to 48 hours**
- **Oven Temperature 350 degrees**
- **Bake 1 hour**

MARINADE
1 cup soy sauce
1/3 cup gin
1/2 cup vegetable oil
5 garlic cloves, minced

BEEF
1 (3-pound) beef tenderloin
Horseradish Sauce (page 166)

Marinated Beef Tenderloin

Elegant

For the marinade, combine the soy sauce, gin, vegetable oil and garlic in a bowl and mix well.

For the beef, pour the marinade over the beef in a shallow dish and cover with plastic wrap. Marinate in the refrigerator for 24 to 48 hours, turning 3 or 4 times. Drain the beef and pat dry. Place on a rack in a roasting pan. Bake at 350 degrees for 1 hour or until medium-rare. Cool immediately in the refrigerator. Cut into thin slices. Serve with Horseradish Sauce.

Beef Stroganoff

Tried and true family recipe

- **Serves 4 to 6**

$^{1}/_{4}$ cup flour
$1^{1}/_{2}$ teaspoons salt
$^{1}/_{4}$ teaspoon pepper
1 pound beef tenderloin, cut into $^{1}/_{4}$-inch strips
$^{1}/_{4}$ cup ($^{1}/_{2}$ stick) butter
$^{1}/_{2}$ cup minced onion
$^{1}/_{4}$ cup water
1 (10-ounce) can chicken broth
1 pound sliced mushrooms
1 cup sour cream
Chopped fresh parsley, chives or dill to taste

Mix the flour, salt and pepper in a bowl. Add the beef and coat well. Brown the beef in melted butter in a Dutch oven. Add the onion. Sauté until tender. Add the water, stirring to deglaze the Dutch oven. Add the chicken broth and mushrooms.

Cook, uncovered, over low heat for 20 minutes or until thickened, stirring constantly. Stir in the sour cream just before serving. Cook until heated through. Sprinkle with parsley. Serve over hot cooked noodles or rice.

Pot Beef Roast with Cranberry Sauce

Makes its own gravy

- **Serves 6 to 8**
- **Oven Temperature 350 degrees**
- **Bake 3 hours**

1 (4- to 5-pound) chuck roast or bottom round roast
1/4 cup (1/2 stick) butter or margarine
1 (16-ounce) can jellied cranberry sauce
3 cloves
1 onion, chopped
1 beef bouillon cube
1 to 2 cups water
Salt and pepper to taste
4 to 6 tablespoons flour
1/4 cup (1/2 stick) butter, melted

Brown the beef in 1/4 cup butter in a Dutch oven. Add the cranberry sauce, cloves, onion, bouillon cube, water, salt and pepper. Mix the flour and 1/4 cup melted butter in a bowl. Add to the beef mixture.

Bake, covered, at 350 degrees for 3 hours or until tender. Remove the beef to a warm platter and slice. Cook the gravy until of the desired consistency, stirring frequently. Serve over the beef.

Italian Beef

Leftovers are tasty too

- **Serves 10 to 12**
- **Oven Temperature 325 degrees**
- **Bake 3 hours**

1 (4- to 5-pound) rump roast, tied
Salt and pepper to taste
2 teaspoons parsley flakes
2 teaspoons basil
2 teaspoons oregano
4 bay leaves
4 garlic cloves, minced
1 large onion, chopped

Place the beef in a Dutch oven. Season with salt, pepper, parsley flakes, basil, oregano and bay leaves. Add the garlic and onion. Add enough water to fill the Dutch oven half full. Bake, covered, at 325 degrees for 3 hours. Cool.

Remove the beef to a platter and cut into thin slices. Return to the liquid. Cook until heated through. Discard the bay leaves. Serve with hard rolls.

MEXICAN STEAK

QUICK FAMILY MEAL

- **Serves 4**
- **Oven Temperature 350 degrees**
- **Bake 45 minutes**

1¼ pounds round steak
2 tablespoons (¼ stick) butter, melted
1 (4-ounce) can chopped green chiles, drained
1 (8-ounce) jar taco sauce
½ cup shredded Monterey Jack cheese

Cut the steak into 4 pieces. Pound until ¼ inch thick. Brown in the butter in a skillet. Place in a greased shallow 2-quart baking dish. Top with the green chiles and taco sauce.

Bake, covered, at 350 degrees for 40 minutes. Uncover and sprinkle with the cheese. Bake for 5 minutes. Serve over hot cooked rice.

Swiss Steak Goes Italian

Working person's answer to dinner

• **Serves 6 to 8**

SAUCE
2 (14-ounce) cans stewed tomatoes
4 large carrots, finely chopped
4 ribs celery, finely chopped
2 medium onions, chopped
1 or 2 fresh tomatoes, chopped

STEAK
2 pounds cubed round steak
1 cup flour
1/4 cup olive oil

For the sauce, simmer the stewed tomatoes, carrots, celery, onions and fresh tomatoes in an electric skillet at 250 degrees.

For the steak, coat the steak with the flour. Pound the steak until 1/4 inch thick. Cut into bite-size pieces. Brown in the olive oil in a skillet; drain and pat dry.

To assemble, add the steak to the sauce. Simmer for 1 hour or until the steak is tender.

Note: Can be simmered in a slow cooker.

J D Steaks

Men will love this

- **Serves 8**
- **Must do ahead**
- **Grill**

10 garlic cloves, pressed
3 tablespoons fresh chopped rosemary
Seasoned salt to taste
1 (10-pound) slab New York strip, trimmed but whole
Dry cedar chips
8 ounces Jack Daniel's or similar bourbon whiskey
1 cup water
2 pounds coleslaw

Mix the garlic, rosemary and seasoned salt in a bowl. Rub the beef thoroughly with the mixture. Let stand for 1 hour.

Soak dry cedar smoking chips in a mixture of the whiskey and water for 1 hour.

Place the slab of beef on a wire rack. Sear over very hot coals for 5 minutes on each side or until blackened. Remove from the heat. Add the soaked wood chips to the fire and reduce the heat to low. Grill the beef, covered, for 2 hours. Cut the beef into ½-inch slices. Serve over a bed of coleslaw.

Barbecued Corned Beef

Very good–easy too

- **Serves 10 to 15**

2 pounds ground beef
1 medium white onion, chopped
1/2 green bell pepper, chopped
2 tablespoons (1/4 stick) butter
1 1/2 cups catsup
1 teaspoon cinnamon
1/2 teaspoon ground cloves
1 (12-ounce) can corned beef

Brown the ground beef in a skillet, stirring until crumbly; drain.

Sauté the onion and green pepper in the butter in a skillet until soft. Add the catsup, cinnamon and cloves. Simmer for 25 minutes, stirring constantly. Add the ground beef and corned beef. Cook until heated through, stirring frequently. Serve on hamburger buns.

Grubby Ducks

Delicious

- **Serves 12**
- **Must do ahead**
- **Oven Temperature 350 degrees**
- **Bake 25 to 30 minutes**

3 pounds ground beef
2 heads cabbage, cut up
6 medium onions, chopped
Salt and pepper to taste
2 loaves fresh or thawed frozen bread dough

Brown the ground beef with the cabbage, onions, salt and pepper in a skillet, stirring until the ground beef is crumbly; drain and cool.

Cut the bread dough into large pieces. Shape into 6-inch squares 1/8 inch thick. Place the cooled ground beef mixture in the center of each. Bring up the corners to enclose the filling and pinch to seal. Place on foil-lined baking sheets. Let rise for 30 minutes. Bake at 350 degrees for 25 to 30 minutes or until brown.

Meat Loaf Olé

Good hot or cold

- **Serves 8**
- **Oven Temperature 375 degrees**
- **Bake 60 to 70 minutes**

MEAT LOAF
1½ pounds ground beef
8 ounces ground pork
2 eggs
1 cup fresh bread crumbs
1 cup taco sauce
1 medium onion, chopped
1 garlic clove, crushed
1 tablespoon chili powder
1½ teaspoons salt
¾ teaspoon cumin
¼ teaspoon pepper

FILLING
1 (16-ounce) can refried beans, heated
1 (4-ounce) can whole green chiles, slivered, drained
1 cup shredded longhorn Cheddar cheese

TOPPING
1 cup crushed tortilla chips

For the meat loaf, mix the ground beef and ground pork in a large bowl. Process the eggs, bread crumbs, taco sauce, onion, garlic, chili powder, salt, cumin and pepper in a blender until smooth. Add to the ground beef mixture and mix well. Shape into a ball. Place between 2 sheets of waxed paper. Roll into an 8x16-inch rectangle.

For the filling, remove the top sheet of the waxed paper. Spread the refried beans to within ½ inch of the edges. Arrange the green chiles over the refried beans. Sprinkle evenly with the cheese. Roll as for a jelly roll, starting at the short end and removing the waxed paper as you roll.

For the topping, place the meat loaf seam side down in a 5x9-inch loaf pan. Sprinkle with the crushed tortilla chips. Bake at 375 degrees for 60 to 70 minutes or until cooked through. Let stand for 15 minutes.

To serve, remove the meat loaf to a serving platter and cut into slices. Serve with shredded lettuce, shredded cheese, chopped onion, sour cream and sliced pitted black olives.

Not Just Any Meat Loaf

Comfort Food

- **Serves 8**
- **Oven Temperature 350 degrees**
- **Bake 1 hour**

2 pounds ground beef
1 egg
3/4 cup barbecue sauce
1/4 cup catsup
1 medium onion, chopped
1 medium green bell pepper, chopped
1 tablespoon pepper, or to taste
1 tablespoon garlic salt, or to taste
1 cup rolled oats

Combine the ground beef, egg, barbecue sauce, catsup, onion, green pepper, pepper, garlic salt and oats in a large bowl and mix well. Shape into a loaf.

Place in a 5x9-inch baking pan. Bake at 350 degrees for 1 hour or until cooked through.

Bleu Cheese Burgers

Spruces up the Ordinary

- **Serves 4 to 6**
- **Grill**

2 pounds ground beef
Seasoned salt to taste
Oregano to taste
1/2 cup crumbled bleu cheese
Salt and pepper to taste
4 teaspoons Worcestershire sauce
4 teaspoons soy sauce

Shape the ground beef into 4 to 6 large patties. Divide each patty into halves; pat each half into thin patties. Season each patty with seasoned salt and oregano.

Place the bleu cheese in the centers of 1/2 of the patties. Place the remaining patties on top, sealing the edge to enclose the bleu cheese. Season with salt and pepper. Place in a shallow dish. Sprinkle with Worcestershire sauce and soy sauce. Let stand for 20 minutes. Place the patties on a grill rack. Grill over hot coals until cooked through, basting with a mixture of additional Worcestershire sauce, soy sauce, salt and pepper.

Codellets de Veau

Your guests will rave and think you slaved

- **Serves 6 to 8**
- **Can do ahead**
- **Oven Temperature 300 degrees**
- **Bake 2 hours**

1/4 cup sliced onion
1 tablespoon butter
2 pounds veal cutlets (at least 2 per person)
Salt and pepper to taste
1 cup coarse fresh bread crumbs
1 cup shredded Swiss cheese
Parsley to taste
1 cup dry white wine
1/4 cup (1/2 stick) butter, melted

Sauté the onion in 1 tablespoon butter in a skillet until translucent. Spread in a 9x13-inch baking dish. Layer the veal over the onion. Season with salt and pepper. Sprinkle with the bread crumbs and Swiss cheese; press to flatten. Sprinkle with parsley.

Make a small channel around the edges of the dish by pushing the layers a little to the center. Pour the wine in the channel around the edges. Drizzle 1/4 cup melted butter over the top. Bake at 300 degrees for 2 hours or until crusty, basting occasionally.

Note: Recipe can be assembled and stored in the refrigerator up to 8 hours ahead of baking.

Veal Scallops Italiano

An easy dish that looks very nice for company

- **Serves 4**
- **Oven Temperature 375 degrees**
- **Bake 15 to 20 minutes**

8 ounces sliced mushrooms
1 tablespoon margarine
1 egg
1/2 cup milk
8 veal scallops, thinly sliced
Flour
1 cup fine cracker crumbs
4 to 5 tablespoons margarine
1 (15-ounce) container marinara sauce
8 slices mozzarella cheese

Sauté the mushrooms in 1 tablespoon margarine in a skillet until brown and tender.

Mix the egg and milk in a bowl. Dip each veal scallop in the flour, egg mixture and cracker crumbs in the order listed.

Heat 4 to 5 tablespoons margarine in a skillet. Add the coated veal scallops. Sauté until brown on both sides. Place in a single layer in a 9x13-inch baking dish. Spread the marinara sauce over each. Place the mushrooms on top of each and cover with a slice of mozzarella cheese. Bake at 375 degrees for 15 to 20 minutes or until the mozzarella cheese melts.

Easy Veal with Pesto

Elegant dish that requires very little time in the kitchen

- **Serves 6**
- **Can do ahead**
- **Oven Temperature 325 degrees**
- **Bake 25 minutes**

PESTO
2 teaspoons chopped garlic
3 tablespoons chopped fresh basil
2 tablespoons chopped pine nuts
1/3 cup olive oil
1 cup (about) grated Parmesan cheese

VEAL AND ASSEMBLY
10 veal scaloppine
Olive oil
1/3 cup white wine (optional)

For the pesto, press the chopped garlic in a mortar with a pestle to release the flavor. Combine the garlic, basil and pine nuts in a bowl. Add 1/3 cup olive oil. Add enough of the Parmesan cheese to form a soft paste, stirring constantly.

For the veal, sauté the veal in a small amount of olive oil in a skillet until light brown.

To assemble, place the veal in a single layer in a 9x15-inch baking dish; do not overlap. Place a dollop of the pesto on top of each. Add the white wine. Bake at 325 degrees for 25 minutes or until heated through.

***Note:** Prepare the pesto ahead by freezing in ice cube trays and storing the pesto cubes in freezer bags in the freezer. Also, keep 2- to 4-person servings of packaged uncooked veal scaloppine in the freezer for unexpected company.*

Grandma Ida's Swedish Stew

"Old Country" recipe with a mild unique flavor

Sauté the celery in 1 tablespoon of the vegetable oil in a 4-quart Dutch oven until wilted. Remove to a bowl. Add the remaining 1 tablespoon vegetable oil to the Dutch oven. Add the veal. Sauté over high heat until the veal is brown and the juices are sealed in. Reduce the heat. Simmer for 10 minutes. Drain, leaving 1 tablespoon of the pan drippings in the Dutch oven. Return the celery to the Dutch oven. Add the potatoes and enough of the 4 cups water to cover. Stir in the bouillon cube until dissolved. Tie the peppercorns in cheesecloth or place in a tea ball. Add to the Dutch oven and season with 1 teaspoon salt. Cook over medium heat for 20 minutes or until the potatoes are tender.

Cook the carrots in 3 cups water in a 2-quart saucepan over medium heat for 15 minutes; drain. Add to the Dutch oven.

Remove 1/2 cup liquid from the Dutch oven and place in a bowl. Add the flour and stir until smooth. Add the milk and mix well. Add gradually to the Dutch oven, stirring constantly. Simmer over low heat until thickened, stirring constantly and adding additional milk as needed for the desired consistency. Add Kitchen Bouquet to darken the color of the stew.

Before serving, remove 6 to 8 potato pieces from the stew and mash with a fork; return to the stew and stir to mix well. Remove and discard the peppercorns. Season with salt and pepper to taste. Ladle into soup bowls. Serve with Swedish hardtack and butter.

- **Serves 8**

3 ribs celery, cut into 1/2-inch pieces
2 tablespoons vegetable oil
2 pounds veal, cut into medium cubes
6 medium potatoes, peeled, cut into medium cubes
4 cups water
1 chicken bouillon cube
10 black peppercorns
1 teaspoon salt
4 large carrots, cut into 1/2-inch pieces
3 cups water
2 tablespoons flour
1/2 cup milk
Few drops of Kitchen Bouquet (optional)
Salt and pepper to taste

Lamb Mandarin

Maestro's mom's favorite

- **Serves 8**
- **Oven Temperature 350 to 375 degrees**
- **Bake 1½ hours**

2 bouillon cubes
1 cup water
8 shoulder or shank lamb chops
1 cup uncooked rice
2 (8-ounce) cans mandarin oranges
Pinch of oregano
1 teaspoon mint (optional)

Dissolve the bouillon cubes in the water in a bowl. Cook the lamb chops in a skillet until brown. Place in a greased 4- to 5-quart baking dish. Add the rice, undrained mandarin oranges and bouillon mixture. Season with oregano and mint.

Bake, covered, at 350 to 375 degrees for 1½ hours or until cooked through, checking occasionally.

Lamb Shanks and Sauerkraut

Enjoy the wonderful flavor

- **Serves 4**
- **Oven Temperature 375 degrees**
- **Bake 2½ hours**

4 lamb shanks
Garlic powder to taste
Salt to taste
1 (10-ounce) can sauerkraut
2 medium onions, sliced
2 potatoes, chopped
¼ cup uncooked instant rice

Season the lamb shanks with garlic powder and/or salt. Place in a heavy baking pan. Bake, uncovered, at 375 degrees for 1½ hours.

Add the sauerkraut, onions, potatoes and rice. Bake, covered, for 1 hour, stirring occasionally.

Grilled Lamb Chops

Simple

- **Serves 2**
- **Grill**

4 (1¼-inch-thick) lamb loin chops
Olive oil
Crushed rosemary

Rub the lamb chops with olive oil. Press the rosemary into the sides of the lamb chops.

Place the lamb chops on a grill rack. Grill over hot coals for 10 to 12 minutes or until medium, turning halfway through the grilling time.

Lamb Casserole

Wonderful

- **Serves 4**
- **Oven Temperature 350 degrees**
- **Bake 1 hour**

1 pound lean lamb, cut into 1-inch cubes
2 tablespoons vegetable oil
1 onion, sliced
1 garlic clove, minced
1 cup canned tomatoes
1 green bell pepper, quartered
2 carrots, sliced
3 lemon slices
1 medium eggplant, cut into 2-inch cubes
2 zucchini, cut into 1-inch cubes
1/2 cup sliced okra (optional)
1/2 teaspoon paprika
1/8 teaspoon cumin
Freshly ground pepper to taste

Brown the lamb cubes in the vegetable oil in a skillet. Add the onion and garlic. Sauté until the onion and garlic are light brown. Add the tomatoes. Cook over low heat for 1 hour, adding a small amount of water if needed.

Pour into a 3-quart glass baking dish. Add the green pepper, carrots, lemon slices, eggplant, zucchini, okra, paprika, cumin and pepper. Bring to a boil and cover tightly. Place in the oven. Bake at 350 degrees for 1 hour or until the vegetables are tender.

Roast Pork Loin with Mushroom Duxelle

Superb

- **Serves 12**
- **Oven Temperature 400 degrees**
- **Bake 30 minutes**
- **Oven Temperature 350 degrees**
- **Bake 30 to 40 minutes**

MUSHROOM STUFFING

1/2 cup finely chopped onion
8 ounces mushrooms, finely chopped
1/4 cup (1/2 stick) butter
3 tablespoons red wine
1 tablespoon lemon juice
2 teaspoons chopped fresh thyme
1 teaspoon salt
1/2 teaspoon freshly ground pepper

PORK AND GRAVY

4 pounds boneless pork top loin
1 (2-ounce) jar roasted red bell pepper, cut into strips
1 1/2 cups water
2 tablespoons cornstarch
2 tablespoons water

For the stuffing, sauté the onion and mushrooms in the butter in a large skillet for 20 minutes. Stir in the red wine, lemon juice, thyme, salt and pepper. Cook until the liquid has evaporated, stirring occasionally.

For the pork, place the pork on a work surface. Place a knife to one side on top of the pork and cut down 2/3 of the way through the pork. Turn the knife in the pork parallel to the work surface and cut across but not through the pork. Open the pork flat, making any additional cuts needed to obtain a flat surface.

To assemble, spread the mushroom stuffing evenly over the pork to within 1 inch of the edges. Arrange the red pepper slices in 3 rows down the length of the pork. Roll up gently and loosely to enclose the stuffing and tie at 3-inch intervals. Weave the ends with wooden picks to enclose the stuffing. Place seam side down on a rack in a roasting pan. Add 1 1/2 cups water to the pan. Bake at 400 degrees for 30 minutes. Reduce the oven temperature to 350 degrees. Bake for 30 to 40 minutes or until a meat thermometer registers 160 degrees when inserted into the thickest portion. Remove the pork from the pan. Let stand for 5 to 10 minutes before slicing.

For the gravy, pour the pan juices into a glass measure. Add enough additional water to measure 2 cups. Pour into a saucepan. Mix the cornstarch with 2 tablespoons water. Add to the saucepan. Bring to a boil and reduce the heat. Simmer for 1 minute or until slightly thickened, stirring constantly. Serve with the pork.

Pork Tenderloin with Rum Chutney

Nice sweet-and-sour sauce

- **Serves 7 or 8**
- **Oven Temperature 400 degrees**
- **Bake 15 minutes**

2 (1-pound) pork tenderloins, trimmed
1/2 teaspoon salt
1/2 teaspoon black pepper
1/2 teaspoon cayenne pepper
2 teaspoons vegetable oil
1/4 cup rum
1 cup mango chutney
Salt and black pepper to taste

Sprinkle the pork with 1/2 teaspoon salt, 1/2 teaspoon black pepper and cayenne pepper. Brown in the vegetable oil in a 10- to 12-inch skillet. Remove the pork to a 9x13-inch baking pan, reserving the drippings in the skillet. Bake at 400 degrees for 15 minutes or until a meat thermometer registers 160 degrees when inserted into the thickest portion. Remove the pork to a serving platter, reserving the pan juices. Let stand for 5 minutes.

Add the rum to the reserved drippings in the skillet. Cook over medium heat, stirring to deglaze the skillet. Add the reserved pan juices from the baking pan and the chutney. Cook over low heat until heated through, stirring constantly.

To serve, cut the pork diagonally into 1/2-inch-thick slices. Season with salt and pepper to taste. Serve with the rum chutney.

Marinated Pork Tenderloin

Perfect for the grill or oven

- **Serves 8**
- **Must do ahead**
- **Marinate 4 hours**
- **Grill**

1/3 cup red wine vinegar
1/4 cup catsup
1 tablespoon Worcestershire sauce
2 tablespoons soy sauce
1/2 teaspoon garlic salt
1/4 teaspoon pepper
1/2 teaspoon dry mustard
1 (2 1/2- to 3-pound) pork tenderloin

Combine the red wine vinegar, catsup, Worcestershire sauce, soy sauce, garlic salt, pepper and dry mustard in a bowl and mix well.

Place the pork in a sealable plastic bag. Pour the marinade over the pork and seal the bag. Marinate in the refrigerator for 4 hours.

Place the pork on a grill rack. Grill until cooked through.

Grilled Pork Medallions with Pineapple Sesame Salsa

Stunning presentation

For the pork, combine the soy sauce, honey, vegetable oil, dry sherry, ginger and garlic in a shallow dish. Cut the pork into ½-inch-thick medallions. Place in the marinade. Marinate, covered, in the refrigerator for 1 hour or up to 3 days. Remove the pork from the marinade and place on a grill rack. Grill for 5 minutes on each side or until cooked through.

For the salsa, combine the pineapple, red pepper, jalapeño pepper, cilantro, scallions, lime juice and sesame oil in a bowl and mix well.

To serve, spoon the salsa over the pork.

Note: Prepare the salsa no more than a few hours before serving and serve at room temperature.

- **Serves 2 to 4**
- **Must do ahead**
- **Marinate 1 hour or up to 3 days**
- **Grill**

PORK
¼ cup soy sauce
¼ cup honey
2 tablespoons vegetable oil
2 tablespoons dry sherry or brandy
1 tablespoon grated fresh ginger
1 garlic clove, minced
1 (14- to 28-ounce) boneless pork loin

PINEAPPLE SESAME SALSA
8 ounces peeled fresh pineapple, cut into ¼-inch pieces
¼ cup finely chopped red bell pepper
1 tablespoon finely chopped seeded jalapeño pepper
1 tablespoon finely chopped cilantro
2 scallions, finely sliced
Juice of 1 lime
1 tablespoon dark sesame oil

MARINATED ROAST PORK AND WINE GRAVY

IMPRESS YOUR GUESTS

- **Serves 8**
- **Must do ahead**
- **Marinate 8 to 12 hours**
- **Oven Temperature 350 degrees**
- **Bake to 185 degrees**

2 cups chopped onions
4 to 5 garlic cloves, minced
1 tablespoon salt
1 teaspoon freshly ground pepper
1/2 teaspoon oregano
1 (6- to 8-pound) center-cut pork loin
3 cups Merlot
3 tablespoons olive oil
3 cups chicken broth
2 tablespoons flour
Cranberry Pecan Stuffing (page 221)

For the pork, mix 2 cups onions, garlic, 1 tablespoon salt, 1 teaspoon pepper and oregano in a bowl. Rub the mixture into the pork. Pour 1 1/2 cups of the wine into a glass dish. Add the pork. Marinate, covered, in the refrigerator for 8 to 12 hours, basting occasionally. Heat the olive oil in a roasting pan. Add the undrained pork. Bake at 350 degrees until a meat thermometer inserted into the thickest portion registers 185 degrees, basting frequently with 2 cups of the chicken broth to keep the pork moist. Remove the pork from the pan, reserving the pan juices. Wrap the pork with foil.

For the gravy, heat the flour and remaining 1 1/2 cups wine in a saucepan, whisking constantly. Heat the reserved pan juices in the roasting pan. Add the remaining 1 cup chicken broth. Bring to a boil, stirring to deglaze the pan. Strain into the flour mixture. Cook until thickened, stirring constantly.

To serve, cut the pork into slices. Spoon the gravy over the pork. Serve with Cranberry Pecan Stuffing.

Cranberry Pecan Stuffing

Serve with Marinated Roast Pork and Wine Gravy

- **Oven Temperature 350 degrees**
- **Bake 30 minutes**

1 cup dried cranberries
1/2 cup orange juice
1 pound bulk mild pork sausage
2 cups coarsely chopped celery
3/4 cup chopped onion
1/4 cup (1/2 stick) margarine
1 (14-ounce) can chicken broth
1/2 teaspoon salt
1/4 teaspoon freshly ground pepper
1/2 teaspoon thyme
1 (6-ounce) package pork stuffing mix
1 tablespoon grated orange peel
1 cup chopped pecans

Combine the dried cranberries and orange juice in a small saucepan. Bring to a boil over medium heat. Remove from the heat and set aside.

Brown the sausage in a large skillet, stirring until crumbly. Drain the sausage, reserving 1 tablespoon of the drippings. Sauté the celery and 3/4 cup onion in the reserved drippings in a skillet over medium heat for 10 minutes. Add the margarine, chicken broth, 1/2 teaspoon salt, 1/4 teaspoon pepper and thyme. Cook for 3 minutes or until the margarine melts, stirring constantly.

Combine the cranberry mixture, sausage, celery mixture, stuffing mix and seasoning packet, orange peel and pecans in a large bowl and mix well. Spoon into a lightly greased 7x11-inch baking dish.

Bake, covered, at 350 degrees for 20 minutes. Bake, uncovered, for 10 minutes longer or until light brown.

Pork Chops with Dried Cherries

Great sauce with other meats

- **Serves 4**

1/4 cup flour
1/2 teaspoon salt
1/2 teaspoon pepper
1/4 teaspoon ground allspice
1/4 teaspoon ground cloves
4 boneless loin pork chops
1 tablespoon unsalted butter
1 tablespoon olive oil
1/4 cup red wine
1/4 cup chicken broth
1/3 cup finely chopped red onion
1/3 cup dried sour cherries
1 (2-inch) strip lemon peel
2 tablespoons minced crystallized ginger
1 teaspoon brown sugar
1/2 teaspoon chopped fresh thyme
1/2 tablespoon balsamic vinegar
1/4 teaspoon salt
1/4 teaspoon pepper

Mix the flour, 1/2 teaspoon salt, 1/2 teaspoon pepper, allspice and cloves in a bowl. Add the pork chops and coat well. Melt the butter with the olive oil in a skillet. Add the pork chops. Cook for 7 to 8 minutes or until cooked through, turning once. Remove the pork chops to a platter and keep warm.

Add the red wine, chicken broth, red onion, dried cherries, lemon peel, ginger, brown sugar, thyme, balsamic vinegar, 1/4 teaspoon salt and 1/4 teaspoon pepper to the pan drippings in the skillet. Cook over high heat for 3 minutes or until thickened, stirring frequently. Discard the lemon peel. Stir in the juices from the pork chops on the platter. Pour over the pork chops.

Company Pork Chops

Easy and Delicious

- **Serves 6 to 8**
- **Oven Temperature 350 degrees**
- **Bake 2½ to 3 hours**

3 cups applesauce
3 tablespoons dry onion soup mix
6 to 8 boneless pork chops
1 (16-ounce) can whole cranberry sauce

Spread the applesauce in a 9x12-inch baking dish. Sprinkle with the onion soup mix. Arrange the pork chops in the prepared dish. Cover the pork chops with the cranberry sauce.

Bake, covered with foil, at 350 degrees for 2 to 2½ hours or until cooked through. Bake, uncovered, for 30 minutes longer or until brown and bubbly.

Grilled Pork Chops

Simple

- **Serves 4**
- **Must do ahead**
- **Marinate 8 to 12 hours**
- **Grill**

⅓ cup soy sauce
⅔ cup Italian salad dressing
4 boneless pork chops

Combine the soy sauce and salad dressing in a sealable plastic bag and shake to mix well. Add the pork chops and seal the bag; shake to coat. Marinate in the refrigerator for 8 to 12 hours.

Drain the pork chops. Place on a grill rack. Grill for 10 to 15 minutes or until cooked through.

CHILENDRON

MOM'S MEMORIES OF CUBA

- **Serves 6 to 8**
- **Must do ahead**
- **Marinate 30 minutes**

6 pounds 3/4-inch lean pork or beef pieces
Vinegar
Salt and pepper to taste
Olive oil
6 medium onions, chopped
6 green bell peppers, chopped
2 garlic cloves, minced
2 pork sausage links, cut into bite-size pieces
2 (11-ounce) cans tomato purée
2 pinches of saffron threads
Dry sherry
2 tablespoons Worcestershire sauce
1/2 cup raisins
1/2 cup blanched almonds
1 cup sliced stuffed olives

Marinate the pork in a mixture of vinegar, salt and pepper in a sealable plastic bag in the refrigerator for 30 minutes; drain. Brown the pork a few pieces at a time in olive oil in a skillet over high heat.

Sauté the onions, green peppers, garlic, sausages, tomato purée and saffron in a skillet until the sausages are cooked through. Combine the pork and sausage mixture in a large stockpot. Add enough sherry to almost cover.

Simmer, covered, for 3 to 4 hours or until the pork is cooked through. Stir in the Worcestershire sauce, raisins, almonds, olives and salt and pepper to taste. Cook for 30 minutes. Serve over hot cooked rice.

Note: May use a combination of lean pork and beef pieces.

Grilled Venison

Different and very easy

- **Yields variable**
- **Must do ahead**
- **Marinate 4 to 24 hours**
- **Grill**

Venison steaks or chops
Garlic salt to taste
1 pound bacon slices, cut into halves

Cut the venison into 2-inch cubes. Layer the venison in a glass dish, sprinkling generously with garlic salt between each layer. Marinate, covered with plastic wrap, in the refrigerator for 4 to 24 hours. Wrap each venison cube with bacon and secure with a wooden pick. Place in a grill basket. Grill until cooked through.

Oriental Venison and Bell Peppers

The Very Best

- **Serves 4 to 6**

1 cup water
1/4 cup soy sauce
1 tablespoon cornstarch
1 tablespoon instant beef bouillon
1 tablespoon sesame oil
1 (4-ounce) can sliced mushrooms
4 garlic cloves, minced
1 teaspoon Chinese five-spice powder
1 pound venison, cut into 1/8x2-inch strips
1 green bell pepper, thinly sliced
1 red bell pepper, thinly sliced
2 small yellow onions, thinly sliced

Combine the water, soy sauce, cornstarch, instant bouillon and sesame oil in a bowl and mix well.

Drain the mushrooms, reserving the liquid. Heat the reserved liquid in a nonstick skillet or wok sprayed with nonstick cooking spray. Add the garlic and five-spice powder. Cook for 15 to 30 seconds. Add the venison. Cook for 5 minutes or until brown, adding additional water if necessary. Add the green pepper, red pepper, onions and mushrooms. Cook for 2 to 4 minutes. Stir in the soy sauce mixture. Cook until thickened, stirring constantly.

Serve over hot cooked rice or noodles.

Note: Can add water chestnuts, bamboo shoots and Chinese pea pods.

Poultry and Seafood

P. J. Hoffmaster State Park features forest-covered dunes along nearly three miles of Lake Michigan shore. It features campsites and ten miles of hiking trails. The Gillette Visitor Center has a variety of programs to help visitors enjoy and understand a unique environment...the Sand Dunes of the Great Lakes.

Chicken Artichoke Cacciatore

Incredible

- **Serves 6 to 8**
- **Oven Temperature 350 degrees**
- **Bake 1 hour**

2 (6-ounce) jars marinated artichoke hearts
1 tablespoon butter
1 (3½- to 4-pound) chicken, cut into pieces
1 cup flour
1 large onion, chopped
8 ounces mushrooms, sliced
3 garlic cloves, pressed
½ teaspoon oregano
½ teaspoon basil
½ teaspoon rosemary
2 pounds tomatoes
½ cup madeira
Salt and pepper to taste
12 to 16 ounces pasta, cooked, drained

Drain the artichoke hearts, reserving the marinade. Simmer the reserved marinade and butter in a skillet over low heat for 10 minutes. Coat the chicken with the flour, shaking off the excess. Add to the skillet. Cook the chicken over medium heat for 25 minutes or until brown on all sides. Remove the chicken to a 9x13-inch baking dish.

Add the onion, mushrooms, garlic, oregano, basil and rosemary to the skillet. Sauté for 10 minutes or until the onion is translucent. Stir in the tomatoes and artichoke hearts. Pour over the chicken, spreading evenly. Bake, covered, at 350 degrees for 50 minutes or until the chicken is tender. Add the wine and salt and pepper. Bake for 10 minutes longer. Serve over the pasta.

***Note:** May substitute one 28-ounce can tomatoes for the fresh tomatoes. May also use boneless chicken breasts instead of chicken pieces.*

Broiled Chicken

Excellent Flavor

- **Serves 4**

1 teaspoon olive oil
2 tablespoons finely chopped shallots and/or garlic
1 tablespoon Dijon mustard
1 tablespoon Worcestershire sauce
1/4 teaspoon cayenne pepper, or to taste
1/2 cup chicken broth
1 tablespoon finely chopped parsley
4 (4-ounce) boneless skinless chicken breasts

Brush an 8x11-inch baking dish with the olive oil. Combine the shallots and/or garlic, Dijon mustard, Worcestershire sauce, cayenne pepper, chicken broth and parsley in a medium bowl and blend well. Add the chicken and coat well.

Arrange the chicken in a single layer in the prepared baking dish. Spoon the remaining broth mixture over the chicken. Broil for 5 to 8 minutes or until the chicken is cooked through. Serve hot or at room temperature.

Creamy Chicken and Broccoli Casserole

It is too good to believe

- **Serves 8**
- **Can do ahead**
- **Oven Temperature 350 degrees**
- **Bake 30 to 35 minutes**

CHICKEN AND RICE
8 boneless skinless chicken breasts
1 teaspoon chicken base
3 cups water
1 1/2 cups converted rice
1 teaspoon salt
1 tablespoon butter

VEGETABLES
1 large bunch broccoli
1 large onion
1 teaspoon salt
1 red bell pepper, julienned

CREAM CHEESE SAUCE
2 cups milk
1 small garlic clove, finely minced
1/4 teaspoon ginger
1/2 teaspoon salt
1/2 teaspoon coarsely ground pepper
16 ounces cream cheese, chopped
3 tablespoons dry sherry
1 cup shredded Parmesan cheese

TOPPING AND ASSEMBLY
1/4 cup grated Parmesan cheese
1/2 cup fine bread crumbs
1/4 cup (1/2 stick) butter, melted
2 tablespoons minced fresh parsley

For the chicken and rice, arrange the chicken in a single layer in a large skillet. Add the chicken base and 3 cups water. Bring to a simmer. Simmer, covered, for 12 to 15 minutes or until the chicken is cooked through. Turn off the heat and let stand for 10 to 15 minutes. Remove the chicken to a platter and tear into large pieces. Strain the broth. Bring 3 cups of the strained broth to a boil in a saucepan. Add the rice and 1 teaspoon salt and stir gently. Simmer, covered, for 20 minutes or until the liquid is absorbed and the rice is tender. Stir in 1 tablespoon butter.

For the vegetables, peel the broccoli stems and julienne. Cut the broccoli crowns into florets. Cut the onion into halves. Cut each half into thinly sliced half rings. Bring enough water to cover the vegetables to a boil in a large saucepan. Add 1 teaspoon salt and broccoli. Cook for 2 minutes. Add the onion and red pepper. Cook for 2 to 3 minutes or until the broccoli is tender-crisp. Pour into a colander to drain. Refresh in cold water and drain. Wrap the vegetables in a towel to absorb the excess moisture.

For the cream cheese sauce, heat the milk, garlic, ginger, 1/2 teaspoon salt and pepper in a double boiler. Add the cream cheese. Heat until the cream cheese melts, whisking constantly. Add the sherry and 1 cup Parmesan cheese and whisk well.

For the topping, combine 1/4 cup Parmesan cheese, bread crumbs and 1/4 cup melted butter in a bowl and mix well.

To assemble, layer the rice, chicken, 1/2 of the cream cheese sauce, vegetables and the remaining cream cheese sauce in a buttered 3-quart baking dish. Sprinkle with the topping. Bake at 350 degrees for 30 to 35 minutes or until heated through. Sprinkle with the parsley.

Note: Can assemble the dish and chill, covered, for 8 to 12 hours. Bring to room temperature before baking.

Poultry

Chicken and Fruit Stir-Fry

Great for Family or Guests

- **Serves 4 to 6**
- **Must do ahead**
- **Marinate 30 minutes**

CHICKEN
2 tablespoons soy sauce
2 tablespoons dry sherry
1 teaspoon finely minced gingerroot
4 boneless skinless chicken breasts, cut into 1-inch pieces

VEGETABLES AND FRUIT
4 green onions, diagonally sliced
1 rib celery, diagonally sliced
1 small green bell pepper, cut into 1/2-inch pieces
8 fresh mushrooms, sliced
1/2 cup sliced water chestnuts
2 cups fresh fruit

SAUCE AND ASSEMBLY
1/4 cup orange juice
2 tablespoons brown sugar
2 tablespoons soy sauce
1 tablespoon vinegar
1 1/2 tablespoons cornstarch
1/2 teaspoon salt
Dash of pepper
3/4 cup chicken broth
6 tablespoons vegetable oil

For the chicken, combine 2 tablespoons soy sauce, sherry and gingerroot in a dish and mix well. Add the chicken and coat well. Marinate, covered, in the refrigerator for 30 minutes.

For the vegetables and fruit, arrange the vegetables on a tray. Chill, covered, in the refrigerator until ready to use. Prepare the fruit just before using.

For the sauce, combine the orange juice, brown sugar, 2 tablespoons soy sauce, vinegar, cornstarch, salt, pepper and chicken broth in a bowl and mix well.

To assemble, heat 2 tablespoons of the vegetable oil in a wok to 375 degrees. Add 1/2 of the chicken. Stir-fry until partially cooked through. Remove to a warm bowl. Add 2 tablespoons of the remaining vegetable oil to the wok and repeat the process with the remaining chicken.

Add the remaining 2 tablespoons vegetable oil to the wok. Add the green onions and celery. Stir-fry for 2 minutes. Add the green pepper. Stir-fry for 1 minute. Add the mushrooms and water chestnuts. Stir-fry for 1 minute. All vegetables should be almost tender-crisp. Return the chicken to the wok. Add the sauce. Cook until thickened and the chicken is cooked through, stirring constantly. Add the fruit. Cook, covered, for 1 minute or until heated through.

***Note:** Use fresh fruit such as apricots, avocados, kiwifruit, mangoes, unpeeled nectarines, papaya, peaches, unpeeled plums, dark sweet cherry halves, grape halves, cubed cantaloupe and cubed honeydew. Green grape halves and purple plums are a good combination to use.*

Chicken Dijon

A Versatile Dish

- **Serves 8**
- **Oven Temperature 350 degrees**
- **Bake 45 to 50 minutes**

1/2 cup (1 stick) butter, melted
1/2 cup vegetable oil
6 tablespoons Dijon mustard
6 tablespoons chopped fresh chives or green onions
1/2 teaspoon basil
Dash of black pepper
Dash of cayenne pepper
8 boneless skinless chicken breasts
2 cups dry bread crumbs

Combine the butter and vegetable oil in a bowl. Add the Dijon mustard, chives, basil, black pepper and cayenne pepper and whisk until thick. Coat the chicken with the mixture. Roll in the bread crumbs.

Arrange in a single layer in a baking dish sprayed with nonstick cooking spray. Bake at 350 degrees for 45 to 50 minutes or until the chicken is cooked through.

Cashew Chicken

Impressive Chinese dish

- **Serves 6**
- **Must do ahead**
- **Marinate 15 to 20 minutes**

2 tablespoons light soy sauce
1 tablespoon cornstarch
1 pound boneless chicken breasts, cut into strips
2 to 3 tablespoons canola oil
Salt to taste
1 medium onion, chopped
1 pound mushrooms, sliced
2 tablespoons canola oil
1 head cabbage, shredded
1 teaspoon sugar
8 ounces unsalted cashews
1 to 2 teaspoons cornstarch
1/4 cup light soy sauce
Chinese fried noodles

Mix 2 tablespoons soy sauce with 1 tablespoon cornstarch in a bowl. Add the chicken strips and coat well. Marinate, covered, in the refrigerator for 15 to 20 minutes.

Heat 2 to 3 tablespoons canola oil and salt in a wok over high heat. Add the chicken. Stir-fry until the chicken is cooked through. Add the onion and mushrooms. Stir-fry for 2 to 3 minutes. Remove to a warm bowl and keep warm.

Add 2 tablespoons canola oil to the wok. Stir in the cabbage and sugar. Stir-fry for 3 to 4 minutes. Return the chicken mixture to the wok. Add the cashews and toss to mix. Stir 1 to 2 teaspoons cornstarch into 1/4 cup soy sauce. Add to the wok and cover. Steam for 1 minute. Cook, uncovered, until the sauce is thickened, stirring constantly. Spoon onto serving plates and sprinkle with Chinese fried noodles.

Chicken Kiev

Wonderful

• **Serves 4**

CHICKEN
4 boneless chicken breasts
1/2 cup (1 stick) butter
1 tablespoon chopped parsley
1 tablespoon chopped green onions
Flour
2 eggs, beaten
1 cup dry bread crumbs
Vegetable oil for deep-frying

MUSHROOM SAUCE
8 ounces fresh mushrooms
3 tablespoons butter
1 tablespoon flour
3/4 cup light cream
1 teaspoon soy sauce

For the chicken, pound the chicken breasts between 2 sheets of plastic wrap. Cut 1/2 cup butter lengthwise into 4 long strips. Place a strip of butter on each chicken breast. Sprinkle with the parsley and green onions. Roll up to enclose the butter and secure with wooden picks. Dip in flour and then in beaten eggs. Roll in the bread crumbs. Deep-fry in vegetable oil in a deep fryer until golden brown.

For the mushroom sauce, brown the mushrooms in 3 tablespoons butter in a skillet. Add 1 tablespoon flour. Stir in the cream and soy sauce. Cook until thickened, stirring constantly.

To serve, pour the mushroom sauce over the chicken.

Chicken Marco Polo

Quick and Easy

- **Serves 4 to 6**
- **Oven Temperature 500 degrees**
- **Bake 10 minutes**
- **Oven Temperature 325 degrees**
- **Bake 10 minutes**

1/4 cup flour
1/4 cup seasoned bread crumbs
1/4 cup grated Parmesan cheese
6 boneless skinless chicken breasts, flattened
1 small jar garden spaghetti sauce

Mix the flour, bread crumbs and Parmesan cheese in a bowl. Add the chicken and coat well, reserving the remaining crumb mixture. Arrange in a 9x13-inch baking dish sprayed with nonstick cooking spray.

Bake at 500 degrees for 10 minutes, turning after 5 minutes. Reduce the oven temperature to 325 degrees. Cover the chicken with the spaghetti sauce. Sprinkle with the reserved crumb mixture. Bake for 10 minutes or until the chicken is cooked through.

Note: Can substitute Romano cheese for the Parmesan cheese.

Indian Chicken

Tasteful

- **Serves 6**
- **Must do ahead**
- **Chill 1 hour**

1 1/2 teaspoons ginger
1 teaspoon each salt, cinnamon and paprika
2 pounds chicken pieces
1 teaspoon saffron threads
1/4 cup lime juice
Vegetable oil for frying
1 medium onion
1 1/2 cups tomato purée
1/2 cup water
3 tablespoons slivered almonds
1 teaspoon each cinnamon, cardamom and vegetable oil
3 tablespoons almonds, finely ground
2 tablespoons poppy seeds, ground

Mix the ginger, salt, 1 teaspoon cinnamon and paprika in a bowl. Rub evenly on the chicken. Chill, covered, for 1 hour. Soak the saffron in the lime juice in a bowl.

Fry the chicken in vegetable oil in a skillet until brown. Add the onion. Cook until the onion is transparent. Add the tomato purée and water. Cook for 1 hour or until the chicken is cooked through, stirring frequently.

Sauté the silvered almonds with 1 teaspoon cinnamon and cardamom in 1 teaspoon vegetable oil in a skillet. Add to the chicken mixture. Stir in the ground almonds and ground poppy seeds. Spoon into a serving dish. Sprinkle with the saffron mixture. Serve hot with rice.

Swiss Chicken

Light and Healthy

- **Serves 6**
- **Can do ahead**
- **Oven temperature 350 degrees**
- **Bake 45 to 55 minutes**

6 boneless skinless chicken breasts
6 slices low-fat Swiss cheese
1 (10-ounce) can reduced-fat cream of chicken soup
1/4 cup dry white wine
3/4 cup herb-seasoned stuffing mix, crushed

Arrange the chicken in a 9x13-inch baking dish sprayed with nonstick cooking spray. Place the cheese on top of each chicken breast. Mix the soup and wine in a bowl. Spoon over the chicken. Sprinkle with the stuffing mix. Spray with butter-flavor nonstick cooking spray. Bake at 350 degrees for 45 to 55 minutes or until the chicken is cooked through.

***Note:** Can be prepared ahead, chilled, covered, in the refrigerator and then baked just before serving.*

Grilled Lemon Chicken

Guests Always Ask for This Recipe

- **Serves 8 to 10**
- **Must do ahead**
- **Marinate 8 to 12 hours**
- **Grill**

8 chicken legs
8 chicken breasts
Garlic powder
Oregano
1 (1-quart) bottle lemon juice

Sprinkle the chicken liberally with garlic powder and oregano. Place the chicken in glass bowls. Pour enough lemon juice in each bowl to cover the chicken. Marinate, covered with plastic wrap, in the refrigerator for 8 to 12 hours.

Drain the chicken, discarding the marinade. Place the chicken on a grill rack. Grill over hot coals for 15 minutes on each side or until cooked through. Serve hot or cold.

***Note:** May grill chicken ahead of time and microwave, covered, on Medium-High for 5 to 15 minutes or until reheated.*

Chicken Oriental

A unique dish

- **Serves 6**
- **Oven Temperature 300 degrees**
- **Bake 1 hour**

CHICKEN
6 boneless skinless chicken breasts
3 tablespoons flour
2 tablespoons vegetable oil
1 garlic clove, chopped
1 small onion, chopped
1 (4-ounce) can sliced mushrooms
1 (4-ounce) can chopped black olives
1/4 cup catsup
1/4 cup soy sauce
1/4 cup dry white wine or vermouth

FRIED RICE
4 ounces bacon, chopped
6 tablespoons chopped green onions
2 tablespoons chopped celery
1/4 cup chopped carrot
1/4 cup chopped green beans
4 teaspoons soy sauce
1 1/2 teaspoons sugar
1/2 teaspoon salt
2 cups cold cooked rice

For the chicken, coat the chicken with the flour. Brown the chicken in the hot vegetable oil in a skillet. Turn over the chicken. Add the garlic and onion. Cook until brown. Remove the chicken to a baking dish. Add the undrained mushrooms, black olives, catsup, 1/4 cup soy sauce and wine to the onion mixture in the skillet and mix well. Pour over the chicken. Bake, covered, at 300 degrees for 1 hour or until the chicken is cooked through.

For the fried rice, brown the bacon in a skillet. Stir in the green onions, celery, carrot and green beans. Add 4 teaspoons soy sauce, sugar and salt. Sauté until the vegetables are tender. Add the rice and mix well.

To serve, spoon the fried rice onto serving plates. Arrange the chicken over the top.

Chinese Smoked Chicken

Experience the Flavor

- **Must do ahead**
- **Marinate 3 days**
- **Grill**

3 tablespoons kosher salt
1 tablespoon Szechuan pepper
1 (3-pound) chicken
$1\frac{1}{2}$ to 2 cups packed brown sugar

Mix the kosher salt and Szechuan pepper together. Rub the chicken inside and out with the mixture. Place the chicken in a sealable plastic bag; place in another plastic bag to prevent leakage and seal tightly. Marinate in the refrigerator for 3 days.

Place a steamer in a large stockpot. Pour enough water into the stockpot so the water level will not touch the chicken through the steamer. Place the chicken on the steamer and cover the stockpot. Steam for 45 minutes.

Place a piece of foil directly on the hot rocks of a gas grill or the coals of a charcoal grill. Sprinkle the brown sugar on the foil, leaving a few lumps. Place the chicken on the grill rack and cover with the grill lid. Grill for 10 minutes, turning occasionally to brown evenly. The brown sugar will burn, giving the chicken a nice caramelized look and a great flavor.

***Note:** Szechuan pepper can be purchased in Asian groceries. Use 1 tablespoon salt and 1 teaspoon Szechuan pepper for each pound of chicken. Can use boneless chicken pieces, but omit the steaming step.*

Classic French Chicken in White Wine Sauce

Memorable

• **Serves 4**

2 tablespoons (1/4 stick) butter
1 (4-pound) chicken, cut into 6 pieces
1 medium onion, finely chopped
1 medium carrot, finely chopped
1/2 rib celery, finely chopped
2 ounces prosciutto or country ham, finely chopped
3/4 cup dry white wine
3/4 cup homemade or low-salt canned chicken stock
3 tablespoons heavy cream, at room temperature
Salt and pepper to taste
Chopped fresh flat-leaf parsley to taste

Melt the butter in a large skillet over medium heat. Add the chicken skin side down. Cook for 15 minutes or until brown. Turn over the chicken. Cook for 5 minutes longer or until brown. Remove the chicken to a warm platter.

Drain the skillet, reserving 2 tablespoons of the pan drippings. Add the onion, carrot, celery and prosciutto to the reserved drippings. Sauté for 8 to 10 minutes or until the onion is brown and the vegetables are soft. Stir in the wine and chicken stock. Return the chicken to the skillet. Bring to a boil and reduce the heat. Simmer, covered, for 20 to 25 minutes or until the chicken is cooked through. Remove the chicken to a warm platter.

Bring the liquid in the skillet to a boil over high heat. Cook for 5 to 7 minutes or until reduced by half and the sauce is of the desired consistency. Stir in the cream. Season with salt and pepper to taste. Remove the skillet from the heat. Arrange the chicken in individual serving bowls. Spoon the sauce over the chicken and sprinkle with parsley.

Garlic Chicken

Excellent

- **Serves 4**
- **Oven Temperature 500 degrees**
- **Bake 35 minutes**

1 (3-pound) chicken, quartered
4 unpeeled potatoes, cut into pieces
Salt to taste
Olive oil
3 to 4 garlic cloves
Juice of 2 lemons
2 tomatoes, quartered

Place the chicken in a baking dish. Arrange the potatoes around the chicken. Season with salt and drizzle with olive oil. Bake at 500 degrees for 30 minutes or until golden brown and the chicken is cooked through.

Peel the garlic and mash in a bowl. Measure the lemon juice in a glass measure; add an equal amount of olive oil. Add the mixture to the garlic and mix well.

Drizzle the chicken with the garlic mixture. Add the tomatoes. Bake for 5 minutes or until heated through. Serve with a salad and rolls.

Sticky Chicken

Family Favorite

- **Serves 4**
- **Must do ahead**
- **Chill 8 to 12 hours**
- **Oven Temperature 300 degrees**
- **Bake 2 to 4 hours**

1 tablespoon salt
2 teaspoons oregano
2 teaspoons paprika
2 teaspoons thyme
1 teaspoon freshly ground pepper or garlic pepper
1 teaspoon garlic powder
1 (3-pound) chicken
1 large onion, chopped

Mix the salt, oregano, paprika, thyme, pepper and garlic powder in a small bowl. Rub the chicken inside and out with the mixture. Place in a sealable plastic bag and seal. Chill in the refrigerator for 8 to 12 hours.

Place the chopped onion in the chicken cavity. Tie the wings and legs if desired. Place on a rack in a roasting pan. Bake, covered, at 300 degrees for 2 to 4 hours or until cooked through, basting occasionally. The pan juices should thicken and caramelize during baking.

Note: May use other seasonings such as seasoned salt, dill, celery seeds, rosemary, basil, etc. May add potatoes and carrots during the last 1½ hours of baking, basting immediately and during baking.

Poultry

Roast Chicken with Rosemary

Simply scrumptious

- **Serves 4**
- **Oven Temperature 375 degrees**
- **Bake 1 hour**

3 garlic cloves, peeled
1 teaspoon (heaping) rosemary
1 (3-pound) chicken
Salt and freshly ground pepper to taste
1/4 cup vegetable oil
1 to 2 tablespoons water

Place the garlic and 1/2 of the rosemary in the chicken cavity. Season with salt and pepper. Rub about 1/2 of the vegetable oil over the outside of the chicken. Sprinkle with salt, pepper and the remaining rosemary.

Place the chicken in the remaining vegetable oil in a roasting pan. Bake at 375 degrees for 1 hour or until brown and cooked through, basting every 15 minutes. Remove the chicken to a warm platter.

Drain the roasting pan, reserving 1 tablespoon of the drippings in the pan. Place the pan over high heat. Add 1 to 2 tablespoons water. Boil until the water evaporates, stirring to deglaze the pan. Pour over the chicken and serve immediately.

Chicken Supreme

Nice buffet dish

- **Serves 4**
- **Can do ahead**
- **Can be frozen**
- **Oven Temperature 350 degrees**
- **Bake 25 minutes**
- **Oven Temperature 200 degrees**
- **Bake 20 to 25 minutes**

4 boneless skinless chicken breasts
1/4 cup (about) flour
Butter, softened
Oregano to taste
Chopped fresh parsley to taste
4 slices Swiss cheese
1 or 2 eggs, beaten
Cracker crumbs
1/2 cup white wine

Coat the chicken with the flour. Pound the chicken until 1/4 inch thick. Spread with butter. Sprinkle with oregano and parsley. Top each with a cheese slice, cutting to fit the chicken. Roll up the chicken. Dip in beaten egg and then in cracker crumbs. Arrange in a single layer in a buttered baking dish.

Bake at 350 degrees for 25 minutes. Pour the wine over the chicken. Cover and reduce the oven temperature to 200 degrees. Bake for 20 to 25 minutes longer or until the chicken is cooked through.

Note: Can be assembled ahead and frozen or baked and frozen. Thaw before baking or extend the baking time, checking frequently. Can also be reheated in the microwave at 80 percent power or reheated in a 350-degree oven for about 15 minutes.

Tarragon Chicken with Mushrooms

Tasty and Tender

- **Serves 8 to 10**

1/2 cup chopped bacon (about 4 slices)
2 chickens, cut into 8 pieces, skinned
1 fresh white onion, or 1 package frozen white onions
2 pounds fresh mushrooms
1 (14-ounce) can chicken broth
3/4 cup dry white wine
2 tablespoons lemon juice
2 teaspoons tarragon
1/2 teaspoon salt
1/4 teaspoon freshly ground pepper
5 tablespoons each flour and water

Brown the bacon in a Dutch oven. Remove the bacon and cool. Cook the chicken in the bacon drippings for 6 minutes or until brown on all sides. Remove the chicken to a warm platter.

Add the onion and mushrooms to the Dutch oven. Sauté until golden brown. Return the chicken to the Dutch oven. Add the chicken broth, wine, lemon juice, tarragon, salt and pepper. Bring to a boil and reduce the heat. Simmer for 40 minutes.

Mix the flour and water in a small bowl. Add 1 cup of the hot broth and mix well. Stir into the chicken mixture. Cook until thickened, stirring constantly. Sprinkle with the cooled bacon.

Baked Yogurt Chicken

You'll Never Know You're Eating Healthy

- **Serves 6**
- **Oven Temperature 375 degrees**
- **Bake 35 minutes**

1 cup bread crumbs
Salt and freshly ground black pepper to taste
1 1/2 teaspoons poultry seasoning
Pinch of cayenne pepper
Pinch of tarragon
1/2 cup nonfat plain yogurt
3 tablespoons mayonnaise or nonfat mayonnaise
3 tablespoons Dijon mustard
1 small garlic clove, minced
1 shallot, minced
1 tablespoon lemon juice
6 chicken pieces

Mix the bread crumbs, salt, black pepper, poultry seasoning, cayenne pepper and tarragon together. Combine the yogurt, mayonnaise, Dijon mustard, garlic, shallot and lemon juice in a bowl and mix well. Coat the chicken with the yogurt mixture. Roll in the bread crumb mixture until covered. Place in a greased 9x13-inch baking dish. Bake at 375 degrees for 35 minutes or until the chicken is cooked through.

Note: Can use boneless chicken pieces, but bake at 425 degrees for 18 to 25 minutes or until the chicken is cooked through.

Jamaican Barbecued Chicken Wings

Extraordinary

- **Serves 6 to 8**
- **Must do ahead**
- **Marinate up to 24 hours**

JERK SEASONING
1/4 cup onion flakes
1/4 cup onion powder
3 tablespoons thyme
3 tablespoons chives
3 tablespoons salt
1 tablespoon coarse ground black pepper
4 teaspoons cayenne pepper
4 teaspoons allspice
1 teaspoon nutmeg
1 teaspoon cinnamon

CHICKEN WINGS
1 cup vegetable oil
2 cups cider vinegar
6 tablespoons dry Jerk Seasoning
1/2 teaspoon white pepper
2 eggs
40 chicken wings

HONEY GINGER DIPPING SAUCE
1 (8-ounce) can sweetened tamarind nectar
1 tablespoon honey
2 to 3 inches fresh gingerroot, grated
1 tablespoon soy sauce
1 tablespoon Jerk Seasoning
1 teaspoon cornstarch
1 teaspoon water

For the jerk seasoning, combine the onion flakes, onion powder, thyme, chives, salt, black pepper, cayenne pepper, allspice, nutmeg and cinnamon in a bowl and mix well. Store, tightly covered, in a glass jar for up to 1 month.

For the chicken wings, blend the vegetable oil, vinegar, 6 tablespoons jerk seasoning, white pepper and eggs in a food processor until smooth. Place the chicken in a single layer in a glass dish. Cover the chicken with 1/3 of the marinade. Marinate, covered, in the refrigerator for up to 24 hours. Drain the chicken, discarding the marinade. Place the chicken on a grill rack. Grill over charcoal with wood chips until the chicken is cooked through, brushing with the remaining marinade. Sprinkle with additional jerk seasoning for spicier chicken.

For the sauce, combine the tamarind nectar and honey in a saucepan. Boil until the mixture is reduced by 1/3. Stir in the gingerroot, soy sauce and 1 tablespoon jerk seasoning. Mix the cornstarch with the water to form a paste. Stir into the tamarind mixture. Cook until thickened, stirring constantly.

To serve, spoon the honey ginger dipping sauce into a serving bowl and place in the center of a large platter. Arrange the chicken around the bowl.

Chicken and Artichoke Supreme

An Easy Recipe with a Gourmet Taste

- **Serves 6**
- **Oven Temperature 350 degrees**
- **Bake 30 to 40 minutes**

1½ cups sliced fresh mushrooms
2 tablespoons (¼ stick) butter
2 (14-ounce) cans water-pack artichoke hearts, drained, chopped
2 cups sliced cooked chicken breasts
1 envelope chicken gravy mix
1 to 1½ cups grated Cheddar cheese
⅛ teaspoon marjoram
2 tablespoons dry sherry
½ cup soft bread crumbs
1 tablespoon butter, melted
1 tablespoon snipped fresh parsley

Sauté the mushrooms in 2 tablespoons butter in a skillet. Layer the artichokes, mushrooms and chicken in a 2-quart baking dish.

Prepare the gravy mix using the package directions. Add the Cheddar cheese and marjoram, stirring until the Cheddar cheese melts. Stir in the wine. Pour over the chicken.

Toss the bread crumbs with the melted butter in a bowl. Sprinkle over the chicken mixture. Bake, uncovered, at 350 degrees for 30 to 40 minutes or until bubbly. Sprinkle with the parsley.

Chicken Asparagus Casserole

Flavorful

- **Serves 8**
- **Oven Temperature 350 degrees**
- **Bake 30 minutes**

2 (15-ounce) cans asparagus
1 (8-ounce) can sliced water chestnuts, drained
¾ cup sliced almonds, toasted
3½ cups chopped cooked chicken
1 (10-ounce) can cream of celery soup
½ cup finely chopped celery
¾ cup mayonnaise
½ cup dry white wine
1 (5-ounce) can evaporated milk
¾ cup shredded Cheddar cheese

Layer the asparagus, water chestnuts, almonds and chicken in a lightly greased 8x12-inch baking dish. Combine the celery soup, celery, mayonnaise, white wine and evaporated milk in a bowl and mix well. Spoon over the chicken. Sprinkle with the Cheddar cheese. Bake at 350 degrees for 30 minutes or until heated through.

Note: Can use 1 pound fresh asparagus spears, trimmed, instead of the canned asparagus. Chopped pimento and/or chopped green bell pepper can be added to the recipe. Recipe can be doubled, but extend the baking time.

M. B.'s Pasties

Keep on hand for a busy day

- **Serves 8**
- **Can be frozen**
- **Oven Temperature 350 degrees**
- **Bake 20 to 25 minutes**

8 ounces cream cheese, softened
1/4 cup (1/2 stick) butter, melted
2 cups chopped cooked chicken
1/2 teaspoon garlic salt
1/2 teaspoon pepper
1/4 cup milk
1 tablespoon chopped green onions
2 (8-count) cans crescent rolls
1 rib celery, chopped, parboiled
1 carrot, sliced, parboiled
1 potato, chopped, parboiled
2 tablespoons (1/4 stick) butter, melted
1 cup crushed seasoned croutons

Blend the cream cheese and 1/4 cup butter in a bowl until smooth. Add the chicken, garlic salt, pepper, milk and green onions and mix well.

Unroll the crescent rolls and separate into 8 rectangles, pressing the perforations to seal. Spoon about 1/4 cup chicken mixture in the center of each rectangle. Sprinkle each with celery, carrot and potato. Bring the 4 corners of each rectangle to the top to enclose the filling and crimp the edges together to seal. Brush with 2 tablespoons butter. Dip in the crushed croutons. Place on an ungreased baking sheet. Bake at 350 degrees for 20 to 25 minutes or until golden brown.

***Note:** Can store the unbaked pasties in the freezer and bake when ready to serve. Can use crushed cheese crackers instead of croutons.*

Cilantro-Marinated Chicken Tenders

Very tender and moist

- **Serves 8**
- **Must do ahead**
- **Marinate 4 hours**
- **Grill**

1 (12-ounce) can frozen limeade concentrate
3/4 cup white Worcestershire sauce
6 garlic cloves, minced
4 pounds chicken tenders
1/2 cup chopped fresh cilantro

Mix the limeade concentrate, Worcestershire sauce and garlic in a sealable plastic bag. Add the chicken and seal the bag. Marinate in the refrigerator for 3 hours. Add the cilantro. Marinate in the refrigerator for 1 hour.

Drain the chicken, discarding the marinade. Place the chicken in a grill basket. Grill over hot coals until the chicken is cooked through. Serve with pineapple salsa.

Chicken Soufflé

Guaranteed to Please

Sauté the mushrooms in the butter in a skillet. Arrange the bread slices over the bottom of a 9x14-inch glass baking dish. Layer the chicken, sautéed mushrooms, water chestnuts, mayonnaise and Cheddar cheese over the bread. Mix the eggs and milk in a bowl. Pour over the cheese. Mix the mushroom soup, celery soup and pimento in a bowl. Spoon over the top.

Chill, covered, for 8 to 12 hours. Bake, uncovered, at 350 degrees for 1¼ hours. Sprinkle with the buttered bread crumbs. Bake for 15 minutes longer.

- **Serves 8 to 10**
- **Must do ahead**
- **Chill 8 to 12 hours**
- **Oven Temperature 350 degrees**
- **Bake 1½ hours**

8 ounces sliced fresh mushrooms
¼ cup (½ stick) butter or margarine
9 slices bread, crusts trimmed
4 cups chopped cooked chicken
1 cup sliced water chestnuts
½ cup mayonnaise
9 slices sharp Cheddar cheese
4 eggs
2 cups milk
1 (10-ounce) can cream of mushroom soup
1 (10-ounce) can cream of celery soup
1 small jar pimento, drained, chopped
2 cups buttered bread crumbs

Healthy Sausage

Nice blend of spices

- **Serves 6 to 8**
- **Must do ahead**
- **Chill several hours**
- **Can be frozen**

1 pound ground turkey or ground chicken breasts
1 tablespoon Butter Buds
1 tablespoon oat bran cereal
1/2 teaspoon basil
1/2 teaspoon thyme
1/2 teaspoon sage
1/4 teaspoon cumin
1/4 teaspoon marjoram
1/4 teaspoon black pepper
1/4 teaspoon oregano
1/4 teaspoon cayenne pepper
1/8 teaspoon garlic powder
1/8 teaspoon nutmeg
1/8 teaspoon ginger

Combine the ground turkey, Butter Buds, oat bran cereal, basil, thyme, sage, cumin, marjoram, black pepper, oregano, cayenne pepper, garlic powder, nutmeg and ginger in a bowl and mix well.

Chill, covered, for several hours. Shape into patties. Grill, bake or fry until cooked through.

Note: May freeze sausage patties before or after cooking.

Roasted Red Pepper Chicken Puff

Great

- **Serves 8**
- **Oven Temperature 400 degrees**
- **Bake 30 to 45 minutes**

4 cups chopped chicken
2 tablespoons rosemary
1 tablespoon each thyme and sage
1 cup roasted red bell pepper
1 (8-ounce) can green chiles, drained
1 cup whole kernel corn
3 packages Alouette garlic and herb cheese spread
2 puffed pastry sheets
1 egg, beaten

Sauté the chicken with rosemary, thyme and sage in a nonstick skillet until cooked through. Combine with the red pepper, green chiles, corn and cheese spread in a bowl and mix well. Spread on ½ of each pastry sheet; fold the remaining half over the filling. Crimp the edges to seal and brush with beaten egg. Place on baking sheets. Bake at 400 degrees for 30 to 45 minutes. Cut into angled sections and serve with a corn salsa.

Note: Can substitute sun-dried tomato cheese spread for the garlic and herb spread.

Honey Apple-Marinated Grilled Chicken

Wonderful

- **Serves 8**
- **Must do ahead**
- **Marinate 8 hours**
- **Grill**

¼ cup apple juice
¼ cup apple cider vinegar
⅓ cup vegetable oil
¼ cup honey
⅓ cup soy sauce
1 teaspoon ginger
1 garlic clove, minced
8 chicken breasts

Mix the apple juice, apple cider vinegar, vegetable oil, honey, soy sauce, ginger and garlic in a sealable plastic bag and mix well. Add the chicken and seal the bag. Marinate in the refrigerator for 8 hours.

Drain the chicken, discarding the marinade. Place the chicken on a grill rack. Grill until the chicken is cooked through.

Cornish Game Hens Cointreau

You will impress your friends with this offering

- **Serves 4**
- **Oven Temperature 450 degrees**
- **Bake 10 minutes**
- **Oven Temperature 300 degrees**
- **Bake 45 minutes**

CORNISH GAME HENS
4 frozen Cornish game hens, thawed
Salt and freshly ground pepper to taste
1/4 cup (1/2 stick) butter

DRESSING
4 ribs celery with leaves, finely chopped
1/4 cup (1/2 stick) butter
2 cups browned bread crumbs
1/2 cup Cognac
2 tablespoons grated orange peel
1 1/2 cups orange juice
1 egg, beaten
Salt and freshly ground pepper to taste
1/4 teaspoon chervil
1 pinch basil

SAUCE
2 pinches rosemary
1 cup dry red wine
1 ounce Cointreau

GRAVY
1/2 cup vegetable stock

For the Cornish game hens, remove the giblets from the Cornish game hens. Rub the game hens with salt and pepper. Coat the hens with 1/4 cup butter.

For the dressing, sauté the celery in 1/4 cup butter in a saucepan for 5 minutes. Stir in the bread crumbs. Cook over low heat for 2 minutes. Remove from the heat. Add the Cognac, orange peel, orange juice, egg, salt, pepper, chervil and basil. Cool slightly.

For the sauce, steep the rosemary in the red wine in a saucepan until faint steam rises from the wine. Remove the saucepan from the heat. Add the Cointreau.

To assemble, stuff the game hens with the dressing and stitch the openings closed. Place in a shallow roasting pan. Bake at 450 degrees for 10 minutes. Reduce the oven temperature to 300 degrees. Bake for 45 minutes longer, basting frequently with the sauce. Baste with the pan drippings after using all the sauce. Remove the game hens to a warm platter and cover with foil to keep warm.

For the gravy, place the roasting pan over low heat. Add the vegetable stock to the pan drippings. Cook until of the desired consistency, stirring constantly.

To serve, pour the gravy over the game hens.

Fish Fillets in White Wine Sauce

A little wine, a little bread, and you think you are in Provence

- **Serves 6**
- **Oven Temperature 350 degrees**
- **Bake 8 to 12 minutes**

FISH FILLETS
2 tablespoons finely minced shallots or green onions
2 1/2 pounds fish fillets
Salt and black pepper to taste
1 1/2 tablespoons butter
1 1/4 to 1 1/2 cups white wine

SAUCE
3 tablespoons butter
1/4 cup flour
Salt and cayenne pepper to taste
1/2 cup cream

ASSEMBLY
2 tablespoons grated Parmesan cheese
Butter

For the fish, sprinkle 1/2 of the shallots in a buttered deep 10-inch baking dish. Season the fish with salt and black pepper. Fold over each fish or roll up. Arrange fish slightly overlapping over the shallots. Sprinkle with the remaining shallots and dot with 1 1/2 tablespoons butter. Pour the wine over the fish. Add enough water to barely cover the fish. Cover the fish with waxed paper. Place the dish on the bottom oven rack. Bake at 350 degrees for 8 to 12 minutes or until the fish flakes easily. Do not overcook.

For the sauce, strain the fish liquid into a bowl. Cover the fish and keep warm. Melt 3 tablespoons butter in a saucepan. Blend in the flour. Season with salt and cayenne pepper to taste. Add about 1 1/2 cups of the fish stock gradually, stirring constantly. Cook over low heat until thickened, stirring constantly. Add the cream. Bring to a boil and remove from the heat.

To assemble, spoon the sauce over the fish. Sprinkle with the Parmesan cheese and dot with butter. Broil until brown.

Grilled Orange Roughy and Vegetable Packets

Low in calories and so good

- **Serves 2**
- **Grill**

1 large sweet apple
1/2 to 3/4 pound orange roughy
1 (1-pound) package frozen snow pea stir-fry with Oriental noodles
1/4 cup chopped green onions
1 cup water
Salt and pepper to taste

Cut the apple into 1/2-inch-thick slices. Cut each apple slice into halves and remove the seeds. Place the apple slices on a large piece of heavy-duty foil.

Cut the fish into 1x2-inch pieces. Combine the fish and frozen snow pea stir-fry in a bowl and toss to mix. Place over the apple slices. Sprinkle with the green onions. Pour the water over the layers. Season with salt and pepper. Bring the foil over the layers and fold the edges to seal, forming a packet. Place the foil packet on a grill rack. Grill over hot coals for 15 to 20 minutes. Open the packet. Continue grilling for 5 minutes longer.

To serve, separate the fish and vegetables from the apples. Sprinkle the apples with brown sugar and/or cinnamon if desired.

***Note:** Can substitute 1/2 cup snow peas, 1/2 cup thinly slivered carrots, 1/2 cup broccoli, 1/2 cup Oriental noodles and 1/4 cup slivered red bell pepper for the frozen snow pea stir-fry.*

Crumb-Coated Salmon Fillets

Perfect every time

- **Serves 4**

¼ cup (½ stick) butter or margarine
1 egg, beaten
1 tablespoon lemon juice
Salt to taste
¾ teaspoon pepper
½ cup dry bread crumbs
2 tablespoons finely chopped almonds
1½ pounds salmon fillets, skin removed, cut into pieces

Microwave the butter in a 9x13-inch glass dish on High until melted. Mix the egg, lemon juice, salt and pepper in a shallow dish. Mix the bread crumbs and almonds on waxed paper. Dip the salmon in the egg mixture; coat with the bread crumb mixture. Arrange the salmon in the melted butter, turning to coat. Drizzle any remaining egg mixture over the salmon; sprinkle with any remaining bread crumb mixture.

Microwave, uncovered, on High for 5 to 6 minutes or until steaming hot. Broil for 2 to 3 minutes or until light brown and the salmon flakes easily.

Grilled Salmon Fillet

Perfect for your Lake Michigan catch

- **Serves 2**
- **Grill**

3 tablespoons butter, softened
1 garlic clove, minced
2 teaspoons dillweed
1 (10- to 12-ounce) salmon fillet

Mix the butter, garlic and dillweed in a bowl. Spread over the salmon. Place the salmon on a grill rack. Grill over medium coals for 15 to 18 minutes or until the fish flakes easily.

Note: Do not substitute margarine for butter in this recipe.

Mango Salmon

Refreshing

- **Serves 4 to 6**
- **Must do ahead**

Salmon

- **Marinate 1 hour**
- **Grill**

Mango Salsa

- **Chill 1 hour or longer**

SALMON
1/4 cup chopped fresh mint
1/4 cup chopped fresh cilantro
2 teaspoons fresh lime juice
1 teaspoon fire oil (see Note)
2 pounds salmon fillet

MANGO SALSA
3 medium mangoes, chopped
1/4 cup chopped fresh mint
1/4 cup chopped fresh cilantro
2 teaspoons fresh lime juice
1/2 cup juice-pack pineapple tidbits

For the salmon, combine 1/4 cup mint, 1/4 cup cilantro, 2 teaspoons lime juice and fire oil in a sealable plastic bag and mix well. Add the salmon and seal the bag. Marinate in the refrigerator for 1 hour.

Place the salmon on a large sheet of foil. Pour the marinade over the salmon. Fold the foil over the salmon and seal the edges to enclose to form a packet. Place on a grill rack. Grill over medium coals for 20 minutes or until the salmon flakes easily.

For the salsa, combine the mangoes, 1/4 cup mint, 1/4 cup cilantro, 2 teaspoons lime juice and pineapple in a bowl and mix well. Spoon into a glass serving bowl. Chill, covered, for 1 hour or longer.

To serve, place the salmon on serving plates. Spoon the salsa beside the salmon. Serve with hot cooked rice.

Note: Fire oil can be found in the Oriental foods section of your grocery.

Baked Salmon Fillets

No pans

For the salmon, sprinkle the salmon with salt and white pepper. Wrap 2 of the salmon at a time tightly in foil. Bake at 400 degrees for 30 minutes.

For the sauce, combine the mayonnaise, sour cream, lemon juice, onion and tarragon in a saucepan. Heat over low heat until warm, stirring constantly.

To serve, place the warm salmon on a serving plate. Spoon the warm sauce over the salmon.

Note: Serve the sauce chilled or at room temperature if serving with cold salmon.

- **Serves 4**
- **Oven Temperature 400 degrees**
- **Bake 30 minutes**

SALMON
4 salmon fillets
Salt to taste
1/2 teaspoon white pepper

TARRAGON SOUR CREAM SAUCE
1/2 cup mayonnaise
1/2 cup sour cream
Juice of 1 lemon
1 tablespoon minced onion
2 teaspoons tarragon

Rolled Sole

You will make it again and again

Dot the fillets with the butter. Sprinkle with salt and paprika. Roll up the fillets and fasten with wooden picks. Place in a 1-quart sauté pan. Add the tomato, mushrooms, green onions, parsley, wine, garlic and salt. Simmer, tightly covered, for 7 to 8 minutes or until the fillets flake easily with a fork. Remove the fillet roll-ups to a warm platter and keep warm.

Boil the tomato mixture for 2 to 3 minutes or until slightly thickened, stirring constantly. Spoon over the fillet roll-ups. Garnish with lemon wedges and sprigs of parsley.

- **Serves 2**

2 sole fillets
1 tablespoon butter or margarine
Salt to taste
Paprika to taste
1 medium tomato, peeled, chopped
1/4 cup sliced mushrooms
2 tablespoons chopped green onions
2 tablespoons parsley
2 tablespoons dry white wine
1 small garlic clove, minced

GARNISHES
Lemon wedges
Sprigs of parsley

Whitefish Grenoble

Magnifique

- **Serves 2**

1 tablespoon capers, chopped
1 medium tomato, peeled, seeded, chopped
1 lemon, peeled, seeded, chopped
2 whitefish fillets (about 8 ounces each)
3/4 cup milk
1/2 cup flour
1/2 teaspoon garlic powder
1/2 teaspoon salt
1/4 teaspoon freshly ground pepper
1/4 cup clarified butter
1 tablespoon butter

Mix the capers, tomato and lemon in a bowl. Soak the fillets in the milk in a bowl for a few minutes. Mix the flour, garlic powder, salt and pepper together. Coat the fillets with the flour mixture, shaking to remove the excess.

Pour the clarified butter into a hot skillet. Add the fillets skin side up. Cook for 1 minute on each side or until brown. Remove to a heated platter.

Heat 1 tablespoon butter in a skillet over medium heat until the butter begins to brown. Add the tomato mixture. Cook for 2 to 3 minutes or until heated through. Spoon over the fillets and serve.

Note: To clarify butter, melt the butter in a small saucepan over low heat until foamy. Remove from the heat and let stand until the milk solids settle to the bottom of the saucepan and the salt crystals settle on the top. Skim off the salt crystals and carefully pour the butter oil into a separate container. Discard the milk solids that have settled in the bottom.

Crab Meat Bayou Teche

Elegant beginning

- **Serves 8**
- **Oven Temperature 350 degrees**
- **Bake 20 minutes**

1/4 cup (1/2 stick) butter, softened
3 hard-cooked egg yolks, sieved
1/2 teaspoon dry mustard
1/4 teaspoon curry powder
1/4 cup dry white wine
3/4 cup heavy cream
3 tablespoons chopped fresh chives
1 pound lump crab meat, picked over
Salt and freshly ground pepper to taste
1 garlic clove, peeled
2 tablespoons (1/4 stick) butter
1/2 cup bread crumbs

Combine 1/4 cup butter and egg yolks in a bowl and mix well. Stir the dry mustard and curry powder into the wine. Add to the butter mixture and whisk well. Beat in the cream. The mixture will look curdled. Stir in the chives and lump crab meat gently. Season with salt and pepper.

Rub 8 scallop shells or ramekins with the garlic clove. Spoon the crab meat mixture into the prepared ramekins. Heat 2 tablespoons butter in a small sauté pan until melted. Add the bread crumbs and stir until coated. Spoon over the crab meat mixture. Bake at 350 degrees for 20 minutes or until bubbly and the tops are brown.

French Bread Shrimp

Nice for luncheon or light dinner

- **Serves 4**

$^{1}/_{4}$ cup chopped scallions
2 teaspoons minced garlic
1 cup (2 sticks) butter, melted
2 pounds shrimp, deveined
1 tablespoon white wine
1 teaspoon lemon juice
$^{1}/_{8}$ teaspoon salt
$^{1}/_{8}$ teaspoon coarsely ground pepper
1 teaspoon fresh dillweed
1 teaspoon chopped fresh parsley
1 loaf French bread, cut into
$1^{1}/_{2}$-inch-thick slices, toasted

Sauté the scallions and garlic in the butter in a skillet. Add the shrimp, wine, lemon juice, salt and pepper. Sauté for 5 to 6 minutes or until the shrimp turn pink. Stir in the dillweed and parsley. Spoon over the toasted bread slices in a serving bowl.

Serve immediately.

Scallops and Shrimp with Dry Vermouth

Rave reviews from all

Peel the shrimp and devein. Rinse in cold water and pat dry. Cut the scallops into halves. Heat the butter in a skillet until melted. Add the shrimp. Sauté for 15 seconds. Add the scallops. Sprinkle with salt and pepper. Sauté for 1 minute. Spoon the shrimp and scallops into a dish.

Add the shallot and vermouth to the pan drippings in the skillet. Cook over high heat until the liquid is reduced by 1/2. Add the cream. Bring to a boil over high heat. Cook until reduced to 2/3 cup, stirring constantly. Return the shrimp and scallops to the skillet. Stir in the basil. Season with salt and pepper.

- **Serves 4**

1 pound shrimp
2 pounds bay or sea scallops
3 tablespoons butter
Salt and freshly ground pepper to taste
1 tablespoon finely chopped shallot
1/3 cup dry white vermouth
3/4 cup heavy cream
12 fresh basil leaves

Seafood Strudel

A Praiseworthy Dish

- **Serves 6 to 8**
- **Must do ahead**
- **Chill 2 hours**
- **Oven Temperature 375 degrees**
- **Bake 47 to 52 minutes**

2 tablespoons (1/4 stick) unsalted butter
2 tablespoons flour
1/2 teaspoon Dijon mustard
Salt to taste
Cayenne pepper to taste
3/4 cup milk, at room temperature
2 tablespoons heavy cream
1 cup bread crumbs
1/4 cup freshly grated Parmesan cheese
1/4 teaspoon dry mustard
8 ounces phyllo pastry sheets
1/4 cup (1/2 stick) butter, melted
1 pound bite-size pieces cooked crab meat, shrimp, lobster or halibut
1/2 cup grated Swiss cheese
2 hard-cooked eggs, chopped
3/4 cup sour cream
1/4 cup chopped parsley
1/4 cup chopped shallots
2 tablespoons chopped chives
1 large garlic clove, minced
3/4 cup (1 1/2 sticks) unsalted butter, melted
2 tablespoons chopped parsley
2 tablespoons freshly grated Parmesan cheese
Minced fresh parsley to taste
Crab or lobster claws

Melt 2 tablespoons butter in a small saucepan over low heat. Add the flour. Heat until the mixture begins to bubble and forms a smooth paste, stirring constantly. Remove from the heat. Add the Dijon mustard, salt and cayenne pepper. Add the milk gradually, stirring constantly. Cook over medium heat until thickened and bubbly, stirring constantly. Add the cream and adjust the seasonings. Chill, covered, for 2 hours or until thick and firm.

Combine the bread crumbs, 1/4 cup Parmesan cheese and dry mustard in a bowl and mix well. Spread a dampened clean dish towel on a work surface. Cover the towel with waxed paper. Unfold the phyllo sheets on the waxed paper. Fold the phyllo sheets in half as for a book. Turn to the first phyllo sheet. Brush with some of the 1/4 cup melted butter and sprinkle with a portion of the bread crumb mixture. Repeat the process until the center is reached. Fold in half again. Work from the back toward the center, brushing each phyllo sheet with the melted butter and sprinkling with bread crumbs. Once the center is reached all phyllo sheets will be stacked.

Layer the seafood evenly on the phyllo stack. Sprinkle with Swiss cheese and chopped eggs. Dot with sour cream. Sprinkle with 1/4 cup parsley, shallots, chives and garlic. Dot with the chilled cream mixture. Roll up as for a jelly roll. Place seam side down on a buttered baking sheet. Brush with some of the 3/4 cup melted butter. Bake at 375 degrees for 12 minutes. Remove from the oven and brush with the melted butter. Cut diagonally with a serrated knife into 1 1/2-inch slices. Push the slices together to retain the loaf. Add 2 tablespoons parsley to the remaining melted butter. Brush the loaf with some of the parsley butter. Bake for 35 to 40 minutes or until crisp and golden brown, brushing 3 times with the parsley butter. Remove the strudel from the oven and brush with the remaining parsley butter. Cool for 10 minutes on the baking sheet. Remove to a warm serving platter using a long spatula. Sprinkle with 2 tablespoons Parmesan cheese and minced parsley to taste. Top with crab or lobster claws.

Desserts

Entrance to
Muskegon Channel
from Lake Michigan

Frankenmuth Bavarian Inn Cheesecake

Absolutely delicious

- **Serves 8**
- **Must do ahead**
- **Chill several hours**
- **Oven Temperature 325 degrees**
- **Bake 35 to 40 minutes**

CRUST

1¼ cups plain or cinnamon graham cracker crumbs

¼ cup (½ stick) butter or margarine, melted

LEMON CREAM CHEESE FILLING

8 ounces cream cheese, softened

½ cup sugar

1¼ tablespoons lemon juice

1 teaspoon lemon peel

½ teaspoon vanilla extract

Dash of salt

2 eggs

SOUR CREAM TOPPING

1 cup sour cream

2 tablespoons sugar

½ teaspoon vanilla extract

For the crust, combine the graham cracker crumbs and butter in a bowl and mix well. Press into a buttered 8-inch pie plate, forming a shell.

For the filling, beat the cream cheese in a mixer bowl until light and fluffy. Add ½ cup sugar gradually, beating constantly. Beat in the lemon juice, lemon peel, ½ teaspoon vanilla and salt. Add the eggs 1 at a time, beating well after each addition.

For the topping, combine the sour cream, 2 tablespoons sugar and ½ teaspoon vanilla in a bowl and mix well.

To assemble, pour the filling into the prepared pie shell. Bake at 325 degrees for 25 to 30 minutes or until set. Spoon the topping over the top. Bake for 10 minutes. Cool. Chill for several hours before serving. Serve with fresh strawberries.

Cannoli

Belissimo!

- **Serves 6 to 8**
- **Must do ahead**
- **Chill 3 to 12 hours**

SHELLS
1¼ cups flour
1½ tablespoons sugar
1¼ teaspoons cinnamon
¼ teaspoon baking powder
Dash of salt
1¼ tablespoons shortening
½ cup plus 1 tablespoon cooking sherry
1 egg white, beaten
Vegetable oil for deep-frying

FILLING
1 (12-ounce) can evaporated milk
4 cups milk
1½ cups sugar
1 cup cornstarch
1 teaspoon vanilla extract
3 or 4 cinnamon sticks
1 extra-large chocolate candy bar, chopped

For the shells, mix the flour, 1½ tablespoons sugar, cinnamon, baking powder and salt in a bowl. Cut in the shortening until blended. Add the wine a small amount at a time, stirring to form a soft dough.

Place a small amount of the dough through a pasta machine set on the number 5 setting; place the dough through again set on the number 3 setting. Repeat with the remaining dough. Place the strips on a floured surface. Cut into 3⅓x4½-inch strips. Place the strips around little metal cylinders. Brush the edges with the egg white to seal. Deep-fry in 400-degree vegetable oil in a deep fryer until light brown. Remove and stand on end over a paper towel. Continue until all the strips are fried.

For the filling, combine the evaporated milk, milk, 1½ cups sugar, cornstarch and vanilla in a large heavy saucepan. Cook over low to medium heat until the mixture just begins to bubble, stirring constantly. Cook for 1 minute. Remove from the heat. Add the cinnamon sticks. Chill in the refrigerator for 3 to 12 hours. Remove and discard the cinnamon sticks. Beat the filling for 2 to 3 minutes. Stir in the chopped chocolate.

To assemble, fill the shells with the filling using a spoon or butter knife.

***Note:** To make cannoli you need little metal cylinders called cannelli, which are about ¾ inch in diameter and about 4 or 5 inches long. Little wooden rods of the same size may also be used.*

Fudge Truffle Cheesecake

A Chocolate Lover's Delight

- **Serves 8 to 12**
- **Must do ahead**
- **Chill**
- **Oven Temperature 300 degrees**
- **Bake 65 minutes**

CHOCOLATE CRUMB CRUST
1½ cups crushed vanilla wafer crumbs
½ cup confectioners' sugar
⅓ cup baking cocoa
⅓ cup butter or margarine, melted

CHOCOLATE FILLING
24 ounces cream cheese, softened
1 (14-ounce) can sweetened condensed milk
4 eggs
2 cups chocolate chips, melted
2 teaspoons vanilla extract

For the crust, combine the vanilla wafer crumbs, confectioners' sugar, baking cocoa and butter in a bowl and mix well. Press into a 9-inch springform pan.

For the filling, beat the cream cheese in a mixer bowl until fluffy. Add the condensed milk gradually, beating constantly. Beat in the eggs. Add the melted chocolate chips and vanilla and beat until smooth. Pour into the prepared pan. Place on a baking sheet. Bake at 300 degrees for 65 minutes or until set. Chill in the refrigerator.

New York-Style Cheesecake

Manhattan's Finest

Process the cream cheese, eggs, sugar, sour cream, vanilla and cornstarch in a blender until smooth. This may have to be processed in batches. Pour into a buttered 9-inch springform pan. Bake at 350 degrees for 1 hour. Turn off the oven and open the oven door a few inches. Let the cheesecake stand in the oven for 1 hour. The cheesecake may have a hollow center, but will level off as it cools. Chill, covered, for 12 hours or longer.

To serve, release the side of the pan and place on a serving plate. Top with strawberry pie filling.

Note: Can substitute cherry pie filling for the strawberry pie filling.

- **Serves 8 to 12**
- **Must do ahead**
- **Chill 12 hours or longer**
- **Oven Temperature 350 degrees**
- **Bake 1 hour**

24 ounces cream cheese, softened
4 eggs
1 cup sugar
2 cups sour cream
2 teaspoons vanilla extract
1 tablespoon cornstarch
1 (21-ounce) can strawberry pie filling

Frozen Chocolate Dessert

Easy to serve

- **Serves 12 to 15**
- **Must do ahead**
- **Must be frozen**

1 cup (2 sticks) margarine, softened
2 cups confectioners' sugar, sifted
4 ounces unsweetened chocolate, melted
4 eggs
2 teaspoons vanilla extract
3/4 teaspoon peppermint extract
1/2 cup vanilla wafer crumbs
Whipped cream

GARNISH
Cherries

Beat the margarine and confectioners' sugar in a mixer bowl until light and fluffy. Add the melted chocolate and beat well. Beat in the eggs until fluffy. Add the vanilla and peppermint extract and beat well.

Sprinkle a thin layer of vanilla wafer crumbs into 12 to 15 muffin cups lined with paper liners. Spoon the chocolate mixture into the prepared cups. Sprinkle with the remaining vanilla wafer crumbs. Freeze until firm. Serve with whipped cream and garnish with a cherry.

Editors Note: In order to avoid raw eggs that may contain salmonella, pasteurize the egg yolk before using. Mix 1 egg yolk with 1 tablespoon lemon juice or vinegar and 1 tablespoon water in a small glass bowl. Microwave, covered, on High for 30 seconds or until the mixture begins to rise. Microwave for 5 seconds longer. Beat with a wire whisk until smooth. Microwave on High for 10 seconds or until the mixture rises again. Beat again. Mixture should be at 200 degrees. Cover the bowl and let stand for 1 minute before using.

White Chocolate Mousse in Chocolate Shells

Make ahead and assemble just before serving

For the chocolate shells, mold plastic wrap over the back of 10 scallop shells 4 to 5 inches in diameter. Place on a foil-lined tray. Melt the bittersweet chocolate in a saucepan over low heat. Stir in the vegetable oil. Brush or spread the chocolate mixture over the prepared shells. Do not brush or spread over the edge. Chill for 2 hours. The shells can be made ahead and frozen.

For the mousse, melt the white chocolate in a saucepan over low heat. Cool slightly. Beat in the egg yolks 1 at a time. Soften the gelatin in the cold water in a glass bowl. Microwave for 3 seconds. Stir until the gelatin is dissolved. Add to the white chocolate mixture and mix well. Fold in the whipped cream. Chill, covered with plastic wrap, for 3 hours before serving. The mousse can be made 1 day ahead.

For the sauce, purée the raspberries in a food processor or blender. Strain into a medium bowl, discarding the seeds. Stir in the sugar and Grand Marnier. Chill for 1 hour or longer. The sauce can be prepared up to 3 days ahead.

To assemble, place the scallop shells chocolate side down on a serving plate. Remove the scallop shells and the plastic wrap carefully. Fill each chocolate shell with the mousse. Drizzle with the sauce. Garnish with fresh whole raspberries and mint leaves.

- **Serves 10**
- **Must do ahead**

Chocolate Shells
- **Chill 2 hours**

White Chocolate Mousse
- **Chill 3 hours**

Raspberry Sauce
- **Chill 1 hour or longer**

CHOCOLATE SHELLS
8 ounces bittersweet chocolate
2 teaspoons vegetable oil

WHITE CHOCOLATE MOUSSE
9 ounces white chocolate
5 egg yolks, at room temperature
2 teaspoons unflavored gelatin
2 tablespoons cold water
2 cups whipping cream, softly whipped

RASPBERRY SAUCE
2 cups fresh raspberries or thawed frozen unsweetened raspberries
1/4 cup sugar
2 tablespoons Grand Marnier or other orange liqueur

GARNISHES
Fresh whole raspberries
Mint leaves

Apple Crisp

An Old Favorite

- **Serves 4**
- **Oven Temperature 375 degrees**
- **Bake 30 minutes**

4 cups sliced apples
3/4 cup packed brown sugar
1/2 cup flour
1/2 cup rolled oats
3/4 teaspoon cinnamon
3/4 teaspoon nutmeg (optional)
1/2 cup (1 stick) butter

Place the apples in a greased 9-inch square baking pan. Mix the brown sugar, flour, oats, cinnamon and nutmeg in a bowl. Cut in the butter until crumbly.

Sprinkle the oat mixture over the apples. Bake at 375 degrees for 30 minutes or until the apples are tender.

Note: Can double the recipe and bake in a 9x13-inch baking pan.

Fruit Cobbler

All Types of Fruit Work Great

- **Serves 10 to 12**
- **Oven Temperature 350 degrees**
- **Bake 1 hour**

1/2 cup (1 stick) butter
1 cup sugar
1 cup flour
2 teaspoons baking powder
3/4 cup milk
1/2 teaspoon vanilla extract
3 cups fresh fruit
3/4 cup sugar

Place the butter in a baking dish. Bake at 350 degrees until melted. Combine 1 cup sugar, flour, baking powder, milk and vanilla in a bowl and mix well. Pour over the melted butter.

Combine the fruit with 3/4 cup sugar in a bowl. Spoon over the top; do not mix. Bake at 350 degrees for 1 hour. Serve warm with ice cream.

Deep-Dish Rhubarb Cobbler

A Winner on All Counts

For the pastry, mix 1 cup flour and salt in a bowl. Cut in the shortening until crumbly. Add the water 1 tablespoonful at a time until the mixture forms a soft dough. Roll the pastry into an 8-inch square. Cut designs in the pastry.

For the filling, combine the rhubarb, sugar, 1/4 cup flour, nutmeg and orange peel in a bowl and mix well. Place in an 8-inch square baking dish. Dot with the butter.

To assemble, place the pastry on top of the filling, sealing and fluting the edges. Bake at 425 degrees for 30 minutes. Garnish with orange triangles.

- **Serves 6**
- **Oven Temperature 425 degrees**
- **Bake 30 minutes**

PASTRY
1 cup sifted flour
1/2 teaspoon salt
1/3 cup shortening
2 to 3 tablespoons water

RHUBARB FILLING
5 cups 1-inch rhubarb pieces
1 1/2 cups sugar
1/4 cup flour
1/8 teaspoon nutmeg
2 teaspoons grated orange peel
2 tablespoons (1/4 stick) butter

GARNISH
Orange slices, cut into triangles

Fruit Compote with Ginger Apricot Sauce

Beautiful and Delicious

- **Serves 8**
- **Can do ahead**

GINGER APRICOT SAUCE
1/2 cup sugar
2 tablespoons cornstarch
1/8 teaspoon nutmeg
1/4 teaspoon ginger
1/2 teaspoon grated lemon peel
1 1/4 cups pineapple juice
12 ounces apricot nectar
1 tablespoon lemon juice

FRUIT
1 pineapple, peeled, cored, cubed
1 pint strawberries, hulled
2 cups fresh or frozen blueberries
2 cups sliced fresh or frozen peaches

GARNISHES
Fresh sweet cherries or strawberries
Sprigs of fresh mint

For the sauce, mix the sugar, cornstarch, nutmeg, ginger and lemon peel in a saucepan. Add the pineapple juice, apricot nectar and lemon juice and mix until smooth. Bring to a boil and reduce the heat. Simmer for 10 minutes or until thickened, stirring occasionally. Can prepare the sauce several days ahead of serving and store in a tightly covered container in the refrigerator.

For the fruit, prepare each fruit early in the day of serving. Chill, covered, in the refrigerator.

To assemble, alternate the pineapple, strawberries, blueberries and peaches in tall glasses. Spoon the sauce over the fruit until covered. Garnish with a cherry and sprig of mint.

Note: Can substitute 4 cups drained canned pineapple for the fresh pineapple. Other fruit combinations can be used.

Lemon Lush Dessert

Try it with chocolate too

For the crust, mix the flour and butter in a bowl until crumbly. Stir in 1/2 cup pecans. Pat into a 9x13-inch baking dish. Bake at 350 degrees for 30 minutes. Let stand until cool.

For the cream cheese layer, beat the cream cheese and sugar in a mixer bowl until light and fluffy. Fold in 6 ounces whipped topping.

For the lemon pudding layer, combine the pudding mix and milk in a bowl and mix until smooth and thick.

To assemble, spread the cream cheese layer over the crust. Spoon the lemon pudding layer over the cream cheese layer. Spread 6 ounces whipped topping over the top. Sprinkle with pecans. Chill until serving time.

Note: Can substitute chocolate instant pudding for the lemon.

- **Serves 10 to 12**
- **Oven Temperature 350 degrees**
- **Bake 30 minutes**

CRUST
1 1/2 cups flour
3/4 cup (1 1/2 sticks) butter or margarine, softened
1/2 cup chopped pecans

CREAM CHEESE LAYER
8 ounces cream cheese, softened
1 cup sugar
6 ounces whipped topping

LEMON PUDDING LAYER
3 (4-ounce) packages lemon instant pudding mix
4 cups milk

TOPPING AND ASSEMBLY
6 ounces whipped topping
Chopped pecans

Lemon Curd

Keeps well in the refrigerator

- **Makes 3 cups**

4 eggs
2 cups sugar
1/2 cup (1 stick) butter
1 1/2 cups lemon juice
1 tablespoon grated lemon peel

Combine the eggs, sugar and butter in a heavy saucepan and mix well. Cook over low heat until smooth, stirring constantly. Add the lemon juice and lemon peel. Simmer for a few minutes or until thickened, stirring constantly.

Use the lemon curd as a filling for tart shells or spread on rusk or toasted English muffins.

LEMON CURD MOUSSE

RICH AND ELEGANT

For the mousse, soften the gelatin in the cold water in a bowl for 10 minutes. Combine the sugar, lemon juice, egg yolks and lemon peel in a heavy saucepan and whisk until blended. Add the butter. Cook over medium heat until the mixture thickens and begins to bubble around the edge, stirring constantly. Remove from the heat. Add the gelatin mixture and stir until the gelatin dissolves. Spoon into a medium bowl. Cover the surface with plastic wrap. Chill in the refrigerator.

Beat the whipping cream in a medium bowl until stiff peaks form. Fold 1 cup of the whipped cream into the chilled lemon mixture, reserving the remainder for the assembly.

For the coconut, place the coconut on a baking sheet. Bake at 350 degrees until toasted. Cool.

To assemble, layer 3 tablespoons blueberries, 3 tablespoons mousse, 1 tablespoon coconut and 3 tablespoons of the reserved whipped cream in each of 8 stemmed 10- to 12-ounce glasses. Repeat the layers. Top each with blueberries and a dollop of whipped cream. Chill until ready to serve.

- **Serves 8**
- **Must do ahead**

Mousse

- **Chill**

Coconut

- **Oven Temperature 350 degrees**
- **Bake until toasted**

MOUSSE
1/2 teaspoon unflavored gelatin
2 teaspoons cold water
1 cup sugar
1/2 cup fresh lemon juice
6 egg yolks
2 tablespoons grated lemon peel
3/4 cup (1 1/2 sticks) unsalted butter, cut into small pieces
1 1/2 cups whipping cream

TOASTED COCONUT
1 cup sweetened flaked coconut

ASSEMBLY
12 ounces fresh blueberries

Heavenly Meringues

Splendid

- **Serves 12**
- **Must do ahead**
- **Oven Temperature 250 degrees**
- **Bake 1 hour**

MERINGUES
6 egg whites, at room temperature
1 teaspoon vinegar
1 teaspoon vanilla extract
Pinch of salt
2 cups sugar

ASSEMBLY
Vanilla ice cream
2 to 3 cups sweetened fruit, such as sliced strawberries, peaches or raspberries

GARNISH
Sprigs of fresh mint

For the meringues, beat the egg whites at medium speed in a mixer bowl until soft peaks form. Add the vinegar, vanilla and salt. Add the sugar a small amount at a time, beating constantly until stiff peaks form. Drop a dollop or 2 for each meringue 2 inches apart onto lightly buttered baking sheets. Make an indentation in the top of each one with the back of a spoon. Bake at 250 degrees for 1 hour. Turn off the oven. Let stand in the closed oven for 8 to 12 hours.

To assemble, place the meringues on individual dessert plates. Spoon vanilla ice cream into each meringue. Spoon the fruit over the ice cream. Garnish with sprigs of fresh mint.

***Note:** Can store the meringues in tightly covered containers. Recipe can be reduced by 1/2 to make 8 small meringues.*

Bread Pudding

Developed decades ago as a good use for day-old bread

- **Serves 6**
- **Baking Temperature 350 degrees**
- **Bake 40 to 50 minutes**

BREAD PUDDING
3 cups cubed bread
2/3 cup sugar
1/4 cup (1/2 stick) butter or margarine, softened
2 eggs
1 cup heavy cream
3 tablespoons raisins
2 1/2 teaspoons vanilla extract

BOURBON SAUCE
3/4 cup sugar
2 teaspoons cornstarch
Dash of cinnamon
Dash of nutmeg
3/4 cup heavy cream
2 tablespoons bourbon

For the pudding, arrange the bread cubes in a single layer in a 2-quart square baking dish or in a 10-inch round baking pan. Beat 2/3 cup sugar and butter in a mixer bowl until creamy. Add the eggs and beat until fluffy. Stir in 1 cup cream, raisins and vanilla. Pour over the bread cubes. Place the baking dish in a larger baking pan. Pour enough water in the larger baking pan to come halfway up the sides of the baking dish. Bake at 350 degrees for 40 to 50 minutes or until set.

For the sauce, combine 3/4 cup sugar, cornstarch, cinnamon and nutmeg in a small saucepan. Stir in 3/4 cup cream. Cook over medium heat until gently boiling and thickened, stirring constantly. Remove from the heat and stir in the bourbon.

To serve, spoon the warm bread pudding into dessert bowls. Spoon the sauce over the bread pudding.

Pecan Croissant Pudding

Mouth-watering

- **Serves 8**
- **Oven Temperature 350 degrees**
- **Bake 45 minutes**

CROISSANT PUDDING
5 croissants
4 eggs, lightly beaten
1 cup sugar
1 1/2 cups 2 percent low-fat milk
1 teaspoon vanilla extract
1 teaspoon almond extract
1/4 cup chopped pecans

PECAN CARAMEL SAUCE
1 cup packed dark brown sugar
1 cup heavy cream
1/2 cup (1 stick) butter
1 cup chopped pecans

For the pudding, cut the croissants into 1/2-inch-thick slices. Layer in a well-buttered 9-inch pie plate using the smaller pieces on the bottom layer. Combine the eggs, sugar, milk, vanilla and almond extract in a bowl and whisk well. Pour over the croissant slices. Sprinkle with 1/4 cup pecans. Bake at 350 degrees for 45 minutes or until set. Cool.

For the sauce, combine the brown sugar, cream and butter in a saucepan. Bring to a boil and reduce the heat. Simmer for 5 minutes. Stir in 1 cup pecans.

To serve, spoon the warm croissant pudding into dessert bowls. Spoon the sauce over the top.

Fresh Strawberries with Toffee Bar Topping

Sensational

Combine the sugar, heavy cream, corn syrup and butter in a saucepan. Bring to a boil. Boil for 2 minutes. Remove from the heat. Stir in the toffee candy. Cool slightly.

Place the strawberries in dessert bowls. Spoon the warm topping over the strawberries. Garnish with sour cream.

***Note:** Can chill the topping in the refrigerator. Reheat and thin with additional heavy cream before serving. The topping is also good on ice cream.*

- **Serves 6 to 8**
- **Can do ahead**

3/4 cup sugar
1/2 cup heavy cream
1/4 cup light corn syrup
2 tablespoons (1/4 stick) butter
5 large toffee candy bars, frozen, finely chopped
2 pints fresh strawberries

GARNISH
Sour cream

Raspberry Trifle

Serve to your special friends

- **Serves 18**
- **Must do ahead**
- **Chill 4 to 12 hours**

Sponge Cake

- **Oven Temperature 325 degrees**
- **Bake 1 hour**

Custard

- **Chill 1 hour**

SPONGE CAKE
1 1/2 cups sifted cake flour
1/4 teaspoon salt
6 egg yolks
1/2 cup cold water
1 1/2 cups sugar
1/2 teaspoon vanilla extract
1/2 teaspoon lemon extract
6 egg whites
3/4 teaspoon cream of tartar

CUSTARD
2 cups milk
6 egg yolks
1 1/2 cups sugar
2 envelopes unflavored gelatin
1/2 cup cold water
1/2 teaspoon vanilla extract
16 ounces mascarpone cheese
6 egg whites, stiffly beaten

ASSEMBLY
16 ounces fresh raspberries or frozen raspberries, thawed, drained

GARNISH
Grated semisweet chocolate

For the sponge cake, sift the cake flour with the salt 3 times. Beat the egg yolks in a mixer bowl until thick and pale yellow. Add the cold water and beat until thick. Beat in the sugar gradually. Beat in the vanilla and lemon extract. Fold in the cake flour mixture a small amount at a time. Beat the egg whites in a mixer bowl until foamy. Add the cream of tartar and beat until moist, glossy peaks form. Fold into the batter, turning the bowl gradually. Spoon into an ungreased 10-inch tube pan. Bake at 325 degrees for 1 hour. Invert pan to cool.

For the custard, scald the milk in a double boiler. Stir a small amount of the hot milk into the egg yolks; stir the egg yolks into the hot milk. Add the sugar gradually, stirring constantly. Cook for 10 to 20 minutes or until thickened and coats a spoon. Remove from the heat. Soften the gelatin in cold water in a bowl. Add to the custard and mix until the gelatin is dissolved. Stir in the vanilla. Cool for 20 to 30 minutes. Fold in the mascarpone cheese. Fold in the stiffly beaten egg whites. Chill for 1 hour.

To assemble, cut the sponge cake into 1/2-inch slices. Reserve a few of the raspberries for garnish. Alternate layers of the custard, sponge cake and raspberries in a trifle dish until all the ingredients are used, ending with the custard. Sprinkle with the reserved raspberries and grated chocolate. Cover with plastic wrap. Chill for 4 to 12 hours before serving.

Note: Can be assembled in a 7x11-inch dish for a tiramisu-type dessert.

Crème Anglaise and Raspberry Sauce

Delicious

For the sauce, purée the raspberries in a food processor. Strain through a sieve into a bowl, discarding the seeds. Add 3 tablespoons sugar and Grand Marnier and mix well. Chill, covered, in the refrigerator for up to 2 days.

For the crème anglaise, place the half-and-half in a medium heavy saucepan. Scrape in the seeds from the vanilla bean; add the vanilla bean. Bring to a simmer. Whisk the egg yolks, 2/3 cup sugar and cornstarch in a medium bowl until blended. Add the hot half-and-half mixture gradually, whisking constantly. Return the mixture to the saucepan. Cook over medium heat for 6 minutes or until thickened. Pour into a bowl. Stir in the Cognac. Chill, covered, in the refrigerator until well chilled or for up to 2 days.

To serve, ladle the raspberry sauce and crème anglaise simultaneously onto each dessert plate. Mound the fruit in the center. Garnish with sprigs of fresh mint.

- **Serves 5**
- **Must do ahead**
- **Chill**

RASPBERRY SAUCE
1 (12-ounce) package frozen unsweetened raspberries, thawed
3 tablespoons sugar
1 tablespoon Grand Marnier or other orange liqueur

CRÈME ANGLAISE
1 1/4 cups half-and-half
1/2 vanilla bean, split lengthwise
3 egg yolks
2/3 cup sugar
3/4 teaspoon cornstarch
1 tablespoon Cognac or bourbon

ASSEMBLY
4 cups assorted fresh fruit, such as sliced bananas, grapes, raspberries, sliced strawberries, sliced kiwifruit and blueberries

GARNISH
Sprigs of fresh mint

Frozen Grapefruit Delight

Refreshing

- **Serves 4**
- **Must do ahead**
- **Chill**
- **Must be frozen**

2 grapefruit, cut into halves
1 teaspoon sugar
1 teaspoon finely chopped fresh lemon thyme or cinnamon basil
4 cups frozen yogurt or vanilla ice cream

GARNISH
Sprigs of lemon thyme, basil or mint

Remove the pulp from the grapefruit halves, reserving the shells and discarding the membranes. Place the grapefruit pulp, sugar and lemon thyme in a saucepan. Heat over low to medium heat for 10 minutes, stirring occasionally. Chill in the refrigerator.

Cut a thin layer of peel from the bottom of each grapefruit shell in order to allow the shell to sit flat. Place in the freezer. Freeze until firm.

To serve, place about 1 cup frozen yogurt into each grapefruit shell. Spoon the grapefruit mixture over the top of each. Garnish with sprigs of lemon thyme.

Fried Ice Cream

Easy

- **Serves 12 to 15**
- **Must do ahead**
- **Must be frozen**

ICE CREAM
1 cup packed brown sugar
1/2 cup (1 stick) butter
2 1/2 cups crisp rice cereal
1/2 cup chopped nuts
1/2 cup shredded coconut
1/2 gallon ice cream, softened

HOT FUDGE TOPPING
1 cup semisweet chocolate chips
2 tablespoons (1 stick) butter
1 (14-ounce) can sweetened condensed milk
3 tablespoons hot water
1 teaspoon vanilla extract

For the ice cream, heat the brown sugar and 1/2 cup butter in a saucepan, stirring until the butter is melted. Add the cereal, nuts and coconut. Reserve 1/2 cup of the crumb mixture for the assembly. Press the remaining crumb mixture in a 9x13-inch dish. Mound the ice cream over the top.

For the topping, heat the chocolate chips, 2 tablespoons butter and condensed milk in a saucepan over medium heat, stirring until the chocolate and butter are melted. Cook for 5 minutes. Stir in the water and vanilla.

To assemble, drizzle the hot fudge topping over the ice cream. Sprinkle with the reserved crumb mixture. Freeze until firm.

Champagne Sorbet

Very light

- **Makes 1 quart**
- **Must do ahead**
- **Chill**
- **Freeze 2 hours**

SUGAR SYRUP
5 cups sugar
4¼ cups water

SORBET
1¾ cups pink or white champagne
1¾ cups cold sugar syrup
¾ cup spring or mineral water
Juice of 1 lemon

For the sugar syrup, combine the sugar and water in a large saucepan and mix well. Cook over high heat until the sugar is dissolved, stirring constantly. Bring to a boil and remove from the heat. Pour into a heatproof container. Chill in the refrigerator. This recipe makes 7 cups.

For the sorbet, pour the champagne, 1¾ cups of the cold sugar syrup, spring water and lemon juice in an ice cream freezer container. Freeze following the manufacturer's directions for 20 to 25 minutes or until frozen; the sorbet will not freeze solid. Spoon into a 5-cup mold or serving dish. Freeze for 30 minutes. Remove from the freezer and stir well. Freeze, covered, for 1½ hours longer or until ready to serve.

Note: This delicate dessert is best served the same day it is made.

Kiwifruit Sorbet

Refreshing—not filling

- **Serves 8**
- **Must do ahead**
- **Chill**
- **Must be frozen**

SORBET
1 cup sugar
1/2 cup water
2 pounds kiwifruit, peeled, chopped (about 9 kiwifruit)

RASPBERRY SAUCE
1 (12-ounce) package frozen unsweetened raspberries, thawed
1/4 cup sugar
2 tablespoons raspberry jam

GARNISH
Kiwifruit slices

For the sorbet, bring 1 cup sugar and water to a boil in a small saucepan over medium heat. Boil until the sugar is dissolved, stirring constantly. Cool. Purée the kiwifruit in a food processor. Reserve 1 cup of the kiwifruit purée. Strain the remaining kiwifruit purée through a fine sieve into a bowl. Combine the reserved kiwifruit purée, strained kiwifruit and sugar syrup in an ice cream freezer container. Freeze using the manufacturer's directions. Spoon into a freezer container. Freeze until firm. Can prepare the sorbet a couple of days ahead and store in the freezer.

For the sauce, purée the raspberries, sugar and raspberry jam in a food processor. Strain through a fine sieve into a container. Store, covered, in the refrigerator.

To assemble, spread the raspberry sauce in the center of each dessert plate. Arrange 1 scoop of kiwifruit sorbet on the raspberry sauce. Garnish with kiwifruit slices.

Chocolate Sauce

Have it on hand for your cravings

- **Makes about 2 cups**

3 (1-ounce) squares unsweetened chocolate
1/4 cup water
1 cup sugar
3 tablespoons white corn syrup
1 1/2 cups sweetened condensed milk
3 tablespoons butter
1 teaspoon vanilla extract

Melt the chocolate in the water in a saucepan. Add the sugar and corn syrup. Cook for 5 minutes or until the sugar is dissolved, stirring constantly.

Add the condensed milk, butter and vanilla. Cook for 5 minutes over low heat, stirring constantly. Cool.

Note: The sauce will thicken as it cools.

Strawberry Topping

Keep on hand for a quickie dessert

- **Makes 3 to 4 cups**
- **Must do ahead**
- **Can be frozen**

4 cups sugar
3 cups water
4 cups whole strawberries
1/4 cup rum

Bring the sugar and water to a boil in a heavy skillet. Boil to 230 degrees on a candy thermometer, spun-thread stage. Add the strawberries. Return to a boil. Simmer for 20 minutes, shaking the skillet back and forth gently; do not stir. Remove from the heat. Cool slightly. Stir in the rum.

Spoon into an airtight container. Chill for 8 to 12 hours. Serve over ice cream or warm and serve the topping over tapioca pudding or cake.

Note: Can store the topping in the freezer. The rum prevents the topping from freezing totally, so it can be spooned directly from the freezer over ice cream.

Apple Cake

Family Favorite

Combine the apples, 3 tablespoons sugar and cinnamon in a bowl and toss to mix well.

Mix the flour, 2 cups sugar, baking powder and salt in a mixer bowl. Add the vegetable oil, eggs, orange juice and vanilla and mix until smooth. Layer the batter and apples 1/2 at a time in a greased 9-inch tube or bundt pan. Bake at 325 degrees for 1 1/2 hours or until the cake tests done. Cool in the pan for 15 minutes. Invert onto a wire rack to cool completely.

Note: Can also be baked in two 5x9-inch loaf pans. The cake is even better 1 to 2 days after baking.

- **Serves 12 to 15**
- **Can do ahead**
- **Oven Temperature 325 degrees**
- **Bake 1 1/2 hours**

4 apples, thinly sliced
3 tablespoons sugar
1 teaspoon (heaping) cinnamon
3 cups flour
2 cups sugar
1 tablespoon baking powder
1/4 teaspoon salt
1 cup vegetable oil
4 eggs, lightly beaten
1/4 cup orange juice
1 tablespoon vanilla extract

Fresh Apple Cake

A good fall treat

- **Serves 12 to 15**
- **Can do ahead**
- **Oven Temperature 350 degrees**
- **Bake 50 to 55 minutes**

CAKE
2 cups sugar
1 cup vegetable oil
4 cups chopped apples
2 cups flour
1 1/2 teaspoons baking soda
1/2 teaspoon baking powder
2 tablespoons cinnamon
1 teaspoon salt
1 cup chopped walnuts

BROWN SUGAR GLAZE
1/3 cup packed brown sugar
1/3 cup sugar
2 tablespoons flour
1 cup water
1/4 cup (1/2 stick) butter
1 teaspoon vanilla extract

For the cake, combine 2 cups sugar, vegetable oil and apples in a bowl and mix well. Let stand for 15 minutes. Mix 2 cups flour, baking soda, baking powder, cinnamon and salt together. Add to the apple mixture and mix well. Stir in the walnuts. Pour into a greased and floured 9x13-inch cake pan. Bake at 350 degrees for 50 to 55 minutes or until the cake tests done.

For the glaze, combine the brown sugar, 1/3 cup sugar, 2 tablespoons flour, water, butter and vanilla in a heavy 3-quart saucepan and mix well. Boil until thickened, stirring constantly.

To assemble, pour the hot glaze over the warm cake.

Buttery Bundt Cake

Great All-Purpose Cake

Combine the eggs, sugar, cake flour, shortening, salt and flavorings in a mixer bowl. Beat for 12 minutes. Pour into a greased bundt pan.

Bake at 350 degrees for 55 to 60 minutes or until the cake tests done. Invert onto a wire rack to cool. Sprinkle with confectioners' sugar.

Note: May serve as a shortcake topped with fresh strawberries and whipped topping.

- **Serves 12 to 15**
- **Oven Temperature 350 degrees**
- **Bake 55 to 60 minutes**

6 eggs
2 cups sugar
2 cups sifted cake flour
1 cup butter-flavor shortening
1/2 teaspoon salt
1/2 teaspoon vanilla extract
1/2 teaspoon lemon extract
1 teaspoon butter flavoring
Confectioners' sugar

Chocolate Angel Cake

Lovely on a Dessert Buffet

- **Serves 8 to 10**
- **Oven Temperature 375 degrees**
- **Bake 35 to 40 minutes**

3/4 cup sifted cake flour
1 1/2 cups sifted confectioners' sugar
1/3 cup baking cocoa
2 teaspoons instant coffee
1 1/2 cups egg whites, at room temperature
1/4 teaspoon salt
1 1/2 teaspoons cream of tartar
1 cup sugar
Confectioners' sugar

Sift the cake flour, 1 1/2 cups confectioners' sugar, baking cocoa and coffee powder together 3 times. Beat the egg whites and salt in a large mixer bowl until foamy. Add the cream of tartar. Beat at high speed until stiff. Fold in the sugar a small amount at a time using a rubber spatula. Fold in the sifted flour mixture a small amount at a time. Do not overmix.

Pour into an ungreased 10-inch tube pan. Cut through the batter with a knife 2 times to eliminate any air bubbles.

Bake at 375 degrees for 35 to 40 minutes or until the cake springs back when lightly touched. Invert the pan on a bottle. Cool for 1 hour. Remove the cake from the pan and invert onto a cake plate. Sprinkle with confectioners' sugar.

Eggless Chocolate Cake

Cholesterol Watcher's Special

- **Serves 9 to 12**
- **Oven Temperature 350 degrees**
- **Bake 30 minutes**

1 cup sugar
1/2 cup baking cocoa
1 1/2 cups flour
1 teaspoon baking soda
Pinch of salt
1 tablespoon vinegar or lemon juice
3/4 cup plus 3 tablespoons milk
1/4 cup vegetable oil
1 teaspoon vanilla extract

Mix the sugar and baking cocoa in a large bowl. Sift the flour, baking soda and salt into the sugar mixture. Mix the vinegar and milk in a 1-cup glass measure. Let stand for a few minutes.

Add the milk mixture, vegetable oil and vanilla to the flour mixture and mix well. Pour into an 8-inch square cake pan. Bake at 350 degrees for 30 minutes.

CHOCOLATE CHIP DATE CAKE

CALORIC INDULGENCE

- **Serves 12**
- **Oven Temperature 350 degrees**
- **Bake 30 to 40 minutes**

1½ cups boiling water
1 cup chopped dates
1 teaspoon baking soda
1¼ cups flour
¾ teaspoon baking soda
1 teaspoon salt
½ cup (1 stick) butter or margarine, softened
1 cup sugar
2 eggs
½ cup sugar
¾ cup chopped walnuts
1½ cups chocolate chips

Pour the boiling water over the dates in a bowl. Add 1 teaspoon baking soda and mix well. Let stand until cool.

Sift the flour, ¾ teaspoon baking soda and salt together. Beat the butter and 1 cup sugar in a mixer bowl until light and fluffy. Add the eggs and beat well. Add the date mixture and mix well. Beat in the flour mixture.

Pour into a greased 9x13-inch cake pan. Sprinkle with ½ cup sugar, walnuts and chocolate chips in the order listed. Bake at 350 degrees for 30 to 40 minutes or until the cake tests done. Serve with a dollop of whipped cream.

Milk Chocolate Cake

Homespun

- **Serves 15**
- **Oven Temperature 375 degrees**
- **Bake 25 to 35 minutes**

1 teaspoon baking soda
1 tablespoon vinegar
2 cups flour, sifted
1/2 teaspoon salt
1/2 cup (1 stick) butter, softened
1 1/2 cups sugar
2 eggs
1 cup sour milk
2 ounces bitter chocolate, melted
1 teaspoon vanilla extract

Dissolve the baking soda in the vinegar in a bowl. Mix the flour and salt together.

Beat the butter in a mixer bowl until creamy. Add the sugar gradually, beating constantly until light and fluffy. Add the eggs 1 at a time, beating well after each addition. Add the sour milk and flour mixture alternately, beating well after each addition. Beat in the chocolate and vanilla. Add the vinegar mixture and beat well.

Pour into a greased 9x13-inch cake pan or 2 greased round cake pans. Bake at 375 degrees for 25 to 35 minutes or until the cake tests done. Serve with whipped cream.

***Note:** This cake is good as a base for a Black Forest Cake. Just spread whipped cream and black cherries between the cake layers.*

GRAHAM CRACKER TORTE

MILE HIGH

- **Serves 12 to 16**
- **Must do ahead**
- **Chill several hours**
- **Oven Temperature 350 degrees**
- **Bake 25 to 30 minutes**

CAKE
8 cups graham cracker crumbs
1 1/2 cups milk
1 cup (2 sticks) margarine, softened
1 1/2 cups sugar
6 egg yolks
1/4 cup flour
2 teaspoons baking powder
1 teaspoon vanilla extract
1 cup finely chopped English walnuts
6 egg whites, stiffly beaten

CREAMY ICING
1 egg white
1 cup sugar
1/2 cup (1 stick) margarine, softened
1/2 cup shortening
3/4 cup lukewarm evaporated milk
1 teaspoon vanilla extract

For the cake, soak the graham cracker crumbs in the milk in a bowl. Beat 1 cup margarine and 1 1/2 cups sugar in a mixer bowl until light and fluffy. Add the egg yolks and graham cracker mixture and beat well. Add the flour, baking powder, 1 teaspoon vanilla and English walnuts and mix well. Fold in 6 egg whites. Spoon into 3 greased and floured 9-inch round cake pans. Bake at 350 degrees for 25 to 30 minutes or until the layers test done. Invert onto wire racks to cool. The layers will shrink some as they cool.

For the icing, beat 1 egg white and 1 cup sugar in a mixer bowl until soft peaks form. Add 1/2 cup margarine, shortening, evaporated milk and 1 teaspoon vanilla and beat until no trace of the sugar remains. This is not a thick icing, so when using in warm weather it may need to be chilled to thicken.

To assemble, spread the icing between the cooled cake layers and over the top and side of the cake. Chill for several hours before serving.

Hummingbird Cake

A Big Hit

- **Serves 12 to 16**
- **Oven Temperature 350 degrees**
- **Bake 25 to 30 minutes**

CAKE
3 cups flour
2 cups sugar
1 teaspoon baking soda
1 teaspoon salt
1 teaspoon cinnamon
3 eggs, beaten
1 cup vegetable oil
1½ teaspoons vanilla extract
1 (8-ounce) can crushed pineapple
2 cups chopped bananas (about 3 bananas)
1 cup chopped pecans

CREAM CHEESE FROSTING
8 ounces cream cheese, softened
½ cup (1 stick) butter or margarine, softened
1 (1-pound) package confectioners' sugar
1 teaspoon vanilla extract

TOPPING
½ cup pecan halves

For the cake, combine the flour, sugar, baking soda, salt and cinnamon in a large bowl. Add the eggs and vegetable oil and stir until the dry ingredients are moistened; do not beat. Stir in 1½ teaspoons vanilla, undrained pineapple, bananas and chopped pecans. Spoon into 2 greased and floured 9-inch round cake pans. Bake at 350 degrees for 25 to 30 minutes or until the layers test done. Cool in the pan for 10 minutes. Invert onto wire racks to cool completely.

For the frosting, beat the cream cheese and butter in a mixer bowl until smooth and creamy. Add the confectioners' sugar and 1 teaspoon vanilla and mix well.

To assemble, spread the frosting between the layers and over the top and side of the cake. Arrange the pecan halves on top of the cake.

BRIDGE CLUB PUDDING CAKE

FANTASTIC

- **Serves 8**
- **Oven Temperature 350 degrees**
- **Bake 35 minutes**

3/4 cup packed dark brown sugar
1 tablespoon flour
3/4 cup sugar
1 1/4 cups flour
1/2 cup chopped pecans
1 tablespoon baking powder
1/4 teaspoon salt
1/2 cup 1 percent low-fat milk
2 1/2 tablespoons butter, melted
1 1/2 teaspoons vanilla extract
1 1/2 cups boiling water
Fat-free whipped topping

GARNISH
Pecan halves

Mix the brown sugar and 1 tablespoon flour in a small bowl. Combine the sugar, 1 1/4 cups flour, chopped pecans, baking powder and salt in a large bowl and mix well. Make a well in the center. Mix the milk, butter and vanilla in a bowl. Add to the flour mixture and stir just until moistened.

Spread in an 8-inch square cake pan. Sprinkle with the brown sugar mixture. Pour the boiling water over the top; do not stir.

Bake at 350 degrees for 35 minutes or until the pudding is bubbly and the cake springs back when lightly touched. Serve warm with whipped topping. Garnish with pecan halves.

Tipsy Orange Cakes

Delicious end to a festive meal

- **Makes 2 cakes**
- **Can do ahead**
- **Can be frozen**
- **Oven Temperature 350 degrees**
- **Bake 55 minutes**

ORANGE CAKE
4 cups flour
2 teaspoons baking powder
2 teaspoons baking soda
2 cups (4 sticks) butter, softened
2 cups sugar
6 egg yolks
2 cups sour cream
Grated peel of 2 oranges
1 cup coarsely chopped walnuts
6 egg whites, stiffly beaten

ORANGE GLAZE
1/2 cup orange juice
1/2 cup light rum
1 cup sugar
2 tablespoons curaçao or other orange liqueur

For the cake, sift the flour, baking powder and baking soda together. Beat the butter and 2 cups sugar in a mixer bowl until light and fluffy. Add the egg yolks 1 at a time, beating well after each addition. Add the flour mixture and sour cream alternately, beating well after each addition. Stir in the orange peel and walnuts. Fold in the stiffly beaten egg whites. Pour into 2 buttered 9-inch tube pans. Bake at 350 degrees for 55 minutes or until the cakes test done.

For the glaze, combine the orange juice, rum, 1 cup sugar and curaçao in a bowl and mix well. Poke holes in the hot cakes. Drizzle with the orange juice mixture. Let stand until cool.

***Note:** Cakes can be wrapped in foil and frozen. Let stand for 2 to 3 hours before serving. Reheat until warm.*

Caramel Frosting

Great on yellow or white cake

- **Makes about 1 cup**

5 tablespoons brown sugar
5 tablespoons evaporated milk
5 tablespoons butter
1 1/2 cups confectioners' sugar

Bring the brown sugar, evaporated milk and butter to a boil in a heavy saucepan. Cook until thickened, stirring constantly. Cook for 5 minutes longer. Remove from the heat. Add the confectioners' sugar and beat until smooth.

Note: Double the recipe for a 9x13-inch cake.

Sugarless Apple Pie

Perfect even without the sugar

- **Serves 8**
- **Oven Temperature 400 degrees**
- **Bake 15 minutes**
- **Oven Temperature 350 degrees**
- **Bake 45 minutes**

1/2 (12-ounce) can apple juice
1 tablespoon cornstarch
6 large tart apples, peeled, sliced
1 (2-crust) pie pastry
3/4 teaspoon cinnamon
2 tablespoons (1/4 stick) butter

Cook the apple juice and cornstarch in a saucepan until thickened, stirring constantly. Mix with the apple slices in a bowl.

Line a 10-inch pie plate with 1 pie pastry. Pour in the apple mixture. Sprinkle with the cinnamon. Dot with the butter. Place the remaining pastry on top, sealing and fluting the edge and cutting vents. Bake at 400 degrees for 15 minutes. Reduce the oven temperature to 350 degrees. Bake for 45 minutes longer.

BEST BLUEBERRY PIE

A MICHIGAN FAVORITE

- **Serves 6 to 8**

4 cups fresh blueberries
3/4 cup sugar
1/2 cup water
2 tablespoons cornstarch
1 tablespoon butter
1/4 cup slivered almonds, toasted
1 tablespoon Cointreau or curaçao
1 baked (9-inch) pie shell
1 cup whipping cream
1/4 teaspoon almond extract
Sugar to taste

Bring 1 cup of the blueberries, 3/4 cup sugar and water to a boil in a saucepan. Cook for 10 minutes or until soft. Let stand until cool.

Combine the cornstarch with a little juice from the blueberry mixture in a bowl and stir until the cornstarch is dissolved. Add to the blueberry mixture. Cook until thickened, stirring constantly. Stir in the butter. Let stand until cool. Add the remaining blueberries, almonds and Cointreau. Pour into the pie shell.

Beat the whipping cream, almond extract and sugar to taste in a mixer bowl until soft peaks form. Spread over the pie, sealing to the edge.

Brownie Tarts

Oh so good

- **Makes about 32**
- **Must do ahead**
- **Chill several hours or up to 3 days**
- **Oven Temperature 350 degrees**
- **Bake 30 minutes**

PASTRY
1/2 cup (1 stick) butter, softened
3 ounces cream cheese, softened
1 cup flour

CHOCOLATE FILLING
4 ounces semisweet chocolate
2 tablespoons (1/4 stick) butter or margarine
2 eggs, beaten
2/3 cup sugar
1/2 teaspoon vanilla extract
Pinch of salt

ASSEMBLY
1/2 cup chopped walnuts

For the pastry, beat 1/2 cup butter and cream cheese in a mixer bowl until light and fluffy. Add the flour and mix to form a ball. Wrap in plastic wrap. Chill for several hours or up to 3 days.

For the filling, melt the chocolate and 2 tablespoons butter in a double boiler. Remove from the heat. Add the eggs, sugar, vanilla and salt and mix well.

To assemble, press a rounded teaspoonful of the pastry dough into each of 1 3/4-inch tartlet pans or miniature muffin cups to form a shell. Sprinkle the walnuts over the pastries. Fill each with the chocolate filling. Bake at 350 degrees for 30 minutes. Remove from the pans to wire racks to cool.

Note: May process the pastry mixture in a food processor.

Coconut Cream Pie

Everyone will want the recipe

For the pie, melt the butter in 2 cups milk in a double boiler. Mix 3/4 cup sugar, cornstarch, flour and salt in a bowl. Place the egg yolks in a 1-cup measure. Add enough milk to measure 1/2 cup. Add to the flour mixture and mix well. Add to the butter mixture. Cook until thickened, stirring constantly. Remove from the heat. Let stand until cool. Add 1 teaspoon vanilla and 1 1/2 cups coconut and mix well. Pour into the pie shell.

For the meringue, beat the egg whites and cream of tartar in a mixer bowl until soft peaks form. Add the sugar gradually, beating until stiff peaks form. Beat in 1/2 teaspoon vanilla.

To assemble, cover the top of the pie with the meringue, sealing to the edge. Sprinkle with 1 cup coconut. Bake at 375 degrees for 10 to 15 minutes or until golden brown, watching carefully to prevent overbrowning.

- **Serves 8**
- **Oven Temperature 375 degrees**
- **Bake 10 to 15 minutes**

PIE
1/4 cup (1/2 stick) butter
2 cups milk
3/4 cup sugar
3 tablespoons cornstarch
1/4 cup flour
1/4 teaspoon salt
3 egg yolks
Milk
1 teaspoon vanilla extract
1 1/2 cups shredded coconut
1 baked (10-inch) pie shell

MERINGUE
3 egg whites
1/4 teaspoon cream of tartar
3 tablespoons sugar
1/2 teaspoon vanilla extract

ASSEMBLY
1 cup shredded coconut

EGGNOG PIE

GOOD ENDING TO A SPECIAL DINNER

- **Serves 8**
- **Must do ahead**
- **Can be frozen**
- **Oven Temperature 450 degrees**
- **Bake 10 to 12 minutes**
- **Chill 6 to 24 hours**

1 (1-crust) pie pastry
1 envelope unflavored gelatin
1/4 cup cold water
1 cup milk
3/4 cup sugar
3 egg yolks
1/4 to 1/3 cup rum
2 cups whipping cream
1 tablespoon sugar
Ground nutmeg to taste

Line a 9-inch pie plate with the pie pastry, trimming and fluting the edge. Prick the bottom and side of the pastry with a fork. Bake at 450 degrees for 10 to 12 minutes or until golden brown. Let stand until cool.

Soften the unflavored gelatin in the cold water in a bowl for 5 minutes. Bring the milk and 3/4 cup sugar to a boil in a medium saucepan. Remove from the heat. Beat the egg yolks and 1/2 cup of the hot milk mixture in a medium mixer bowl; add to the remaining hot milk mixture in the saucepan and beat well. Cook over medium heat until the mixture coats a metal spoon, stirring constantly. Do not boil. Remove from the heat. Stir in the softened gelatin and rum. Pour into a mixer bowl. Chill until the mixture begins to set.

Beat 1 cup of the whipping cream in a large mixer bowl until soft peaks form. Fold into the chilled gelatin mixture. Chill until the mixture mounds when dropped from a spoon, stirring occasionally.

Spoon into the cooled pie shell. Chill, covered, for 6 to 24 hours or until set. Beat the remaining 1 cup whipping cream and 1 tablespoon sugar in a mixer bowl until stiff peaks form. Spread or dollop the whipped cream over the pie. Sprinkle with nutmeg.

Lemon-Layered Ribbon Pie

Cool and Refreshing

Melt the margarine in a medium saucepan. Stir in the lemon juice, sugar and salt. Cook until the sugar dissolves, stirring constantly. Pour 1/2 of the hot mixture into the beaten eggs; stir the eggs into the hot mixture. Cook until thickened, stirring constantly. Remove from the heat. Chill in the refrigerator.

Spread 1/2 of the ice cream in the graham cracker pie shell. Freeze until firm. Spread 1/2 of the chilled lemon mixture over the ice cream. Freeze until firm. Repeat with the remaining ice cream and lemon mixture. Freeze until firm. Garnish with fresh strawberries or raspberries. Cut with a sharp warm knife to serve.

- **Serves 8**
- **Must do ahead**
- **Freeze until firm**

1/4 cup (1/2 stick) margarine
1/3 cup fresh lemon juice
3/4 cup sugar
Dash of salt
3 eggs, lightly beaten
1 quart vanilla ice cream, slightly softened
1 (9-inch) graham cracker crust

GARNISH
Fresh strawberries or raspberries

Shaker Lemon Pie

Old-Fashioned Goodness

- **Serves 8**
- **Must do ahead**
- **Chill 8 to 12 hours or up to 2 weeks**
- **Oven Temperature 400 degrees**
- **Bake 1 hour**

2 cups sugar
2 tablespoons hot water
2 lemons, very thinly sliced
4 eggs
1 unbaked (10-inch) deep-dish pie shell

Dissolve the sugar in the hot water in a bowl. Add the lemon slices. Chill, covered, in the refrigerator for 8 to 12 hours or up to 2 weeks.

Beat the eggs in a mixer bowl until light and fluffy. Add the lemon mixture and mix well. Spoon into the pie shell. Bake at 400 degrees for 1 hour.

Note: Peel 1 of the lemons if using between Christmas and spring.

Margarita Pie

Tangy

- **Serves 8**
- **Must do ahead**
- **Chill 5 hours**

1 envelope unflavored gelatin
1/4 cup cold skim milk
1/2 cup boiling skim milk
1 (8-ounce) container egg substitute
2/3 cup sugar
1/3 cup lime juice
2 to 3 tablespoons tequila
1 teaspoon grated lime peel
1 to 2 drops green food coloring
1 cup whipped topping
1 baked (9-inch) pie shell

GARNISHES
Lime slices
Whipped topping

Sprinkle the unflavored gelatin over the cold milk in a blender container. Let stand for 2 minutes. Add the hot milk. Process for 2 minutes or until the gelatin is completely dissolved. Add the egg substitute, sugar, lime juice, tequila, lime peel and food coloring. Process at high speed for 1 minute or until blended. Pour into a large bowl.

Chill for 1 hour or until the mixture mounds when dropped from a spoon, whisking with a wire whisk occasionally. Fold in the whipped topping. Pour into the pie shell.

Chill for 4 hours or until firm. Garnish with lime slices and a dollop of whipped topping.

- **Serves 8**
- **Oven Temperature 325 degrees**
- **Bake 1 hour**

6 to 8 fresh peaches
1 unbaked (10-inch) pie shell
1/3 cup margarine, softened
1 cup sugar
1 egg, beaten
1/4 teaspoon vanilla extract
1/3 cup flour

Peach Pie

Traditional

Peel the peaches. Cut into slices. Place the peaches in the pie shell.

Beat the margarine and sugar in a mixer bowl until light and fluffy. Add the egg, vanilla and flour and mix well. Spread over the peaches. Bake at 325 degrees for 1 hour.

Chocolate Pecan Pie

Not for the Calorie Counter

Beat the eggs in a medium bowl until well beaten. Add the sugar, corn syrup, flour, salt and vanilla and beat until combined. Stir in the butter and pecans. Pour into the pie shell.

Bake at 350 degrees for 1 hour or until the center is set when the pie is gently shaken. Sprinkle the hot pie with the chocolate chips. Let stand until cool. Chill in the refrigerator before serving. Serve with whipped cream.

- **Serves 8**
- **Chill**
- **Oven Temperature 350 degrees**
- **Bake 1 hour**

4 eggs
1 cup sugar
1 cup light corn syrup
1½ teaspoons flour
¼ teaspoon salt
1 teaspoon vanilla extract
¼ cup (½ stick) butter, melted
2 cups pecan halves
1 unbaked (9-inch) pie shell
1 cup chocolate chips

Pumpkin Pie

Scrumptious

- **Serves 8**
- **Oven Temperature 400 degrees**
- **Bake 15 minutes**
- **Oven Temperature 300 degrees**
- **Bake 40 to 50 minutes**

1 cup cooked pumpkin
1 cup packed brown sugar
1 teaspoon cornstarch
1 teaspoon cinnamon
1/2 teaspoon ginger
1/4 teaspoon salt
2 eggs, beaten
1 tablespoon butter, melted
1 1/2 cups hot milk
1 unbaked (10-inch) pie shell
Whipped cream
Crushed gingersnaps

Combine the pumpkin, brown sugar, cornstarch, cinnamon, ginger, salt, eggs and butter in a bowl and mix well. Add the hot milk and mix well. Pour into the pie shell.

Bake at 400 degrees for 15 minutes. Reduce the oven temperature to 300 degrees. Bake for 40 to 50 minutes or until set. Do not overbake. Let stand until cool. Top with whipped cream and sprinkle with gingersnaps.

Guilt-Free Pumpkin Ice Cream Pie

Absolutely divine

- **Serves 8**
- **Must do ahead**
- **Freeze until firm**

1/4 cup honey
3/4 cup canned pumpkin
1/2 teaspoon cinnamon
1/2 teaspoon ground cloves
1/4 teaspoon ginger
1/8 teaspoon nutmeg
1/4 teaspoon salt
1 quart sugar-free, fat-free vanilla ice cream, slightly softened
1 (9-inch) graham cracker pie shell
3/4 cup chopped pecans

Combine the honey, pumpkin, cinnamon, cloves, ginger, nutmeg and salt in a saucepan and mix well. Bring to a boil, stirring constantly. Cool completely.

Add the ice cream and mix well. Spoon into the pie shell. Sprinkle with the pecans. Freeze until firm.

Raspberry Crème Pie

First-rate

- **Serves 8 to 10**
- **Oven Temperature 350 degrees**
- **Bake 10 minutes**
- **Chill**

1½ cups graham cracker crumbs (1 package)
3 tablespoons sugar
⅔ cup butter, melted
1 cup confectioners' sugar
8 ounces cream cheese, softened
1 cup whipping cream, whipped
1 teaspoon vanilla extract
4 cups raspberries
3 tablespoons cornstarch
¾ cup sugar
½ cup water

Mix the graham cracker crumbs, 3 tablespoons sugar and melted butter in a bowl. Press over the bottom and slightly up the side of a 9-inch pie plate. Bake at 350 degrees for 10 minutes. Let stand until cool.

Beat the confectioners' sugar and cream cheese in a mixer bowl until smooth. Fold in the whipped cream and vanilla. Chill in the refrigerator.

Mash 1 cup of the raspberries in a small saucepan. Add the cornstarch, ¾ cup sugar and water. Cook over medium heat until thickened, stirring constantly. Let stand until cool. Stir in the remaining 3 cups raspberries.

Reserve 2 to 3 tablespoons of the baked graham cracker crust for topping. Spoon the cream cheese mixture into the remaining crust. Spoon the raspberry mixture over the top. Sprinkle with the reserved graham cracker topping.

Note: Can substitute blueberries for the raspberries.

Best-Ever Pie Pastry

Nice to have on hand

Mix the flour, sugar and salt in a bowl. Cut in the shortening until crumbly. Add the egg, vinegar and water and mix until the mixture forms a ball. Fit into two 10-inch pie plates, trimming and fluting the edge. Use immediately or freeze, covered, until ready to use.

- **Makes 2 pie pastries**
- **Can be frozen**

2 cups flour
1 1/2 tablespoons sugar
1 teaspoon salt
1 cup shortening
1 egg, beaten
1 1/2 tablespoons vinegar
1/4 cup water

Pie Pastry

Quick and Easy

- **Makes 1 pie shell**
- **Oven Temperature 375 degrees**
- **Bake 15 minutes**

1½ cups flour
1 tablespoon sugar
Pinch of salt
½ cup vegetable oil
2 tablespoons water

Mix the flour, sugar and salt in a 9-inch pie plate. Make a well in the center. Mix the vegetable oil and water in a bowl. Pour into the pie plate and mix until the mixture forms a ball. Pat to line the pie plate, trimming and fluting the edge.

Bake at 375 degrees for 15 minutes or until golden brown, or bake as directed in your favorite pie recipe.

Cookies and Candies

The Frauenthal Performing Arts Center

After a 7.5-million-dollar renovation, the theater is the performance hall for the West Shore Symphony, as well as many professional performances.

German Anise Cakes

Different

- **Makes 2 dozen**
- **Must do ahead**
- **Chill 12 hours**
- **Oven Temperature 350 degrees**
- **Bake 10 minutes**

2 cups flour, sifted
1 teaspoon baking powder
3 eggs
1 cup sugar
1/2 teaspoon vanilla extract
1 1/2 tablespoons anise seeds, crushed

Sift the flour and baking powder together. Beat the eggs in a mixer bowl until light and fluffy. Add the sugar gradually, beating well after each addition. Add the flour mixture, vanilla and anise seeds and beat well.

Drop by tablespoonfuls onto well-greased cookie sheets. Chill for 12 hours to dry. Bake at 350 degrees for 10 minutes or until the edges are golden brown. Cool on wire racks.

Danish Pastry Apple Bars

An apple lover's cookie

- **Makes 3 dozen**
- **Oven Temperature 375 degrees**
- **Bake 50 minutes**

2 1/2 cups sifted flour
1 teaspoon salt
1 cup shortening
1 egg yolk
Milk
1 cup cornflakes
8 cups sliced peeled tart apples
3/4 to 1 cup sugar
1 teaspoon cinnamon
1 egg white
1 cup sifted confectioners' sugar
3 to 4 teaspoons milk

Combine the flour and salt in a large bowl. Cut in the shortening until crumbly. Beat the egg yolk in a 1-cup measure. Add enough milk to measure 2/3 cup and mix well. Stir into the flour mixture.

Divide the dough into 2 equal portions. Roll 1 portion into a 12x17-inch rectangle on a floured surface. Fit into a 10x15-inch baking pan. Sprinkle with the cornflakes. Layer the apples over the cornflakes. Sprinkle with a mixture of sugar and cinnamon. Roll the remaining dough into a 10x15-inch rectangle. Place over the apples, sealing the edges and cutting vents.

Beat the egg white until frothy. Brush over the pastry. Bake at 375 degrees for 50 minutes. Combine the confectioners' sugar with enough of the 3 to 4 teaspoons milk to make of a glaze consistency. Drizzle over the warm pastry. Cut into bars.

Chocolate Walnut Biscotti

Great for a Coffee Break

Mix the flour, baking cocoa, baking powder and salt together. Beat the butter and sugar in a mixer bowl until light and fluffy. Add the egg, orange peel and orange juice and beat well. Stir in the flour mixture to form a stiff dough. Stir in the walnuts.

Shape the dough into two 9-inch logs on a buttered large cookie sheet. Bake at 350 degrees for 13 minutes or until slightly firm to the touch. Cool on the cookie sheet on a wire rack for 15 minutes. Cut each log diagonally into 1/2-inch-thick slices using a serrated knife. Arrange cut side down on cookie sheets. Bake for 15 minutes or until crisp. Cool on a wire rack.

Note: Can prepare biscotti 1 week ahead of time and store in airtight containers. Biscotti can also be prepared and frozen for up to 1 month ahead of time.

- **Makes 3 dozen**
- **Can do ahead**
- **Can be frozen**
- **Oven Temperature 350 degrees**
- **Bake 28 minutes**

1 cup flour
1/4 cup Dutch-process baking cocoa
3/4 teaspoon baking powder
1/2 teaspoon salt
1/4 cup (1/2 stick) unsalted butter, softened
1/4 cup plus 2 tablespoons sugar
1 egg
1 tablespoon freshly grated orange peel
1 tablespoon fresh orange juice
1/2 cup chopped walnuts, toasted

Jeweled Biscotti

Super

- **Makes 4 dozen**
- **Oven Temperature 350 degrees**
- **Bake 30 minutes**
- **Oven Temperature 275 degrees**
- **Bake 30 minutes**

3/4 cup dried cranberries
2 1/4 cups flour
1 teaspoon baking powder
1/4 teaspoon baking soda
1/4 teaspoon salt
1/2 cup chopped dried apricots
1/2 cup chopped dried pears or apples
3/4 cup pecan pieces
2 eggs
3/4 cup sugar
1/2 cup corn oil
2 tablespoons brandy or orange juice

Combine the dried cranberries with enough boiling water to cover in a small bowl. Let stand for 30 minutes; drain and pat dry.

Mix 2 cups of the flour, baking powder, baking soda and salt in a large bowl. Stir in the dried cranberries, apricots, pears and pecans. Beat the eggs and sugar at medium-high speed in a mixer bowl until thick and pale yellow. Add the corn oil and brandy and blend well. Add the flour mixture and beat until combined, beginning at low speed and increasing to medium speed. Knead on a lightly floured surface, adding enough of the remaining flour to form a soft nonsticky dough. Add additional flour if needed. Shape into two 2x12-inch logs. Place 2 inches apart on a lightly greased cookie sheet. Bake at 350 degrees for 30 minutes or until light brown. Cool for 15 minutes. Reduce the oven temperature to 275 degrees.

Cut each log diagonally into 1/2-inch-thick slices using a serrated knife. Arrange cut side down on 2 ungreased cookie sheets. Bake for 15 minutes. Turn over the slices. Bake for 15 minutes longer or until golden brown. Remove to wire racks to cool completely. Store at room temperature in an airtight container.

Out-of-This-World Chocolate Brownies

Very Gooey

For the brownies, bring the water, 1 cup butter, 1/4 cup baking cocoa and sea salt to a boil in a saucepan. Combine the flour and sugar in a bowl. Add the chocolate mixture and mix well. Stir in the buttermilk, eggs, baking soda and 1 teaspoon vanilla. Pour into a greased and floured 9x13-inch baking pan. Bake at 400 degrees for 20 minutes.

For the frosting, beat 1/2 cup butter, 1/4 cup baking cocoa, milk and 1 teaspoon vanilla in a mixer bowl until blended. Add the confectioners' sugar and beat until smooth.

To assemble, spread the frosting over the warm brownies. Cut into bars or squares.

- **Serves 20**
- **Oven Temperature 400 degrees**
- **Bake 20 minutes**

BROWNIES
1 cup water
1 cup (2 sticks) butter
1/4 cup baking cocoa
1/2 teaspoon sea salt
2 cups flour
2 cups sugar
1/2 cup buttermilk
2 eggs, beaten
1 teaspoon baking soda
1 teaspoon vanilla extract

CREAMY CHOCOLATE FROSTING
1/2 cup (1 stick) butter, softened
1/4 cup baking cocoa
6 tablespoons milk
1 teaspoon vanilla extract
3 2/3 cups confectioners' sugar

Chocolate Buttersweets

A TREAT FOR THE CHOCOLATE LOVER

- **Makes 3 dozen**
- **Oven Temperature 350 degrees**
- **Bake 12 to 15 minutes**

COOKIES
1/2 cup (1 stick) butter
1/2 cup confectioners' sugar
1/4 teaspoon salt
1 teaspoon vanilla extract
1 to 1 1/4 cups flour

CREAMY WALNUT FILLING
3 ounces cream cheese, softened
1 cup sifted confectioners' sugar
2 tablespoons flour
1 teaspoon vanilla extract
1/2 cup chopped walnuts
1/2 cup flaked coconut

CHOCOLATE FROSTING
1/2 cup semisweet chocolate chips
2 tablespoons (1/4 stick) butter
2 tablespoons water
1/2 cup sifted confectioners' sugar

For the cookies, beat 1/2 cup butter in a mixer bowl until smooth. Add 1/2 cup confectioners' sugar, salt and 1 teaspoon vanilla and beat until light and fluffy. Add 1 to 1 1/4 cups flour gradually, beating constantly. Shape the dough by spoonfuls into balls. Place on ungreased cookie sheets. Make an indentation in the center of each. Bake at 350 degrees for 12 to 15 minutes or until brown.

For the filling, beat the cream cheese, 1 cup confectioners' sugar, 2 tablespoons flour and 1 teaspoon vanilla in a mixer bowl until smooth. Stir in the walnuts and coconut.

For the frosting, melt the chocolate chips and 2 tablespoons butter with the water in a saucepan over low heat, stirring occasionally. Add 1/2 cup confectioners' sugar and beat until smooth.

To assemble, spoon the filling into the warm cookies. Let stand until cool. Spread the frosting over each filled cookie.

Note: This recipe can easily be doubled or tripled.

Clipper Chocolate Chip Cookies

Sinfully delicious

Mix the flour, baking soda and salt in a small bowl. Beat the butter, sugar, brown sugar, vanilla, Frangelico and coffee liqueur in a large mixer bowl until light and fluffy. Add the eggs and beat well. Add the flour mixture and mix well. Stir in the chocolate chips, walnuts, pecans and macadamia nuts.

Drop by 1/4 cupfuls 2 inches apart onto ungreased cookie sheets. Bake at 325 degrees for 16 minutes or until light brown. Cool on wire racks.

- **Makes about 3 dozen**
- **Oven Temperature 325 degrees**
- **Bake 16 minutes**

2 1/2 cups flour
1 teaspoon baking soda
1/2 teaspoon salt
1 cup (2 sticks) unsalted butter, softened
3/4 cup sugar
3/4 cup packed light brown sugar
1 tablespoon vanilla extract
1 tablespoon Frangelico (hazelnut liqueur)
1 tablespoon coffee liqueur
2 eggs
4 cups milk chocolate chips
1 cup chopped walnuts
1/2 cup chopped pecans
1/2 cup chopped macadamia nuts

Spicy Christmas Cookies

A Tradition

- **Makes 5 to 7 dozen**
- **Must do ahead**
- **Chill briefly or 8 to 12 hours**
- **Oven Temperature 350 degrees**
- **Bake 10 to 13 minutes**

COOKIES
4 cups flour
1/2 teaspoon salt
1 tablespoon cinnamon
2 teaspoons ginger
2 teaspoons ground cloves
2 cups (4 sticks) butter, softened
1 1/2 cups sugar
1 egg
2 tablespoons molasses
1 tablespoon dark corn syrup
2 teaspoons baking soda
2 tablespoons hot brewed coffee

CHRISTMAS ICING
2 egg whites
1 3/4 cups confectioners' sugar
1/8 teaspoon cream of tartar
1/2 teaspoon vanilla extract

For the cookies, sift the flour, salt, cinnamon, ginger and cloves together. Beat the butter in a mixer bowl until creamy. Add the sugar and beat until light and fluffy. Beat in the egg, molasses and corn syrup. Dissolve the baking soda in the coffee. Add to the batter and mix well. Beat in the flour mixture. Chill the dough briefly or for 8 to 12 hours. Return almost to room temperature. Roll the dough on a lightly floured surface. Cut into desired shapes. Place on nonstick cookie sheets. Bake at 350 degrees for 10 to 13 minutes or until brown. Cool on wire racks.

For the icing, beat the egg whites with 1/4 cup of the confectioners' sugar in a mixer bowl for 3 to 4 minutes. Add the remaining confectioners' sugar, cream of tartar and vanilla gradually, beating at high speed until a knife inserted in the frosting comes out clean. Keep lightly covered with a damp towel to prevent drying out.

To assemble, spread the icing on the cooled cookies. Decorate as desired.

Friendship Cookies

Rich and Flavorful

- **Makes 15**
- **Oven Temperature 350 degrees**
- **Bake 25 to 30 minutes**

1 cup (2 sticks) butter, softened
2½ cups rolled oats
1 cup sugar
1 cup flour
¼ cup sugar
1 tablespoon cornstarch
1 cup undrained crushed pineapple
1 teaspoon lemon juice

Combine the butter, oats, 1 cup sugar and flour in a bowl and mix well. Pat ½ of the mixture in a 9x13-inch baking pan.

Combine ¼ cup sugar, cornstarch and pineapple in a saucepan. Cook over low heat until thick and clear. Stir in the lemon juice. Let stand until cool. Pour into the prepared pan.

Crumble the remaining oat mixture over the top. Bake at 350 degrees for 25 to 30 minutes. Cool and cut into squares.

Macadamia Coconut Cookies

Rich and Good

- **Makes 6 dozen**
- **Oven Temperature 350 degrees**
- **Bake 12 minutes**

1 cup (2 sticks) butter, softened
1 cup packed brown sugar
2/3 cup sugar
2 eggs
1 teaspoon vanilla extract
2 cups flour
1 teaspoon baking soda
1 teaspoon baking powder
1/2 teaspoon salt
1 cup shredded coconut
2 1/2 cups old-fashioned oats
1 cup macadamia nuts
1 1/2 cups chocolate chips

Beat the butter, brown sugar and sugar in a mixer bowl until light and fluffy. Add the eggs and vanilla and beat well. Beat in the flour, baking soda, baking powder and salt. Stir in the coconut, oats, macadamia nuts and chocolate chips.

Drop by spoonfuls 2 inches apart onto nonstick cookie sheets. Bake at 350 degrees for 12 minutes. Cool on wire racks.

Honey Macaroons

You'll need to eat at least two

- **Makes 2 to 3 dozen**
- **Oven Temperature 350 degrees**
- **Bake 15 to 20 minutes**

1½ cups quick-cooking rolled oats
½ cup flaked coconut
½ cup chopped walnuts
½ cup flour
¾ cup packed brown sugar
½ cup (1 stick) butter or margarine
2 tablespoons honey
36 red or green candied cherries (optional)

Combine the oats, coconut, walnuts and flour in a large mixer bowl and mix well. Combine the brown sugar, butter and honey in a saucepan. Bring to a boil, stirring frequently. Pour over the oat mixture and mix well. Press 1 level tablespoonful dough at a time into greased 1¾-inch muffin cups. Top each with a candied cherry.

Bake at 350 degrees for 15 to 20 minutes or until brown. Cool in the pans for 10 minutes. Remove to wire racks to cool completely.

Note: For a crisper cookie, bake in 2-inch muffin cups.

Mexican Wedding Cookies

"I do" love these

- **Makes 4 dozen**
- **Must do ahead**
- **Chill 2 hours**
- **Oven Temperature 350 degrees**
- **Bake 10 to 12 minutes**

1 cup (2 sticks) butter, softened
1 cup ground walnuts
6 tablespoons confectioners' sugar
1½ cups flour
½ teaspoon vanilla extract
Confectioners' sugar

Beat the butter in a mixer bowl until light and fluffy. Add the walnuts, 6 tablespoons confectioners' sugar, flour and vanilla and mix well. Divide into 2 equal portions. Roll each portion into a log 1 inch in diameter. Wrap each in waxed paper. Chill for 2 hours. Cut into ¼-inch slices. Place on ungreased cookie sheets.

Bake at 350 degrees for 10 to 12 minutes; do not let the edges brown. Cool for 2 minutes on the cookie sheets. Coat each cookie with confectioners' sugar. Let stand until cool. Coat each cookie again with confectioners' sugar.

Tropical Oatmeal Scotchies

Wonderful orange flavor

- **Makes 2 dozen**
- **Oven Temperature 375 degrees**
- **Bake 7 to 8 minutes**

1 cup butter-flavor shortening
3/4 cup sugar
3/4 cup packed brown sugar
2 eggs
1 teaspoon orange extract
1 teaspoon baking soda
1/2 teaspoon salt
1/2 teaspoon cinnamon
1 1/4 cups flour
3 cups rolled oats
1/2 cup shredded coconut (optional)
1 cup butterscotch chips
1 cup white chocolate chips

Beat the shortening, sugar and brown sugar in a mixer bowl until light and fluffy. Add the eggs and orange extract and mix well. Beat in the baking soda, salt and cinnamon. Add the flour gradually, beating well after each addition. Stir in the oats and coconut. Stir in the butterscotch chips and white chocolate chips.

Drop by spoonfuls 2 inches apart onto nonstick cookie sheets. Bake at 375 degrees for 7 to 8 minutes or until brown. Cool on wire racks.

Candy Bar Cookies

You'll crave more

- **Makes 5 dozen**
- **Oven Temperature 350 degrees**
- **Bake 10 to 12 minutes**

COOKIES
3 cups flour
1 teaspoon baking powder
1 teaspoon baking soda
1 cup (2 sticks) butter, softened
1 cup creamy peanut butter
1 cup sugar
1 cup packed brown sugar
2 eggs
2 teaspoons vanilla extract
60 miniature Snickers candy bars

CHOCOLATE GLAZE
1 cup confectioners' sugar
2 tablespoons baking cocoa
Hot water

For the cookies, mix the flour, baking powder and baking soda together. Beat the butter, peanut butter, sugar and brown sugar in a mixer bowl until light and fluffy. Add the eggs and vanilla and beat well. Fold in the flour mixture. Shape a rounded teaspoon of dough around each candy bar to form a ball; make sure the candy bars are completely covered. Place on ungreased cookie sheets. Bake at 350 degrees for 10 to 12 minutes or until light brown. Let stand until cool.

For the glaze, mix the confectioners' sugar and baking cocoa in a bowl. Add enough hot water to make of a glaze consistency.

To assemble, drizzle a small amount of the chocolate glaze over each cookie.

Raspberry Ribbons

Melts in your mouth

- **Makes 4 dozen**
- **Must do ahead**
- **Chill 2 to 12 hours**
- **Oven Temperature 350 degrees**
- **Bake 20 minutes**

1/2 cup (1 stick) butter, softened
1/2 cup shortening
1/2 cup confectioners' sugar
1 egg yolk
1 teaspoon vanilla extract
2 1/4 cups flour
1/4 teaspoon salt
1/2 cup seedless raspberry jam
1 recipe confectioners' sugar icing

Beat the butter, shortening, confectioners' sugar, egg yolk and vanilla at medium speed in a mixer bowl until light and fluffy. Add the flour and salt. Beat at low speed until blended. Divide the dough into 4 equal portions and shape into disks. Chill, wrapped in plastic wrap, for 2 to 12 hours or until firm.

Shape each disk into a 12-inch rope. Arrange 2 inches apart on ungreased cookie sheets. Flatten each rope until 5/8 inch thick. Make a 1/4-inch-deep groove lengthwise down the center of each rope using the handle of a wooden spoon. Bake at 350 degrees for 12 minutes. Remove from the oven and gently press the grooves again. Stir the jam in a bowl until smooth. Fill the grooves on the ropes with the jam. Bake for 8 minutes or until light golden brown around the edges. Cool on the cookie sheets for 10 minutes. Remove to wire racks to cool completely. Drizzle each rope in a zigzag pattern with confectioners' sugar icing. Cut each rope diagonally into 1-inch slices.

Rhubarb Bars

Delicious

- **Makes 1 to 1½ dozen**
- **Oven Temperature 375 degrees**
- **Bake 30 minutes**

2 tablespoons cornstarch
1/4 cup water
3 to 4 cups 1/4- to 1/2-inch rhubarb pieces
1 1/2 cups sugar
1 teaspoon vanilla extract
1 (3-ounce) package raspberry or strawberry gelatin
1 1/2 cups flour
1 1/2 cups rolled oats
1 cup packed brown sugar
1/2 teaspoon baking soda
1/2 cup chopped nuts
3/4 cup (1 1/2 sticks) margarine, softened

Dissolve the cornstarch in the water in a saucepan. Add the rhubarb and sugar. Cook until thickened, stirring constantly. Add the vanilla and raspberry gelatin and mix well.

Combine the flour, oats, brown sugar, baking soda, nuts and margarine in a large bowl and mix until crumbly. Pat 3/4 of the crumb mixture into a 9x13-inch baking pan. Pour the rhubarb mixture into the prepared pan. Top with the remaining crumb mixture. Bake at 375 degrees for 30 minutes. Cool and cut into bars.

***Note:** Can also serve as a dessert topped with whipped cream or whipped topping.*

Rocky Road Fudge Bars

Wonderful

- **Serves 15**
- **Oven Temperature 350 degrees**
- **Bake 27 to 32 minutes**

BAR LAYER
1/2 cup (1 stick) margarine
1 ounce unsweetened chocolate
1 cup sugar
1 cup flour
2 eggs
1 teaspoon vanilla extract
1/2 to 1 cup chopped walnuts

FILLING
6 ounces cream cheese, softened
1/2 cup sugar
2 tablespoons flour
1/4 cup (1/2 stick) margarine, softened
1 egg
1/2 teaspoon vanilla extract
1/4 cup chopped walnuts
1 cup chocolate chips
2 cups miniature marshmallows

CHOCOLATE CREAM CHEESE FROSTING
1/4 cup (1/2 stick) margarine
1 ounce unsweetened chocolate
2 ounces cream cheese
1/4 cup milk
3 cups confectioners' sugar
1 teaspoon vanilla extract

For the bar layer, melt 1/2 cup margarine and 1 ounce chocolate in a saucepan over low heat. Add 1 cup sugar, 1 cup flour, 2 eggs, 1 teaspoon vanilla and 1/2 to 1 cup walnuts and mix well. Spread in a greased and floured 9x13-inch baking pan.

For the filling, combine 6 ounces cream cheese, 1/2 cup sugar, 2 tablespoons flour, 1/4 cup margarine, egg and 1/2 teaspoon vanilla in a mixer bowl. Beat for 1 minute or until smooth and fluffy. Stir in 1/4 cup walnuts. Spread over the bar layer. Sprinkle with the chocolate chips. Bake at 350 degrees for 25 to 30 minutes. Remove from the oven. Sprinkle with the marshmallows. Bake for 2 minutes longer.

For the frosting and assembly, combine 1/4 cup margarine, 1 ounce chocolate, 2 ounces cream cheese and milk in a saucepan. Cook over low heat until melted, stirring frequently. Stir in the confectioners' sugar and vanilla. Pour immediately over the marshmallows. Cool and cut into bars. Store in the refrigerator.

Millionaire's Shortbread

Worth every calorie

- **Makes 4 dozen**
- **Oven Temperature 350 degrees**
- **Bake 35 to 40 minutes**

FIRST LAYER
1/2 cup packed brown sugar
1/2 cup sugar
2 cups (4 sticks) butter or margarine, softened
4 cups flour

SECOND LAYER
1 cup (2 sticks) butter or margarine, softened
1 cup packed brown sugar
1/4 cup light corn syrup
2/3 cup sweetened condensed milk
1/2 teaspoon vanilla extract

THIRD LAYER
1 (12-ounce) package miniature milk chocolate chips

For the first layer, beat 1/2 cup brown sugar, sugar and 2 cups butter in a mixer bowl until light and fluffy. Add the flour 1 cup at a time, beating until blended after each addition. Press into a 10x15-inch baking pan. Prick with a fork. Bake at 350 degrees for 35 to 40 minutes or until golden brown.

For the second layer, combine 1 cup butter, 1 cup brown sugar, corn syrup and condensed milk in a saucepan. Heat over low heat until the brown sugar is dissolved. Bring to a boil. Boil for 7 minutes, stirring constantly. Remove from the heat and add the vanilla. Beat until smooth and glossy. Pour over the first layer. Let stand until cool and set.

For the third layer, melt the chocolate chips in a double boiler over hot water. Spread over the second layer. Cool until set. Cut into 2-inch bars.

Sugar Cookies

Crisp

- **Makes 1½ dozen**
- **Oven Temperature 300 degrees**
- **Bake 20 minutes**

1 cup (2 sticks) margarine, softened
3/4 cup sugar
3/4 teaspoon baking soda
1 1/2 cups flour
1 teaspoon white vinegar
1 teaspoon vanilla extract

Beat the margarine, sugar and baking soda in a mixer bowl for 10 minutes. Add the flour, white vinegar and vanilla and mix well. Drop by teaspoonfuls onto nonstick cookie sheets.

Press down with the bottom of a glass that has been buttered and dipped in sugar. Bake at 300 degrees for 20 minutes. Cool on wire racks.

Swedish Creams

Melts in Your Mouth

- **Makes 4 dozen**
- **Must do ahead**
- **Chill**
- **Can be frozen**
- **Oven Temperature 375 degrees**
- **Bake 7 to 9 minutes**

COOKIES
1 cup (2 sticks) butter, softened
1/2 cup heavy cream
2 cups flour
Sugar

VANILLA FILLING
1/2 cup (1 stick) butter, softened
1 1/2 cups confectioners' sugar
2 egg yolks
2 teaspoons vanilla extract

For the cookies, combine 1 cup butter, cream and flour in a bowl and mix well. Chill in the refrigerator. Roll the dough a portion at a time 1/8 inch thick on a floured cloth-covered board. Cut with a 1 1/2-inch round cookie cutter. Dip in sugar, turning to coat well. Place on ungreased cookie sheets. Bake at 375 degrees for 7 to 9 minutes; do not brown. Cool on a wire rack.

For the filling, combine 1/2 cup butter, confectioners' sugar, egg yolks and vanilla in a mixer bowl and beat until light and fluffy.

To assemble, spread the filling on 1/2 of the cookies. Top with the remaining cookies.

Note: Can use raspberry jam as the filling.

Editors Note: In order to avoid raw eggs that may contain salmonella, pasteurize the egg yolks before using. Mix 1 egg yolk with 1 tablespoon lemon juice or vinegar and 1 tablespoon water in a small glass bowl. Microwave, covered, on High for 30 seconds or until the mixture begins to rise. Microwave for 5 seconds longer. Beat with a wire whisk until smooth. Microwave on High for 10 seconds or until the mixture rises again. Beat again. Mixture should be at 200 degrees. Cover the bowl and let stand for 1 minute before using.

Thumbprint Cookies

Paint Your Season

- **Makes 2 dozen**
- **Oven Temperature 375 degrees**
- **Bake 13 minutes**

1/4 cup shortening
1/4 cup (1/2 stick) butter, softened
1/4 cup packed brown sugar
1 egg yolk
1/2 teaspoon vanilla extract
1 cup flour
1/4 teaspoon salt
1 egg white, lightly beaten
Finely chopped walnuts
1 cup prepared white frosting

Beat the shortening, butter, brown sugar, egg yolk and vanilla in a mixer bowl until light and fluffy. Add the flour and salt and beat well. Roll into 1-inch balls. Dip in the egg white; roll in the walnuts. Place 1 inch apart on ungreased cookie sheets. Bake at 375 degrees for 5 minutes. Make an indentation in each ball using a thimble or small spoon. Bake for 8 minutes longer. Remove to wire racks to cool.

Divide the frosting into portions and tint as desired. Fill the cookies with the tinted frosting.

Note: Frosting tint could match the seasons or a party theme. For example, tint the frosting in pastel colors for Easter.

Vanilla Pretzels

Fabulous

- **Makes about 3 dozen**
- **Can be frozen**
- **Oven Temperature 325 degrees**
- **Bake 10 minutes**

COOKIES
5 egg yolks
1 cup plus 2 tablespoons sugar
2 teaspoons vanilla extract
3 cups flour
1 cup (2 sticks) butter, softened, cut into pieces

VANILLA ICING
1 cup sifted confectioners' sugar
1½ teaspoons vanilla extract
1 to 2 teaspoons water

For the cookies, beat the egg yolks and sugar in a mixer bowl until thick and pale yellow. Stir in 2 teaspoons vanilla. Mix the flour and butter in a large mixer bowl. Add the egg mixture and mix until smooth and no longer sticky. Roll a small amount of dough at a time into strips ½ inch thick and 6 to 7 inches long using floured hands. Shape each into a pretzel shape on a cookie sheet. Bake at 325 degrees for 10 minutes or until the edges are just beginning to brown. Cool slightly.

For the icing, combine the confectioners' sugar and 1½ teaspoons vanilla in a small bowl. Add enough water to make of a thick cream consistency, adding additional water if needed.

To assemble, brush the vanilla icing over the warm cookies. Cool completely. Store in airtight containers.

Baby Ruth Bars

Watch them disappear

- **Makes 3 dozen**

½ cup sugar
½ cup packed brown sugar
1 cup light corn syrup
1 cup peanut butter
6 cups cornflakes
1 cup salted peanuts
1 (7-ounce) milk chocolate candy bar, melted

Bring the sugar, brown sugar and corn syrup to a boil in a saucepan, stirring constantly. Stir in the peanut butter, cornflakes and peanuts.

Press into a greased 9x13-inch dish. Spread the melted chocolate over the top. Let stand until cool. Cut into bars.

Candies

Coconut Joys

Really good

- **Makes 1½ pounds**
- **Must do ahead**
- **Chill until firm**

½ cup (1 stick) butter, melted
3 cups (packed) shredded coconut
2 cups confectioners' sugar
2 (1-ounce) squares unsweetened baking chocolate, melted

Combine the butter, coconut and confectioners' sugar in a bowl and mix well. Drop by small scoopfuls onto a baking sheet. Make indentations in each. Pour a small amount of melted chocolate into each indentation. Chill until firm.

Florida Orange Balls

Unusual, great flavor

- **Makes about 3 dozen**
- **Can be frozen**

1 (11-ounce) package vanilla wafers, crumbled
¼ cup orange juice concentrate
¼ cup Grand Marnier
¾ cup (scant) confectioners' sugar
¾ cup shredded coconut (optional)
½ cup chopped pecans
Confectioners' sugar

Combine the vanilla wafers, orange juice concentrate, Grand Marnier, ¾ cup confectioners' sugar, coconut and pecans in a large bowl and mix well. Shape into 1-inch balls. Roll in additional confectioners' sugar. Store in the refrigerator.

Note: May store in an airtight container in the freezer.

Toffee

You'll need more than one piece

• **Makes about ½ pound**

Pecan pieces
1/2 cup (1 stick) butter
3/4 cup packed brown sugar
2 (1 1/5-ounce) chocolate bars

Line a 9-inch pie plate with foil. Spread the pecans in the prepared pie plate. Bring the butter and brown sugar to a boil in a heavy saucepan over medium heat. Boil for 7 minutes, stirring constantly. Pour over the pecans.

Arrange the chocolate bars over the top and cover. Let stand for 3 minutes or until the chocolate melts. Spread the chocolate over the top. Let stand until cool. Break into bite-size pieces.

Orange Chocolate Truffles

Great for Gift Giving

- **Makes about 2 pounds**
- **Must do ahead**
- **Chill**

1 pound semisweet chocolate
$1/2$ cup (1 stick) butter
1 cup heavy cream
Zest of 1 orange
$1/4$ cup orange liqueur
$1/4$ cup baking cocoa
1 cup confectioners' sugar

Melt the chocolate and butter in a double boiler. Add the cream, orange zest and orange liqueur and mix well. Chill in the refrigerator.

Sift the baking cocoa and confectioners' sugar into a bowl. Scoop the chilled chocolate mixture into balls; roll in the confectioners' sugar mixture.

Note: May roll in ground toasted walnuts or pecans.

Quick and Easy Truffles

Nice Gift for Your Hostess

- **Makes $1\frac{1}{2}$ pounds**
- **Must do ahead**
- **Chill 1 to $1\frac{1}{2}$ hours**

2 cups semisweet chocolate chips
$1/4$ cup Godiva liqueur
1 cup chocolate fudge frosting
Ground nuts, confectioners' sugar, baking cocoa, sprinkles or shredded coconut

Melt the chocolate chips in a saucepan over low heat, stirring frequently. Remove from the heat. Stir in the liquor and fudge frosting. Chill for 1 to $1\frac{1}{2}$ hours or until firm enough to handle.

Scoop into 1-inch balls; roll in ground nuts. Place in foil candy cups. Chill in the refrigerator until firm.

White Chocolate Crunch

Addictive

- **Makes 15 cups**
- **Can do ahead**

1 pound white chocolate
6 cups rice Chex
3 cups Cheerios
2 cups pretzel sticks
2 cups cashews
2 cups "M & M's" Plain Chocolate Candies

Melt the white chocolate in a double boiler or in the microwave. Mix the rice Chex, Cheerios, pretzel sticks, cashews and candies in a large bowl. Spread in a large flat baking pan. Pour the white chocolate over the mixture. Cool until firm. Break into bite-size pieces. Store in an airtight container.

Note: Can be prepared up to 3 days ahead of time.

Swedish Nuts

They will just disappear

- **Makes 1 pound**
- **Oven Temperature 325 degrees**
- **Bake 30 minutes**

1 pound pecan halves
3 egg whites
Dash of salt
1 cup sugar
1 cup (2 sticks) butter

Spread the pecans on a baking sheet. Bake at 325 degrees until light brown. Let stand until cool.

Beat the egg whites and salt in a mixer bowl until foamy. Add the sugar gradually, beating until stiff peaks form. Fold in the cooled pecans.

Melt the butter in a 10x15-inch baking pan. Spread the pecan mixture over the butter. Bake at 325 degrees for 30 minutes or until light brown, stirring every 10 minutes. Let stand until cool. Break into pieces.

Friends of the Symphony Publications
P.O. Box 1603 • Muskegon, Michigan 49443

Please send me ________ copies of *More Enchanted Eating* at $23.95 each $ ________________
Add postage and handling at $3.50 each $ ________________
Michigan residents add 6% sales tax at $1.44 each $ ________________
Total $ ________________

Name ________________
Address ________________
City ________________ State ________ Zip ________

Method of Payment: [ ] MasterCard [ ] VISA [ ] Check payable to Friends of the Symphony Publications

Account Number ________________ Expiration Date ________

Signature ________________

More Enchanted Eating

Friends of the Symphony Publications
P.O. Box 1603 • Muskegon, Michigan 49443

Please send me ________ copies of *More Enchanted Eating* at $23.95 each $ ________________
Add postage and handling at $3.50 each $ ________________
Michigan residents add 6% sales tax at $1.44 each $ ________________
Total $ ________________

Name ________________
Address ________________
City ________________ State ________ Zip ________

Method of Payment: [ ] MasterCard [ ] VISA [ ] Check payable to Friends of the Symphony Publications

Account Number ________________ Expiration Date ________

Signature ________________

Photocopies will be accepted.